John Keble, Edward Bouverie Pusey

Ten Sermons During a Retreat for Clergy and a Mission for the People

At S. Saviour's Church, Leeds, in the Octave of its Consecration 1845. Third Edition

John Keble, Edward Bouverie Pusey

Ten Sermons During a Retreat for Clergy and a Mission for the People
At S. Saviour's Church, Leeds, in the Octave of its Consecration 1845. Third Edition

ISBN/EAN: 9783337003210

Printed in Europe, USA, Canada, Australia, Japan

Cover: Foto ©Lupo / pixelio.de

More available books at **www.hansebooks.com**

TEN SERMONS

DURING

A RETREAT FOR CLERGY AND A MISSION FOR THE PEOPLE

AT S. SAVIOUR'S CHURCH, LEEDS,

IN THE OCTAVE OF ITS CONSECRATION 1845,

BY

THE REV. E. B. PUSEY, D.D.

WITH

EIGHT SERMONS
BY THE
REV. JOHN KEBLE, M.A. REV. C. MARRIOTT, M.A.
REV. W. U. RICHARDS, M.A. REV. ISAAC WILLIAMS, B.D.

TURN THOU ME AND I SHALL BE TURNED;
FOR THOU ART THE LORD MY GOD.

THIRD EDITION.

SOLD BY

JAMES PARKER AND CO., OXFORD,
AND 377, STRAND, LONDON;
RIVINGTONS,
LONDON, OXFORD, AND CAMBRIDGE
1877.

PREFACE.

The deep and kind interest which many, both of the clergy and laity, took in the Consecration of S. Saviour's, as well as the love of the poor people for whom the Church was intended, seemed to furnish an occasion which ought not to be neglected, for essaying, by the blessing of Almighty God, to fix the feelings which that Solemnity called forth, even beyond the impressive service of the day of Consecration. The expectation, also, that many of the clergy would be present, seemed a reason the more, why they should not disperse, without an attempt, in what way they might, to benefit the place where they were for the time gathered. Any thing too, which might be done, seemed the more natural and less of an effort, as flowing out of the circumstance of their being brought together. The Editor, accordingly, (with the aid of his valued friend the Rev. C. Marriott who afterwards, although absent in body, assisted in the work, and whose society he was at the time enjoying), formed a plan for a course of Sermons, beginning with very solemn and aweful subjects, which might, they hoped, by God's mercy, be the means of awakening in some a sense of the end and awefulness of their being, the deadliness of sin, the nothingness of all beside God, the necessity for repentance for sin, the love of God in Christ Jesus our Lord, and of deepening and fixing these thoughts in others. A general outline of the plan was transmitted to the Bishop of the diocese, with the assurance that nothing was further from the mind of the Editor than to enter upon controversy; his one object being to bring solemn truths before the hearers, with the hope and prayer that God would bring them home to their souls. The simple aim to benefit the souls committed to his care could not but obtain the concurrence [a] of the chief Pastor of the diocese, (whose anxiety for the spiritual benefit of his diocese it would ill become such as the writer to speak of,) as well as of his friend the devoted and laborous Vicar of the parish. The Editor was much cheered by the words, "I heartily pray God to bless the efforts to convert and build up souls which will then be made."

As the time drew near, trial seemed to hang over the plan. Heavy distress, still more for the Church's sake than for his own, broke at last suddenly on the writer; and for the first time he had to go forth to his labour, apart from the friend of above twenty-two years, who was to him as his own soul, with whom had been shared the little he had himself been enabled to do for God's service in our Church, and whose counsel had been to him for the last twelve years, in every trial, the greatest earthly comfort and stay. Of those also, to whom he looked to assist him in the plan, some who would kindly have shared in it, were hindered; and of those who did aid most effectually, three were visited with sickness, either in those very near them or in themselves. Still, what was undertaken simply for the Glory of God and the good of souls, it seemed wrong to abandon; and the plan was continued, in trust in Him, to Whom, it was hoped, souls might thereby be won.

It has seemed necessary to explain thus much, because it might seem to some unfitting that in the midst of those first distresses, the Editor should any where be taking any prominent part, (although he trusts that it was altogether of the Good Providence of God,) while those other

[a] Some of the subjects were altered, in consequence of the change of the day of Consecration, (some legal forms having been delayed,) through which All Saints' Day fell on the ensuing Saturday. It became necessary to bring the austerer subjects into a narrower space. Other changes were involved by the hindrances alluded to.

distresses compelled him actually to take a much larger share in the plan, than he had originally thought of, and in appearance, a yet larger. For, unwilling to lose the concurrence of those whose bodily presence was hindered by sickness or attendance upon a sick-bed, he himself delivered the Sermons of those who were thus hindered [b]. He did thereby greatly gain both by their help and their prayers while absent, and himself meditating on what he had of their's to deliver; and he felt even the more united with them, in that every thought of their's which he had to deliver, became his own.

With regard to his own Sermons, he has thought it best to say, that the Sermon on All-Saints' Day had been previously preached before the University of Oxford, the great pressure of occupation preventing him from preparing any thing anew for that Festival. It stands nearly as it was originally preached, except that some things local, and others, slightly controversial, were omitted in the delivery, and are not now inserted. Of the other Sermons, he may just say, that in the three "on the Bliss of Heaven," he thought that, after the very solemn subjects of the preceding days, he might safely venture to speak upon the very deep mysteries, which he has there dwelt upon. For his own sake as well as for his hearers, he employed, in so doing, the words and thoughts [c] of holy writers, rather than his own.

[b] It becomes necessary in consequence to distinguish the Sermons, lest the Editor should claim what is not his. The 2d and 3d Sermons, then, are the contribution of the Rev. C. Marriott; the 4th, 5th, and 6th, of the Rev. John Keble; the 7th of the Rev. W. U. Richards; the 9th of the Rev. Isaac Williams, as also the 8th, although unfinished in consequence of severe illness; the rest are by the Editor. In delivering those of others, the Editor found that he could not but add something of his own, following out their thoughts, or closing some of the Sermons as seemed natural to himself. These additions at the close have been retained, and marked by an † prefixed.

[c] Many of these are distinguished in the notes; others were perhaps too much interwoven in his own mind to distinguish; and to attempt to mark all might have tended to distract the mind of many readers from the solemn subjects themselves.

Since then the thoughts are mostly not his own, he may venture to say, that the reverential attention, with which these very solemn subjects were listened to, shewed that our congregations would dwell with benefit on such contemplations of Almighty God. This he may say the rather, because he has, for many years, had a very deep conviction, that we undergo very great loss and risk, through not dwelling more upon the Mysteries of the Faith, as brought out in the Nicene and especially the Athanasian Creed. We undergo loss; for it has been observed by S. Augustine, how God, "Who useth to good even the evil," overrules even heresies to the benefit of the Church, in that, in order to defend sacred truth against "the crafty restlessness of heretics," "many[d] things belonging to the Catholic Faith are both considered more diligently, and understood more clearly, and preached more earnestly; and thus the question raised by the adversary becomes an occasion of learning." Especially upon the sacred doctrine of the Holy Trinity, heretical error has been, through the goodness of Divine Providence, of great benefit to devotion, by occasioning the Church, through the aid of God's Holy Spirit, to clear many points upon which we might otherwise be in doubt, and thus to enlarge the rich pastures in which the soul might safely range, even while she was drawing a boundary around them, which is not to be passed. We are then losing a portion of our inheritance, if we avail not ourselves of this benefit; while, at the same time, so natural is heresy to the human mind, (for it is the very produce of the natural man,) we must be in great peril of falling into it, if we are not on our guard against it. To have no fears of it, is but too sure a road to it; to follow one's own thoughts in Divine Truth, is to go astray.

It may just be said further, that the Editor has added

[d] De Civ. Dei xvi. 2. § 1. see Conf. vii. § 25. Oxf. Tr. De vera relig. § 15. et al.

notes in some places in which he has introduced such high doctrine, lest to any who might not happen to be acquainted with the Θεολογία, he might seem to be entering upon subjects which would be "too high for him," had he not herein been following the steps of the Fathers. But, in meditating upon these solemn subjects, it would be evidently misplaced to dwell upon controversy even with heretics, and such notes had therefore then best be passed by.

With regard to the course generally, an order of subjects has been introduced, which was broken in the delivery [e], chiefly through the fear, lest such very awful subjects coming so close upon each other, three times in the day, might have an oppressive effect [f] upon tender minds. The more comforting subjects were accordingly intermingled with those which must, of necessity, be distressing. And this was the more necessary, since the congregation consisted, at first, in great degree, of strangers. The case might be different, if it should seem good to any to adopt any similar plan, at solemn seasons, in places where all the flock should be known to their Clergy.

And indeed, there seems no reason for withholding that it was the hope of the Editor that, should the blessing of Almighty God rest upon this plan, others might be encouraged to attempt the like, who might be better qualified than himself for that great office, "to preach the Gospel to the poor." Not that there is any thing new in the plan. It was but the employment of the daily services of our Church, daily Communion, frequent Sermons, so as to occupy the minds of those who had leisure, in a series of prayer, hearing of Holy Scripture, meditation on

[e] The days upon which the several Sermons were preached, have been noted at the wish of some, who were desirous of recurring to them, in connection with the memory of that blessed, peaceful, week.

[f] The dread of this occasioned the suggestions at the end of the first, and the beginning of the sixth Sermon. The like invitation to any distressed in mind was also premised at the beginning of what is now the third Sermon.

solemn subjects, and the great Act of Christian Worship and Communion, at periods through the day. It was hoped that they who could thus retire to be with their Lord might return to their duties in the world, with more fervent devotion to Him; while on others, who were less prepared or were unprepared for the whole extent of services so continuous and so sacred, impression, it was hoped, might, by God's mercy, be made by the solemnity of the subjects preached upon. Thus, "by the dew of His blessing," might, it was hoped, both the faithful grow, and sinners be converted. Private intercession on the part of the Clergy engaged could not but form a part of the plan; and the prayers of distant friends were asked and obtained. More than they asked, they had through the mercy of their God, and the Christian love of their brethren.

Indeed, there was nothing peculiar or distinctive in the plan; the only circumstance, in which it perhaps went beyond what had been usual of late, was the frequency of the services [g]. Courses of Sermons on special subjects have been, in the Church, a great instrument in the revival [h] of religion in the United States. In this country also, Lent and Advent Sermons are, of course, frequent. Indeed it seems to have been felt, for some time, that Sermons, confined to the Sunday, are more calculated for tending those who are already within the fold, than to bring in those yet astray. Whatever impression is made, occurs at too great intervals; and mostly they who need to be aroused from an habitual sinful state are not there to hear. Some

[g] Morning Prayer was at 7; then later, the Holy Communion with a Sermon; and prayers and Sermons in the afternoon and evening. The Holy Communion was celebrated at the later hour, since many, who came from a distance, would have been unable to attend at the earlier; daily prayers were in other Churches.

[h] The Writer was much impressed many years ago by an account given to him by Bishop Mc Ilvaine. He mentioned that, on such occasions, the only external attraction used, was a public notice of a course of Sermons, specially relating to some class, as "on the duties of young men." Of 80 converts, at one such season, two only, many years afterwards, had apparently gone back.

feeling of this kind has probably suggested the evening lectures, which have for some years been introduced; and if this has too often been done at the cost of morning devotion, especially of the Litany, this, of course, cannot be necessary. Rather, the more, persons are awakened out of a lethargic state, the more they would value and be upheld by daily devotional services, especially our more penitential, those of the Wednesday and Friday. Yet, so far, we owe thanks to those who have zealously used preaching as a means of conversion. Rightly viewed, it is a great gift of Him Who saith, "It is not ye that speak, but the Spirit of your Father Which speaketh in you," " not in words which man's wisdom teacheth, but which the Holy Ghost teacheth." It needeth not to depreciate any gift of God in order to exalt another.

On the late occasion, God did bless very visibly the solemn services. There seemed, so to say, to be an atmosphere of blessing hanging around and over the Church. How should not one hope it, when, besides those gathered there, many were praying Him, in Whose Hands are the hearts of men, and Who turneth not away the face of those who seek Him? It was the very feeling of those engaged, that God was graciously in a Heavenly manner present there. He seemed, amid the solemn stillness of those services, to speak in silence to the soul of each; and many hearts were there by His secret call, and through the Holy Eucharist which we were permitted daily to celebrate, stirred to more resolute devoted service. To Him be the praise, Whose was the gift.

The single object of the plan of the Editor was the conversion of souls among those for whom the Church was built. The Clergy who, in very large numbers, out of love and sympathy, were present, made it a retreat for themselves.

In conclusion, the Editor hopes that the purpose to avoid controversy, and to speak that only which might bear directly on the souls of the hearers, has been steadily kept in view. This, amid our manifold distresses, is the strong ground of present hope, and of looking for brighter days, that God is stirring in their very depths the souls of men, and calling them to serve Him more earnestly and more early. It seems hopeless, for the time, that many of us can understand one another. It will be a great gain if (except, of course, in cases of plain heresy) we censure not one another. There are enemies enough abroad, moral and intellectual, which may gain possession of the citadel, while our attention is drawn off in another direction. This is no new device of Satan. Even, in human affairs, the presence of a common enemy brings those together, who before were alienated. There are too many tokens of the presence of the enemy of all Faith, and of a fiercer subtler assault than the Faith has undergone hitherto. There are too many forms of idolatry set up and worshipped; idolatry of wealth, luxury, power, intellect. If we, as Christ's faithful soldiers, are, within and without, in earnest warfare against His enemies, we shall, in the very warfare itself, the armour we bear, His watchword, His gracious help, His love, the more readily recognise those whom He vouchsafes to call "My friends." God give us grace more and more to seek Him; so, if we find Him, we shall in Him find each other who shall have sought Him our common Centre; we shall in His light and love at length understand one another; we shall see in one another the work of His grace, and love one another in Him, and Him in one another.

O Lord, we beseech Thee, incline Thy merciful ears to our prayers, and enlighten the darkness of our minds by the grace of Thy Visitation, Who livest.

E. B. P.

CHRIST CHURCH,
ADVENT EMBER WEEK, 1845.

CONTENTS.

SERMON I.
LOVING PENITENCE.
(Evening of the Consecration.)

S. LUKE vii. 47.

"*I say unto thee, Her sins which are many, are forgiven, for she loved much.*" . . . . . pp. 1—22.

SERMON II.
THE NATURE OF SIN.
(Wednesday Morning, Oct. 29. [Rev. C. M.])

S. JOHN xv. 24.

"*Now have they both seen and hated both Me and My Father.*" . . . . . . pp. 23—47.

SERMON III.
THE SINNER'S DEATH.
(Friday Afternoon, Vigil of All Saints. [Rev. C. M.])

PHIL. iii. 18, 19.

"*The enemies of the Cross of Christ. Whose end is destruction.*" . . . . . . pp. 48—69.

SERMON IV.

GOD'S MERCIFUL VISITATIONS BEFORE JUDGEMENT.

(Wednesday Afternoon, Oct. 29. [Rev. J. K.])

1 KINGS xvii. 18.

"And she said unto Elijah, What have I to do with thee, O thou man of God? art thou come unto me to call my sin to remembrance, and to slay my son?" pp. 70—84.

SERMON V.

THE LAST JUDGEMENT.

(Thursday Morning, Oct. 30. [Rev. J. K.])

REV. xxii. 12.

" And, behold, I come quickly, and my reward is with Me, to give to every man according as his work shall be."
pp. 85—103.

SERMON VI.

HELL.

(Thursday Afternoon, Oct. 30. [Rev. J. K.])

S. MARK ix. 47, 48.

"If thine eye offend thee, pluck it out; it is better for thee to enter into the Kingdom of God with one eye, than having two eyes to be cast into hell-fire: where their worm dieth not, and the fire is not quenched." pp. 104—122.

SERMON VII.

LOVE OF CHRIST FOR PENITENTS.

(Wednesday Evening, Oct. 29. [Rev. W. U. R.])

S. LUKE xv. 1, 2.

"*Then drew near unto Him all the publicans and sinners for to hear Him. And the Pharisees and Scribes murmured, saying, This Man receiveth sinners, and eateth with them.*" . . . . . pp. 123—144.

SERMON VIII.

TEMPER OF THE RETURNING PRODIGAL.

(Monday after the Consecration, Nov. 3. [Rev. I. W.])

S. LUKE xv. 18, 19.

"*I will arise and go to my Father, and will say unto Him, Father, I have sinned against Heaven, and before Thee, and am no more worthy to be called Thy son.*"
pp. 145—167.

SERMON IX.

VIRTUE OF THE CROSS THROUGH LOVE.

(Friday Morning, Vigil of all Saints. [Rev. I. W.])

GAL. vi. 4.

"*But God forbid that I should glory, save in the Cross of our Lord Jesus Christ, by Whom the world is crucified unto me and I unto the world.*" . pp. 168—185.

SERMON X.

LOOKING UNTO JESUS, THE GROUNDWORK OF PENITENCE.

(Friday Evening, Vigil of all Saints.)

HEB. xii. 2.

"*Looking unto Jesus, the Author and Finisher of our faith.*"
pp. 186—207.

SERMON XI.

LOOKING UNTO JESUS, THE MEANS OF ENDURANCE.

(Monday Evening after the Consecration, Nov. 3.)

HEB. xii. 2.

"*Looking unto Jesus, the Author and Finisher of our Faith, Who, for the joy which was set before Him endured the Cross, despising the shame, and is set down at the right hand of the throne of God.*" . . pp. 208—229.

SERMON XII.

UNION WITH CHRIST INCREASED THROUGH WORKS WROUGHT THROUGH HIM.

(Saturday Morning, the Feast of All Saints.)

S. JOHN xv. 9, 10.

"*As the Father hath loved Me, so have I loved you: continue ye in My love. If ye keep My commandments, ye shall abide in My love; even as I have kept My Father's commandments, and abide in His love.*" pp. 230—260.

SERMON XIII.

HOPES OF THE PENITENT.

(Saturday Evening, the Feast of All Saints.)

S. LUKE xv. 7.

"*I say unto you, that likewise joy shall be in heaven over one sinner that repenteth, more than over ninety and nine just persons, which need no repentance.*" pp. 261—280.

SERMON XIV.

BLISS OF HEAVEN, "WE SHALL BE LIKE HIM."

(Sunday Morning, Nov. 2.)

1 S. JOHN iii. 2.

"*Beloved, now are we the sons of God, and it doth not yet appear what we shall be: but we know that, when He shall appear, we shall be like Him; for we shall see Him as He is.*" . . . . . . pp. 281—300.

SERMON XV.

BLISS OF HEAVEN, "WE SHALL SEE HIM AS HE IS."

(Sunday Afternoon, Nov. 2.)

1 S. JOHN iii. 2.

"*Beloved, now are we the sons of God, and it doth not yet appear what we shall be; but we know that, when He shall appear, we shall be like Him; for we shall see Him as He is.*" . . . . . . pp. 301—319.

SERMON XVI.

BLISS OF HEAVEN—GLORY OF THE BODY.

(Sunday Evening, Nov. 2.)

PHIL. iii. 20, 21.

"*Our conversation is in heaven, from whence also we look for the Saviour, the Lord Jesus Christ, Who shall change our vile body, that it may be fashioned like unto His glorious Body, according to the working whereby He is able even to subdue all things unto Himself.*" . pp. 320—343.

SERMON XVII.

PROGRESS OUR PERFECTION.

(Tuesday Morning, Octave of the Consecration, Nov. 4.)

PHIL. iii. 15, 16.

"*Let us therefore, as many as be perfect, be thus minded; and if in any thing ye be otherwise minded, God shall reveal even this unto you. Nevertheless, whereto we have already attained, let us walk by the same rule, let us mind the same thing.*" . . . . pp. 344—368.

SERMON XVIII.

DAILY GROWTH.

(Tuesday Afternoon, Nov. 4.)

Ps. cxxxix. 15, 16.

"*Thine Eyes did see my substance, yet being imperfect, and in Thy book were all my members written, which day by day were fashioned, when as yet there was none of them.*"
pp. 369—391.

SERMON I.

LOVING PENITENCE.

(Evening of the Consecration.)

S. LUKE vii. 47.

"I say unto thee, Her sins, which are many, are forgiven, for she loved much."

Joyous must ever be these days, when Almighty God vouchsafes to receive these offerings at our hands; and He Who filleth heaven and earth deigns in a special way to be present in these temples made with hands, where two or three are gathered together in His Name: joyous and solemn is it, when a fresh abode on earth is set apart to echo on from day to day our Redeemer's praise, until those who in truth sing it, in heart as in voice, shall be caught away one by one, to hear the new song and endless Halleluiahs, whereof we learn the first faint preludes here; solemn, especially, is this first day, on which our Lord has here vouchsafed to feed those hungry and athirst for Him with His own Body and Blood. Yet to-day has its own special source of joy, not less precious in the sight of our Redeemer, because it relates to one single soul; for so great was His love, that

He died for love of each of us, as if there had been none beside; and so not less precious is it in the sight of the holy Angels, who joy over one sinner that repenteth, nor, with them, in yours.

You know, my brethren, that this day's offering differs from most beside, that it is the offering of a penitent. You know not from what sin recovered; but you will have read, as you entered, his own confession of unworthiness, and have given him the prayers he asked for; and, whether you have been preserved from deeper or from subtle ensnaring sin, by His same grace Who, we trust, has restored this His prodigal son, or whether you too have been recovered from some state of sin and negligence, you will have rejoiced with and over him, who, we trust, has been sought and found. It is an Angel's joy; yea, in rejoicing over him, you share the joy of our Lord, Who invites His friends and neighbours, those who ever do His will and stand near Him, to joy over His sheep which was lost. As yet, indeed, this stray sheep is not laid up in the everlasting fold; the piece of silver is not replaced in the everlasting treasury; yet, through the prayers here offered, may he hope the more to be brought unto the end, to have his soiled face cleansed by the abundance of the grace of God, and that Royal Image, which sin had marred, again by penitence renewed.

To-day, then, is a festival of penitence and love. He hath, in this, done what he could out of love, imperfect as it must be, to Him Who first loved him; and you will pray, that He Who has this day accepted his offering, will, for our loving Redeemer's sake, accept himself, will bind up the wounds which yet remain, pour into them the austere wine of penitence, and if it seem good to Him, the oil of His consolations, at least the healing Unction of His Spirit, and restore to his soul some portion of the grace and beauty which by sin it lost.

And although he does not wish to be spoken of in this holy place, which he feels himself deeply unworthy to have offered to the praise of his Redeemer, yet it may just be said, that in all the beautifying of this house, one thought, which God, he hoped, had worked into his soul, was before him, how to set forth the doctrine of the Cross, the Cross borne for us, and now, as good soldiers or as penitents, to be borne by us. He wished the Cross, every where to meet the eye, inviting the soul to rest in love on Him Who bore it; that lifted up toward Him here, by His Agony[a], His Cross and Passion, we might through His mercy be brought to the glory of His Ascension, and be received into the everlasting Arms which He stretched out on the Cross for us, and in ascending, lifted up to bless us.

On this day then, of the acceptance of the offering of a penitent, it seemed the more fitting to speak of God's acceptance of loving penitents; and since on the following, such of us as remain, hope to meditate on some of the most solemn subjects which can fill the soul, it seemed disposed by God's Providence,

---

[a] The Agony of our Lord and His Sacred Passion, the Bearing of the Cross, and the Crucifixion are subjects of the three large windows in S. Saviour's. At the East end is that of the Ascension. The object of this position was to inculcate that by His Cross and Passion must we be brought, if we are brought, to the glories of the Ascension.

we might hope, that we should first begin with thoughts of His love.

The sinner, to whom our Lord thus spake, is the very image of penitents. She is the picture of the Gentile Church[b], sunk, ere they were called, in open, putrifying, sins, yet, while the Jews in false righteousness despised them, called in penitence to love. And, in herself, she is in her actions the model of penitence after deep abiding sin, as David is in the deep groans of the penitential Psalms, and S. Peter in his continual bitter tears. "When I think of the penitence of Mary," says S. Gregory[c], "I had rather weep than speak! Whose heart so stony, that the tears of this sinner should not soften him after the pattern of her penitence?" Who, my brethren, could in mind stand beside that penitent, and not catch some feeling of her penitence? All was against her, except that look or word of her Lord which melted her, and the secret grace which drew her to the Fount of grace. She was, as we know, wealthy. As soon as she was converted, she ministered to our Lord of her substance. You know how difficult it is to be penitent among riches, comfort, and ease. She comes with the precious ointment, the instrument of her luxury. You know how luxury deadens and closes up the soul. Death was still far from her; Scripture tells us of a portion of her beauty, when it, the instrument of sin, whereby she took souls prisoners, had become hallowed by touching the Feet of our Lord in penitence. Yet how does promise of

[b] S. Greg. in Evang. Hom. 33. § 5. S. Cyr. Al. in Joann. 11, 6; and to the same effect Orig. in S. Matt. Tr. 35, and S. Ambr. ad loc.   [c] l. c.

life delay penitence, day by day! She was then affluent, at ease, luxurious, fair, the world before her, flattered doubtless, perhaps scarcely feeling her own shame; we know at least, how in this Christian land, such outward things as birth and wealth will fence off public shame. Such was she without, and what within! "A sinner," with that sin which most destroys every spark of life, an adulteress, and, it is thought, a widow, with none to reproach, none to call her to herself. One more fearful thing Holy Scripture tells, more or less true still of all, who are guilty of her sin; for where the Holy Spirit dwells not, that body is the dwelling-place of unclean spirits, trampled under foot of devils, "a cage of every unclean and hateful bird." But as she had reached the height of evil, she humbled herself to the depth of penitence. "Out of whom," Scripture tells us shortly after, "Jesus cast out seven devils." Our Lord Himself tells us that there were different kinds of this miserable dominion of Satan, when He says of one, "This kind goeth not out, but by prayer and fasting." We are apt to think of those miserable cases of possession by Satan, as though those so held must needs always have had those outward marks of trouble and disquiet, which some we read of in the Gospel had. But Satan holds not in one way only. Perhaps his surest hold is the most secret. Even now, in those cases which bear most likeness to it, there is often no outward shew of violence. Inwardly restless they must ever be! Our Lord speaks of the unclean spirit as seeking rest and finding none. How can he be at rest, who has no love, no hope, no God; but is all hate? And they whom he influences, or in whom he dwells, can have no rest, having lost the centre, in Whom Alone there is rest, God. But their unrest does not always shew itself without. There is, even now, often deep unrest within, which is soothed in a manner, as it was in the unclean spirit, by going in a way out of itself. Wretched people are often goaded on to wickedness, to get rid of the pressure of this inward unrest. Restless [d] is the very name of the wicked in the language which was formed by God. Such then seems to have been the Magdalene. Actually indwelt by devils, but those leading not to outward violence but to sins. And as in Holy Scripture we read of different spirits, according to the different sins to which they tempt men, (as a spirit of jealousy, a lying spirit, a spirit of fornications, an evil or malicious spirit,) so it seems likely that the seven devils cast out of her held her captive heretofore to seven deadly sins. "What," says S. Gregory, "are pointed out by the seven devils, but the whole range of sin? For since all time is comprised in seven days, a whole is figured by seven. Mary then had seven devils, who was full of all sins." And not merely was she thus given up to sins, not sin alone dwelt in her, but the very authors of sins had mastery over her body, and (as we see in some measure even now) moved her limbs and ruled her.

Such then was she. All fair without, within all decayed; nothing without to impel her to penitence, nothing within (of which we know) to draw her; in the mastery of Satan and possessed by seven devils. Nothing was there within, except that which alone is of avail, the constraining grace of Christ. He Who

[d] רשע.

made her, saw, in this her hopeless state, the capacity of penitence, and, at once, remade her. By what look, what words, we know not, on what outward occasion, or by what inward drawings! She stands before us, the more as a model of all penitents, in that of the special history of her conversion, we are told nothing. One mightier than the strong man was there, had taken from him the armour wherein he trusted, and spoiled his house. The dwelling-place of devils was become the abode of love. She who had lived in deeds of darkness, was in the presence of the Light; she, in whom had been seven devils, was at the Feet of Jesus in her right mind. All was changed. She shrank from nothing, heeded nothing, but Him Alone, Whose love had brought her to herself and to Him. Love is stronger than shame, which people fear more than death. All, humility, contrition, faith, fervour, knowledge, love, trust, were poured into her at once; all stand out in that one act. All else vanished from her sight, all love of pleasure from her heart; she saw Him, on Whom her being hung, and all besides fell off, as wax melteth at the fire, as she was drawn to Him. She, who had been before the idol of others, makes herself the mark of shame. Among those who held themselves righteous and despised others, who would have shrunk from her touch, as they thought her Lord should, she (marvelling, doubtless, at His condescending love far more than they) stood an unbidden guest, a sinner, marring their self-pleasing feast with a sinner's tears. But what has the penitent to do with any save Him, the Fountain of mercy, her Redeemer and her God? She knew by that inward drawing, that He Who knew her heart so as to draw her, heard her speechless prayer, and would receive with tenderness herself, whom in mercy He had drawn. She stood at His Feet. She dared not as yet meet His Eye. She, who with a holy shamelessness shrank not from the scorn of men, shrank with a holy awe and fear at the Eye of God. We feel, as penitents, that we must come to God; and yet, when penitents, then is it aweful to come into that Presence, which awed us not in sin. And how would we stand, my brethren, in that blessed, but aweful, Presence? May such of us as have been in any degree like her, so stand with her, until we too hear those blessed words, "Thy faith hath saved thee; go in peace." How does every word betoken her humility! She came to pour on Him, in token of her love, the gifts she had hitherto wasted on herself. But she does not, at once, approach Him. She stood behind Him weeping. "Christ sat at meat there," says a father*, "not to receive chalices flavoured with honey, perfumed with flowers, but from the very fountain of her eyes to drink the tears of a penitent. God hungereth after the tears of offenders; He thirsteth for the tears of sinners." His Feet had gone in search of her who was astray; the dust clave to them, even as He bore our sins upon Him, although He was harmless, separate from sin; they could not touch His all-holy Soul. But with that simple love, wherewith she would afterwards embalm His Body, now would she remove from His feet the dust which, in seeking her, had gathered round them. And then, when she found that they disdained not a sinner's tears, when tears

* S. Chrys.

from her were allowed to rest upon them, how was all the fervour of her love unlocked! And even so, we too doubtless have felt, that when, by some token of inward peace, He accepts, as we hope, some gush of sorrow, or deep abhorrence of ourselves, which He has given, then have we seemed, like her, able to pour ourselves forth in penitence! "Blessed tears," again to speak in a father's words [f], "blessed tears, which not only can wash our sins, but even bedew the footsteps of the Divine Word, so that His goings should abound in us! Blessed tears, in which is not only the redemption of sinners, but the refreshment also of the righteous; for it was a righteous man who cried, 'My tears have been my meat day and night.'" Oh how well it must have been with her then! How gladly would we ever remain with her at His Feet, though as yet He were silent to us! How blessed that our tears might rest upon them, even if we might not touch them! But what when, yet more, He allowed her to wash His Feet with her tears, and wipe them with the hair of her head, and kiss His Feet, and anoint them with the ointment? But He Who gave to a sinner such love, shall we wonder that He received the love He gave? First, love made her offer to her Redeemer all which she had hitherto abused to sin, and then through her offering He kindled in her new love. "What she had unworthily employed on herself," so sums up a father [g], "now she laudably offered unto God. With her eyes she had coveted things of earth; now she wore them out with tears of penitence. Her hair she once displayed to set forth her face: now with her

[f] S. Ambr. ad loc. L. 6. § 18.   [g] S. Greg. ad loc.

hair she was wiping the tears. With her mouth she had spoken proud things; now, kissing the Feet of the Lord, she pressed it to the Footsteps of her Redeemer. Whatever enjoyments she had in herself, so many offerings she devised of herself; she turned every sin into a virtue, that whatsoever of her had despised God in sin, might wholly serve God in penitence." How He would make her a model to us sinners both in her penitence and His love! The first tears of sorrow had but just, at His bidding, gushed from the stony heart He had melted, and she is admitted to the privilege of the Bride. She had but just washed off the dust of her sins, and she is allowed to kiss the Feet of God. Her sin-defiled lips stain not the Holy, but the cleansing touch of that Flesh Which He gave for the life of the world, hallows them. He, from the hem of Whose garment Virtue had gone forth to heal; He, Who was Himself that living purifying Form of fire, His Sacred Manhood, filled with His Godhead Which is a consuming Fire, touched her lips, and her iniquity is taken away and her sin purged [h]. The lips which she had profaned were the very instruments of her acceptance: the kiss is the very token of reconciliation, the pledge of love; her sins had separated her from her God; now she may touch Him. O wondrous love, which would thus teach us sinners, how He would receive our returning love, and not endure only, but praise the penitent's love which He had given! He Who called her to His Feet, Who gave her the grace, there in humility to remain, in perseverance to cleave, speaks not of His own but of her love, "Since I came,

[h] Is. vi.

she hath not ceased to kiss My Feet." O blessed portion! To touch her Physician, to hold Him that He leave her not; to rest her weary head as the footstool of those glorious Feet which brought life to the world, which were wearied; to give rest to the heavy-laden and the weary; in washing them, herself to be washed from her sins; in wiping them, to have the stains of her soul removed; anointing them, to be anointed with that Blessed Spirit,

>Whose blessed Unction from above,
>Is comfort, life, and fire of love.

Such was the outward change; but who can tell the inward, whereof these were the tokens? Who of us could trust himself to speak of the depth of that inward faith and love, which Christ in an instant accepted fully, for which He, at once, blotted out all the past with His own gracious sentence, "Thy sins are forgiven thee," sent her away, free from the past, in peaceful hope for the future, her heart guarded by that peace which passeth all understanding, until at last, she should lay her down and take her rest in Him Who is our Peace? "Thy faith hath saved thee; go in peace." Who shall measure that faith, which knew her Physician Whom the Pharisee, who would honour Him, knew not, which knew that He had the power to forgive sins, knew that He was not a "man" and a "prophet" only, but "Who" He was that "forgiveth sins also," God and Man? Her very action shews that she knew and believed in Him Who could read her inmost thoughts, "knew who and what manner of woman she was who touched Him;" and so she spake to Him Who knew her wants, in silence by her devotion and her tears, heard the yet unuttered sentence of forgiveness in His silent permission that such as she should touch His Feet, yea felt that she had more than she dared to ask from Him Who is more ready to give than we to pray, that she was not forgiven only, but restored and loved. And so, both forgiven much, she loved much, and her much love completed the fulness of her forgiveness. "Her sins which are many are forgiven her; for she loved much." Oh who shall tell the depth of that love which He shed abroad in her heart, which He, the Maker of the heart and its Judge, pronounced "much love?" He Who said to S. Peter, on his penitence, "Simon son of Jonas, lovest thou Me," and asked for a three-fold love to efface the three-fold denial, and that he should, as it were, gather into himself a manifold love, to requite the manifold forgiveness, Himself bears witness to her, the chief of sinners, that she "loved much." What can be "much" in the sight of God? Could the Seraphim's burning love to Him the Fount of love, from Whom all love flows forth, yet dwells fully only in Himself, the Co-equal Trinity, yea is Himself? He tells us of others whom He hath loved, the beloved disciple, and, as it seems, this very Mary and her sister Martha and Lazarus, (and they must much have loved Whom He so loved,) and Moses He pronounces "faithful in all His house," and Abraham He calls "His friend;" and yet, to teach us sinners, how, if penitent, we may ourselves hope to love, He has kept this praise in store for one who was a grievous sinner; of the woman who was a sinner, alone does He bear witness, "she loved much." Well might that inward fire of love burn out of the

Loving penitence. 13

soul the dross of sin, which He Who came on earth to kindle it, called "much."

Such was her change. We need not then be startled to think that she, who "chose the good part which shall not be taken from her," the sister of Martha, of whom it is said, "Jesus loved Martha and her sister and Lazarus," is the same [i] as this blessed, holy, penitent. We have pictured to us Mary, sitting at the Feet of Jesus, pious, devout, child-like, calm, peaceful, contemplative, and can hardly think that she who so chose, had ever so miserably chosen the world and the flesh, or that Jesus so loved one once so fallen. Yet this were to doubt the power of grace. Is it strange that she who stood at our Lord's Feet, should, when restored, sit in thankful adoration at those blessed Feet, where she had received her pardon? or what God had cleansed, should it be any longer common or unclean? Could not His Word remake what He had made? or He Whom His love for sinners brought down from Heaven to the likeness of our sinful flesh, is it strange that He so loved the sinner whom His love had cleansed, to whom He had given such glow of love? "The love of God," says a holy man [k], "readily followeth our love which it forecometh. For how should He be slow to love again, whom, as yet not loving, He loved?"

And so Holy Scripture in one blessed convert, of the number of those whose conversion is, humanly, least hopeful, shews us the depth both of penitent and forgiven love, and in both the depth of the love of God. Blessed is the thought after deep sin, that we shall one day put off the body wherein we have

[i] See note A. at the end.   [k] S. Bern. Ep. 107.

sinned, that the members, once the instruments of unrighteousness, shall be wholly laid aside, though in dishonour, and we shall receive them, anew, we hope, in glory; blessed tokens of decay, which are the cock-crowing of the resurrection in purity conformed to our Lord's. But the history of this penitent brings us nearer hopes of present restoration, calm brightness of joy, holy aspirations, and even the secret intercourse of our Lord with the soul which loves Him. For we see her, so deeply, once so hopelessly, stained, admitted to His friendship, sitting at His Feet, in holy contemplation, hearing from His mouth the words of life, the object of His tender love, so that when, on her brother's death, Jesus saw her weeping and the Jews also weeping, which came with her, He "groaned in the spirit and was troubled," and we are told "Jesus wept." We see her, a sinner, who two years before had stood at His Feet, in shame and tears, admitted to anoint His Sacred Head, (yet then too not forgetting to anoint in humility the Feet whereat she had received mercy,) her act a hidden prophecy, anointing His Body for His Burial, owned as "a good work wrought upon" Himself; proclaimed as a memorial of her, wherever the Everlasting Gospel is preached. And when for us He hung upon the Cross, where He said He should draw all unto Him, while others, who yet loved Him and ministered to Him of their substance, "stood afar off," she, amid the scoffing, blaspheming, multitude, (as before amid the contempt of the Pharisees, at the feast,) is drawn again alone to Him by His love, to its very foot. There, in that sacred, solemn nearness, there stand only His Virgin Mother, His

Loving penitence. 15

Mother's sister, His virgin beloved disciple, and this deep penitent. There we love to imagine her, as Christian feeling is wont to paint her to our eyes, enfolded round the Cross, as near as she could, still to His sacred Feet. To Him yet living on the Cross, she clave; His Divine Body she watched, laid in the tomb; earliest by the tomb, on Easter Morning, is the penitent; she, when even the beloved disciple and S. Peter went away to their homes, believing, remained by the tomb, weeping; with tears she had first found Him, with tears anew she seeks Him; she cannot leave the empty tomb; she cannot believe she shall not see Him; she sought and found Him not; she sought with persevering tears and found Him; she looked in (as love is wont) even when she had seen that He was not there, and she saw angels; but angels gave her no comfort, for she sought Him Alone Whom her soul loved, the Lord of angels and her own; and Whom her love sought she saw, and He called her by name, as He doth His own sheep, and made a penitent the first witness of the Resurrection, the apostle to His Apostles, the herald of life, the announcer of His Ascension and His Glory. And since this were little to her love, (for she sought no office even about Him, but only Himself,) while He said to her "Touch Me not, for I am not yet ascended," He promised her a time when she should touch Him, the earnest and first-fruits of His Presence in mystery after the Resurrection; throughout eternity, the fulness of sight and of fruition. "Then," says a father[1], "He began in an ineffable way to be nearer in His Divinity, as He became further in His

[1] S. Leo Serm. 2 de Ascens. Dom. c. 4.

Humanity. Then began more instructed faith to approach to the Son, Coequal to the Father, by the step of the mind, and not to need the touch of the bodily Substance in Christ whereby He was less than the Father, since, while the Nature of His glorified Body remained, the faith of believers was thither called, where not by the hand of flesh, but by spiritual perception, is the Only-Begotten, Equal to the Father, touched." "I will not," He saith, "that thou come to Me in a bodily way, nor own Me by thy bodily senses; I put thee off, to give thee higher things; greater things I prepare for thee. When I ascend unto My Father, then shalt thou touch Me more perfectly and more truly, apprehending what thou touchest not, and believing what thou seest not." And as, to those who love much, our Lord does vouchsafe from time to time, distincter, though passing, tokens of His Presence, so it is a beautiful thought that this blessed penitent may, through her life, have ever been seeking and finding, ever mourning that she had once been so displeasing unto Him Whom now she loved, ever longing for His Presence, visited by His consolations, and then again longing, and again comforted.

My brethren, if we think against what light we have sinned, although we may have not committed her actual sin, who shall say that he is not such as she once was? She sinned not against such grace; she was not, ere she sinned, the Temple of the Holy Ghost; she knew not that God had become Man in order to make her anew an image of Himself; she had not been made a member of Himself; she knew not how dear a Price her redemption was to cost, or what she was wasting; she counted not the Blood of the covenant wherewith she was sanctified, an unholy thing, nor did despite to the Spirit of grace, nor (words which one could not utter but that they are the words of God) "trod under foot the Son of God, crucified Him afresh, and put Him to an open shame." She loved Him Who pardoned her, ere she knew how He loved her, for she knew not the Price, whereat He had purchased her pardon; she loved the Heavenly Physician Who healed her, though she knew not that the medicine was His own precious Blood. We, especially if we have been guilty of some deep though subtle sin, have sunk lower than she. And shall we not long to rise with her? If you have not begun already, you would now begin; you would wish to know the sweetness of her tears; you would wish to be admitted near your Saviour's Feet; you, nay we, would all long to hear His mild forgiving voice, "Thy sins are forgiven thee, thy faith hath saved thee, go in peace;" or far more than any peace on earth, we would long to have that foretaste of endless bliss, "much to love" Him Who has so patiently borne, so long foreborne, Who, when we deserved only Hell, still holds open to us the gates of Heaven.

Would any begin? "To whom little is forgiven, the same loveth little." The first step earnestly to return, is to know where we have been. Think you not, that, as the Magdalene stood at her Saviour's Feet, all the foulness of her life stood out before her, in one aweful view, by the holiness and majesty of Him, to Whom she was come? The beginning of penitence, then, is to review our whole life, with prayer to God to reveal it to us, and confess it, at least, at the Foot of His Cross. It is often a ghastly sight, which could only be borne at our Saviour's Feet. If it is too aweful to bear alone, or does any thing weigh heavily, or need we counsel, or long we for peace through His pardoning words, our Church has taught us how to obtain it, by "opening our grief to some discreet and learned minister of God's word." Great grace is so bestowed by God on those who seek it, for His forgiveness and His love.

Our first step then is to contemplate our sins by the light of His love. Darkness seems blacker when over against the light. Yet not even thus can we gain contrition or love. Could we, by any thoughts on God's mercy, gain love, this would be to convert ourselves. His look melted Magdalene's icy heart, His word cast out the seven devils; and would we have the fire of love kindled in us, or the demons of our sins cast out, we must pray Him to give us power to pray, ask for His gracious look to bring us to ourselves, wait in His Presence, seek Him, desire Him, grieve, for love of Him, that we have offended Him, desire to grieve, not for ourselves alone, not so much that we have deserved Hell, not for the glory we have forfeited, not that we are the wrecks of what we might, by His grace, have been, but that we have sinned against Him Who so loved us, and, as far as in us lay, done dishonour to Him, our Redeemer and our God. Great is the power of love with God; for it is His chief gift, since God is love. "Her sins which are many are forgiven, because she loved much." It seems a bold word which holy

Loving penitence.

men [m] have said, " When a sinner, rising again from his sins and wholly turning away from them, purposes for ever to serve God and to live to Him Alone, He, that Eternal and boundless Goodness, shews Himself as gracious to him, as if he had never fallen into sin. For He perfectly remitteth to him all his sins, nor will He ever impute them to him, were they as many as all mankind together have committed, if he but grieve from the heart purely to the glory of God, and hate his sins chiefly on this ground, that they displease God. For that very fervent love, from which that sorrow flows, consumes all the rust of sins, if but that love and contrition be great enough, and, as it ought, with his whole strength." It seems a bold word; yet He Himself has taught it us, Who fell at once on the neck of the returning prodigal, and clothed him with the best robe; He, although He continued the merciful chastisement, said at once to David, "The Lord also hath put away thy sin." He, when He gives much love, owns, at once, the love He gave. He put no delays, He teaches us to say in the Psalms to Himself, " I said, I will confess my sins unto the Lord, and so Thou forgavest the iniquity of my sin." He hath said, " Turn unto Me, and I will turn unto you." He hath said, " If the wicked turn from his sin, and do that which is lawful and right, none of his sins which he hath committed shall be mentioned unto him; he shall surely live, he shall not die." No bounds hath the infinite mercy of God, but what we set by our want of contrition and of love.

[m] Rusbroch. de præcip. quibusd. virt. c. 10. Opp. p. 184. Thauler. Inst. spirit. c. 20.

But love of God cannot co-exist with self-love, or want of love to man. And therefore true penitents have ever sought, with Magdalene, to break off self-indulgence, to turn the instruments of sin and luxury into means of penitence; as they had used things unlawful, to deny self things lawful, at times at least, as God shall put into the power of each; to shew love to Christ's poor, in order in them to shew love to Himself. We cannot now wash His Feet, nor wipe them with our hair, nor anoint them, but He, when He withdrew His bodily Presence, left us those in whom to minister to Himself. "The poor ye have always with you." "We wash His feet with tears," says a father[n], "if we are moved with compassion to any the lowest members of our Lord, and count their sorrow our own. We wipe our Lord's Feet with our hair, when we shew pity to His saints, (with whom through pity we suffer,) even by cutting off things superfluous to us. We kiss the feet we wipe, if we love earnestly whom through our bounty we relieve, not feeling the needs of our neighbour a burden to ourselves, nor giving with the hand, while the heart is chilled to love."

We are met, my brethren, to joy in such an act of a penitent; you who can rejoice over him with an Angel's joy, will not deny yourselves a portion of his joy. Blessed and hopeful sign of love were it, if this day's united effort might, at least, go far to rear such an house to our Redeemer's praise, as this which He has to-day vouchsafed to make His own; a joy to him, with whom you sympathize, that his penitent love has called forth yours; a joy to Angels,

[n] S. Greg. ad. loc. § 5.

who joy when the lost are found; yea, I may dare to say, a joy to our glorified Redeemer, since He vouchsafes to say, "Rejoice with Me, for I have found the sheep which I had lost." God hath mercy upon us, that we may have mercy on those, upon whom, with us, He would have mercy. Whether He has preserved you from deeply falling, or raised you, when fallen, you, if you now love Him, will long that all should, together with you, love Him, with that love with which you love Him, yea rather with which He has loved you. "If thou place thy hope in God," says a father [o], "what office hast thou, but to praise Him Whom thou lovest, and make others love Him with thee?—Lay hold on Him, whoever can, whoever shall possess Him; not too narrow is He; no bounds wilt thou place in Him; Him shall ye each possess wholly, Him shall ye all have wholly."

First then and chiefest, brethren, (for such is the choicest gift,) in purpose of heart, give yourselves. Your souls are they, which He, the Good Shepherd, seeks. Wide-open is the Bosom of His Almighty, all-containing, love; wide did He stretch His Arms upon the Cross, that He might encompass within His love, the sins and sorrows of the whole world. Think we over with sorrow the sins of our youth; weep we for them, at least, with burning inward shame at His Feet; and He will not shrink at our sin-defiled touch; He will account our penitence as innocence, our grief for our sins as purity; more gladly will He forget our sins, than we willingly remember them. He will not suffer us only to wash

[o] S. Aug. in Ps. 72. § 34.

His Feet, but Himself will wash us anew in His own Blood; He will not only admit on His Sacred Feet a sinner's kiss, but He Himself has said, He will fall upon the neck of His returning prodigals and kiss them; while we stand at His Feet weeping, He will gather us into His Bosom, He will hide us in His wounded Side, He will place us near His Almighty Heart, the Fountain opened for sin and uncleanness; He will hush our sorrows, and compensate our brief tears with His endless joy; where with the Father and the Holy Ghost He liveth and reigneth, One God, to Whom &c.

SERMON II.

THE NATURE OF SIN [a].

(Wednesday Morning, Oct. 29.)

JOHN xv. 24.

"*Now have they both seen and hated both Me and My Father.*"

THERE are things in this world too great for us to take into our minds. We hear of them, and believe them, and know them, and feel them, but there is more in them than we can reach, and thought is lost when it would take hold of them. Many such things there are for our good, but there is not only a 'mystery of Godliness,' but likewise a 'mystery of iniquity.' *Man* let *sin* into the world, but he knew not what he did, nor can he know, save in eternity. Sin is around us and within us, embitters our life, affrights us in death, haunts us day and night,—but what is it? On the one hand it is grounded in unsearchable nothingness. In all creation, it alone God created not; the "rich wisdom of the Word [b]" made not it, and therefore it is a nothing. It hath

[a] [To p. 37. Rev. C. Marriott.]   [b] S. Prosper.

no life, for it is death; no substance c, for it is a corruption only and spoiling of what God made "very good." It is a departure from the unchangeable Good, the Source of all being, and so tending to not-being. It issues not in life, but in death, even though that death is deathless. It is a disordering of nature, not nature itself; a privation, a defect, which, when it is healed, ceases to be. What then is that which God created not, which is the absence of all which He Is, Holiness, Righteousness, Love, which existeth only as beings are apart from Him, which, when in penitence we return to Him, He blotteth out, so that it is no more? What is it that we sin for? When we do evil, where is our reward? There is indeed something that hangs before us and draws us toward it; but when we come to it, and try to see clearly what it is, where is it to be found? If we gain pleasure, where is it but in the moment? Search for it after, and it is gone, and the soul is left empty and alone and desolate, with nothing to lean upon, and nothing to feed upon. We may turn again to it like a dog to his vomit, but once again all is gone, and it is a vanity, an emptiness at last. So it is with riches, if we try to think

c S. Aug. Conf. vii. p. 122. Oxf. Tr. "If things shall be deprived of all good, they shall no longer be. That evil then, as to which I enquired, whence it is, is not any substance, for, were it a substance, it should be good." cont. Sec. Manich. c. 11. "When the mind stoopeth aside to the body, it doth not become a body, and yet through its desires, sinking away from its End, in a manner partakes of the fleshly nature, (corporascit,) so also the lofty nature of Angels, when over-pleased with its lordship over itself, it turned away its affection to what was less [than God is] both began less to be than it was, and in its degree, tended to nothing." et passim. [Ed.]

what they are; and with the world's praise, 'vanity of vanities! all is vanity!'

One thing in sin is real. One thing abides, and stares us in the face when we think of it, though this also is out of our reach, and above the mastery of our minds. We cannot take it in and know it all. The truth of it glares upon us, look which way we will, but we cannot grasp it and overcome it or put it aside.

One thing in sin is real—that it sets man against his Maker.

O aweful truth! O deep and unsearchable gulf of misery beneath! But what eye shall dare to look into the boundless height above, and to search what it is, to be at strife with the Almighty? Yet this we must learn to think of, if we would know our own dangers, and seek our only safety. How fearful a thing sin is, we cannot find out, any more than we can measure the power and goodness of God. But we must open our eyes to what is before us, and turn them outward and inward to see what we can, lest we be like the rich man, who saw not things in their true light, until 'in hell he lift up his eyes, being in torments.'

Strange it is that such weak fleeting beings as we are should have it put in their power to set themselves against the Almighty. Yet they cannot freely choose to be His and to serve Him, without having the power also to refuse His service. The choice is given them not to entrap them into evil, but, on their choosing aright, to give them the greatest good. What He has prepared for them we know not, but we know that it is their part to choose the good, and to make trial of His goodness, and not of their own power against His.

It were enough, that sin puts out the laws and order of God's work, which He made ' very good.' Strange and sorrowful it is, that the beings He has made, and set in highest place in this world, should so misuse all that He has put into their hands. Good and beautiful was its order as He appointed it, and even now, as it is after man's first transgression, beautiful would be its order, if man did but obey His laws. But sin mars all. The good fruits of the earth are not received with thankfulness and dispensed with justice and mercy, but grasped or grasped at with greediness, and grudgingly dealt out, or sottishly wasted. The common blessings of the light and air, almost too pure in themselves to afford matter of abuse, are made to serve the purposes of wickedness and disorder, are stinted or embittered to the weak by oppression, are forfeited or made tasteless to the low-minded by intemperance. The active mind of man is misapplied to schemes of ambition, violence, gain, fraud, deceit, or to the indulgence of accursed imaginations, that make men discontented with God's real gifts. The relation of man and woman, that should be sanctified in the family, is made an occasion of vile and hurtful lust. Children, that ought to be brought up in ways of peace and godliness, are left to be the slaves of passion, or taught little, save the art of getting certain earthly gains, nothing of the behaviour that is right for them as members of God's family on earth. They are brought up in the ways of their fathers, weak, headstrong, self-pleasing, envious, false, vain, greedy; and are likely rather to undo what remains of God's good order in the world, than to build up what has been pulled in pieces by those before them.

This is not a true picture of all Christian men and families, but of the common course of sin, when it has its way. There are those, blessed be God, for whom the gifts of holiness are effectual, though with imperfection. There are those, even without the highest gifts of the Church, who set themselves against sin according to their knowledge. But I spoke of sin, as it is where people do not strive against it *as sin;* and but a little of its foul, corrupting, undoing, deforming work did I pourtray.

Let even one who has striven against it look back on it in his own heart and life, and think of the good it has spoiled and undone, the love it has broken off, the purity it has sullied, the holy sanctuaries of thought and feeling it has profaned, and he will most likely find cause for even a deeper hatred of it, than he would learn from knowing the outward lives of criminals and vagabonds.

And the reason why he will find more cause to hate sin from looking within than without is, that which really makes sin what it is.

There are those who see no more in sin than a putting things out of a certain order which is best for the happiness of all. But they miss of its real nature. Sin is a turning away of the mind and heart from God their true good, after things that are, one and all, vanity.

Man will have himself to himself, out of the hand of his Maker. *There* is the foundation of sin. Then he will have other creatures to himself, in himself, not in and for his Maker and theirs. He thinks to be his own master, and master of what more he can get. He becomes the slave of his own lust, and of the next thing he cannot get. He may seem happy outwardly, and may not offend the world by his conduct. But his slavery, and wretchedness, and corruption are within. The misery is that an immortal spirit, made for the knowledge and love of God, should be turning away from Him, madly to set up itself, and as madly to give itself up to things beneath it.

And this turning away from Him, and taking of His creatures for self-willed use, sets man even against Him. It is going to war with Him, and trying to seize from Him a part of His kingdom. Vain purpose indeed, so vain that one can hardly think of it as really entertained; yet such is the aim of multitudes of men.

Now, for the present, God does not shew Himself so much without as within. His works indeed tell of Him, and proclaim His power; still they are but His handywork, not Himself. Those who do not know Him otherwise see but little of Him in them. They talk of vast power, every where diffused, and of infinite and yet most minute intelligence, but they scarce think of His holy will, His all-wise election, His hatred of evil, His everlasting Love, His marvellous government.

He must be known within, if we would really know Him. Sought far and wide, looked-for in the fire, felt-for in the earthquake, listened-for in the mighty wind, there at last the devout soul finds Him, speaking with gentle but awful utterance; a still small voice, in the depth of its own being. There it is that He makes things known to us, as they truly are, and there that we must deal with Him for life or death. There He offers to be with us, and we welcome or scorn His Presence. There it is, therefore, that we must look, if we would see what sin is. Conscience there is His court, and, if we listen, there His Law is declared. Even there, indeed, we cannot so find Him, as actually to fasten even the eyes of the mind upon His very substance. But there we meet Him unseen in such wise, that it is Himself and not any mere image or shadow, to Whom we bow down our will, and to Whom we uplift our love and thankfulness.

Our own soul is created in His Image, and within that Image, itself the inmost thing we can steadily behold, we worship the Living God, or, if we worship not, we bring our sin into His very Presence, where it is self-condemned, and all its foulness comes to view, if there is an eye to see it. And those who are used to look for God within, have an eye to see it, and they detect it there, and loathe their own inward corruption as seeing it in the light of eternity, and in the presence of Himself, the very Beauty of Holiness.

Here it is that sin takes its last and true character; here it is seen as *setting itself against God*. In the outward world it seems only to set itself against His law and order, and the course and well-doing of His works. But within the heart it confronts and defies Himself. Such is the perfect act of sin, and such becomes the character of him who gives himself up to it. Defiance of God, persevered in, is hatred of Him.

Thus does sin in man work its way back to the

source of all sin, and complete in him the likeness of Satan. Little is taught us in Holy Scripture of the beginning of *his* fall, yet perhaps we may gather it from the following connection of different passages, so taken by holy Fathers. Satan is called the prince of this world, and the king of Babylon is one of his types. Our Lord says of Satan, "I saw Satan like lightning fall from heaven." Of the king of Babylon Isaiah sings [d], "How art thou fallen from heaven, O Lucifer, son of the morning! How art thou cut down to the ground, which didst weaken the nations! For thou hast said in thine heart, I will ascend into heaven, I will exalt my throne above the stars of God: I will sit also upon the mount of the congregation, in the sides of the north. I will ascend above the heights of the clouds; I will be like the Most High. Yet shalt thou be brought down to hell, to the sides of the pit."

This has been taken to shew the character of the sin by which Satan fell, and it agrees with the character of the sin to which he tempted our first parents. "Ye shall be as gods, knowing good and evil." The will to be a god to himself is the very essence of sin in a created being. This principle of evil runs through all sins great and small, but it is more seen in some than in others. We see it most simply in the description of Satan, in the sin of man's fall, and in the extreme cases that go before God's heavy judgements in Holy Scripture. But in every sin it is really present, and working toward death eternal.

To see what it really is, look at those cases. Satan, a mighty angel in the very presence of and amidst

[d] Is. xiv. 12—15.

The nature of sin.

the glory of the Most High, once makes the choice of setting up himself against his Maker, and is condemned to the blackness of darkness for ever, cast out and fallen for eternity. One choice of sin turns an angel, perhaps the very first of angels, into a devil, for ever accursed, for ever banished from the face of God, for ever to be subject to His utmost wrath.

And even man, who in his very punishment finds mercy, for him what is the punishment of one transgression? Grace withdrawn from himself and his whole race. Death to himself and all his offspring, and after death, unless he be restored, no hope. The power of the Wicked one over him, dragging him toward the second death. What a change is this to be made in the good work of the Creator! What must we think of the act, that brought down this judgement from Him, Whose mercy is over all His works?

I speak of this now, not in order to stir up the fear of punishment, but to open to our minds the thought of sin's real nature, and its accursedness before God. By these signs we may faintly see how He regards it, and if we cannot bring ourselves to perceive how much it is to be abhorred, we may yet learn to know, that we do not enough abhor it, and that there is some mystery about it, that our eyes are not pure enough to see. This conviction may be one step towards a clearer sight, especially if it leads us to correct ourselves, and to undo the ill-doing that has blinded us, and to feel after Him Whom we have left, and mourn that we have left Him. This alone, well considered, is enough to shew us that sin is really a setting one's self against God. He has His way for us, and that way He cannot forego. It would be an undoing of His own creation. He will not make us a fool's paradise, when we will not have true blessedness. His work began in Truth and must end in Truth. Good must have its perfect work, and they that will not have good must have their way to the full. Man's ways are not as His ways. Men would go on halting between two opinions, one while leaning towards God, another while toward the world and self-will, and expect mercy to spare them, because they did not wholly reject their Creator. But He must have a perfect work. Sin must be condemned in the flesh, if it can be only by God made Flesh. Since evil has come into His creation, the world must see the aweful sight of perfect goodness in the midst of evil, and outwardly bowed down under it to the utmost. Still His work is perfect; and the very heavens new-made, when all the morning stars sung for joy, were not so pure in His sight, as shall be the New Jerusalem, the City of God, the Bride of the Lamb, when finally united to Him. Pure indeed she had not been of herself, but this again is more aweful, that she is washed and made white in the Blood of the Lamb. He dies, that He may be made perfect in His members that are upon earth. Good and evil are mixed now, but the good that is to be brought out is perfect.

Away then with every thought of bearing with sin for a little, and taking it easily, and letting it have its way in lesser matters. A little sin may be made great by indulging such unholy weakness. His will is, that we should be pure and holy and without

The nature of sin.

spot, and we must have no other will. Many, indeed, are our infirmities, and we cannot attend to all equally. But we spoil our work, if, while we attend to one especially, we make up our mind to give way in another. We may be tempted and give way, and yet we must not give it up. Making up our mind to spare a sin, is making up our mind against God. In this sense every sin is deadly, for we can make it deadly by obstinately keeping to it against Him. Every act of sin is not deadly, because, in some acts, sin is not fully chosen. But in proportion as we make up our mind to do such acts, we do fully choose it to ourselves, and so set ourselves against God. The first thought of sin may not be deadly, because it is not wilful, but when the thought is persisted in, till it becomes thoroughly wilful, it becomes even as the deed, a deadly sin. We count the deed worse than the thought, because it makes it clear that the will consents, and because in general the thought has gone before besides, and because, in it, the whole man works together for evil. But the thought may be so chosen and wilfully maintained, as to make it as truly an act of the man as the outward word or deed. And every degree of approach to this is an approach toward setting ourselves against God, and declaring that we will not be ruled by Him, nor have Him for our portion. It is not easy to speak on this subject without giving occasion to the slothful to take comfort in some false hope that their sins may not be deadly, because they have some feeling against them, and some wish to give them up. But we must say the truth, that there is a difference in acts of sin, and that some are really much more acts of infirmity, and some are really much more wilful than others. Men will take the easy side with themselves, and we can only warn them to take, instead, the safe side, and rather to judge themselves for an infirmity, as if it had been wilful, than run any risk of letting wilfulness pass for mere infirmity.

There is a wilfulness of sloth and self-indulgence, that passes itself off for infirmity, to the ruin of many souls. It is, when a man will not make the effort of shaking off a bad habit. He says he 'cannot,' when after all he could, if he would, submit himself to God. "The carnal mind is enmity against God, for it is not subject to the law of God, neither indeed can be." He 'cannot' make it as pleasant to his carnal nature to be bound by the rule of right as to follow his own will and passions. Of course he cannot. But he can, by the Spirit, subdue the carnal mind, and bring it captive to the law of Christ.

How miserable is it then to go on from day to day, and from year to year, doing things which we know are against the will of God, even half against our own will! Why can we not rouse ourselves to look upon them as though we saw Him present, as though we were borne for a moment out of ourselves, and could see the foolish, perverse, ungrateful wretch, busied with his own little fancies of the moment, holding up his head against his fellows, discontented at every thing that is not at his beck, and all the while fretting if he is expected to be careful, and to wait a few moments, or to forego a paltry indulgence, for the sake of more exactly and punctually fulfilling the end of his being, proposed by his Maker?

The nature of sin. 35

How would many a man turn in disgust from a mere likeness of himself and his own crooked ways livelily set before him! What ugliness would he find even in the less bold and open forms of sin, where people call it by mild names, and hardly fancy any guilt that can be laid up against them for judgement! Who is sufficient to speak of these things? Who, but must say, if he would speak the truth, words that ought to cut deep into his own heart? Excuse ourselves as we will, so it is, that very many of us set ourselves against God in this way. He would have us work earnestly at making our life and conversation better. We find it easier to leave it as it is, and we in fact refuse to work. Conscience calls on us, and we turn and bow to it, much like the son to whom his Father said, "Go and work in my vineyard," and he said, "I go, Sir," and went not. We go on idling, as if we trusted that conscience would go some other way, or drop asleep, and we might loiter away the next hour or two without fear of another rebuke. At last we come to fancy that we really are doing all that is required of us, and that the rebuke we have now and then from conscience merely tells us of what must be the case while we are subject to human infirmity. Thus do sins grow old upon us, that are really abominable in the sight of God, and frightful to any one who looks on them really as in His presence. We get used to them, and think nothing of them, and deal gently with them, and think we are serving our Maker, while we are on good terms with His enemies.

I speak not only of good men, who may be taken to task perhaps by the wicked, as David was by

Joab, when he let his own affection prevail over his duty as the king and judge of Israel. Many there are who think perhaps that this is their case, but who are rather like Saul when he spared Agag, and brought home the Amalekitish cattle. Let it never be forgotten, that sloth and negligence are one acknowledged form of deadly sin. We are bid destroy the enemy, and it is then wilfulness to spare. Never can it be well with us till we are heartily and boldly at work, warring against *all* the enemies of our King. It may be, that one requires our first collected strength, and almost undivided attention, but the others must not therefore have peace. We may leave them till they attack us, while we go forward to storm the fenced city of another, but we must make no friendship with them, nor even let them come peaceably to us. They are against our God, and we must be against them, or we cannot be wholly for Him.

We Christians are His soldiers, and must not shrink from carrying out His orders. If we make terms with sin, we are traitors to Him Who requires that we should be ready to resist even unto blood, and proclaims, "he that findeth his life shall lose it, but he that loseth his life for My sake shall find it." We cannot be as those who have not known Him and His will, nor even as those who rejected Him when they had only seen Him outwardly as the Son of Man, though of them He says that they hated the light, and came not to the light, lest their deeds should be reproved. If we hold off from opening ourselves to His searching, we are like them in not coming to the light, but we are worse, because we 'say we see' in a sense in which even they did not.

The nature of sin.

They said 'we see,' thinking the light of the Law enough. We say we see in the light of the Gospel. Worse then will it be with us than with them, if we will not come to that light, through any affection we have toward the things it would reprove.

O let it shine full upon all your ways! Hold back nothing! Bring every thought, word, look, motion, under its pure and searching light; and wink not, when your most favourite fancies and pursuits are before it. Look them through and through, if by any means you may detect in them the least spot of the canker of sin, and when you have found it, magnify it in your own eyes by a concentrated attention as though with a microscope, till you can see its horrid and monstrous shapes, and its incalculable growths and multiplications, and till you are not only emboldened to cast it from you, but loathe it, and loathe your very self for having borne it about you.

All that you can see is but a faint image of the malignity that inspires sin, of the spiritual wickedness against which you have to wrestle, and which sets itself utterly and wholly against God, and against all that is good and holy, and would turn the whole creation into loathsomeness and corruption. With this you take part, so far as you allow sin. For your souls' sake, and for the love of your Creator, your Redeemer, your Sanctifier, beware of such fellowship!

† And yet such companionship you do choose, if you knowingly allow a single sin, if you suspect it even, and take not pains to uproot it. Aweful as it is, willingly to remain in one single sin, is to choose

Satan, and reject God. That soul is not chaste, which loves any thing besides God. All else is matter of degree. There are heavier degrees of sin, and, in God's aweful justice, deeper degrees of damnation, as, in His loving-kindness, measures of bliss, all but infinitely exceeding each other. Sins do not indeed come alone, as we may see in the aweful history of others, or in our own miserable waste of grace. Sins, seemingly wide apart from one another, are held together by a mysterious band, as are graces. If then we know or suspect of any one sin, against which we are not earnestly combating, we may with reason believe that we have many more, which we less suspect. But this is to say that it is worse with us than we suspect, not that one sin may not be fatal. Many sins are probably bound up in that one. In many a heart which little thinks of it, there are the germs, at least, of all the deadly sins. Take the most common, and what seems the slightest. How common is it for persons to have too good an opinion of themselves; how very uncommon to be really humble; how few have set themselves in earnest even to seek real humility, or have made any great effort to gain it, or see whether they have it; and yet if they have it not, the very foundation of their spiritual building is wanting. Without humility, they cannot dig down to build on the Rock, a lowly Saviour, God become Man, to heal man's pride. Yet sins, as you know too well, spring up of themselves; graces are obtained with toil and prayer. If we suspect not our own want of lowliness, we have probably not begun to acquire it. What we have, is too likely a gift of nature, not of grace. And then all besides is probably but seeming virtue; at best, the fruit of imperfect grace, not the deep, inworked, transforming, grace of Christ. We speak of such sin slightly as though a little thing, that " such an one thinks too well of himself;" but with this one sin, how subtly will other sins entwine themselves, until there be a deep unknown labyrinth of sin ! How, e.g. with this one sin will there follow censoriousness, wrong dislikes, evil-speaking and with it slanders, then half-falsehood, detraction, readiness to believe evil, gladness at another's evil, (dreadful as this is, yet in order to keep up self-esteem), doubting or denying the grace of God in another, acting more or less consciously for the love of the praise of man rather than of God, impatience, hard unloving words, if affronted, and then lasting breaches of love ; making self the end, instead of God; how will such and many more spring up from one sin, so common as undue self-esteem. And yet in this list of subtle sins, there are the germs not of deadly sin only, or deadly sins, but forerunners of the sin against the Holy Ghost, eating out the love of God and of man, sins which, where they have gained the mastery, have ended, as in the Pharisees, in entire unbelief, and of whose number single sins have alone brought damnation.

This is a specimen only of the deadly evils, which will gather in every unsifted, uncleansed, conscience. People who are not strict with themselves are at ease, because their sinful tempers do not burst out in shocking overt acts. Evil acts strengthen and fix and give substance to evil tempers; but is it not frightful enough that these tempers should be within us, should be wrought into our souls, should shew their existence, if in no worse way, by slight words, or in the first spontaneous feelings of the mind, or when by some sudden emotion or more vehement disturbance, restraint is taken off and the lurking evil puts itself more forth? Single occasions in which men give way, prove more the existence of the secret evil, than a long period passed without any outbreak does its absence. Then only are we safe, when the evil is subdued; and subdual implies conscious struggles through the grace of God and victory. But who shall tell that hidden consumption of the soul, when all seems right, simply because the evil within is unexplored? The inward home of life is set thick with the seeds of death; yet men are secure, because the disease is not yet developed into strong active virulence.

Sin is, perhaps, never fully developed here; it will not be fully developed, except in hell. And this may give us, the more, some thought of the intensity of the evil of sin, and by God's grace make us stand in awe of ourselves. Even if we saw the extremest working of the most dreadful sin, which we cannot, (we see but some outbreaks only, some lurid gleams of a smothered, raging, pent-up fire,) we could see it only, as softened by humanity. Most, blessed be God, bad as they may be, have some grace left, through which they may be converted; there is some smouldering spark left; at the worst, they are as yet men; they are not, in the extremest sense, devils. Even Judas, after our Blessed Lord had pronounced of him, 'One of you is a devil,' had that in him, through which, had he used the grace given him, he might have been saved. When he had betrayed his Lord, and was going (in the aweful language of Holy Scripture) "to his own place," he had some human feelings left. He knew not what he did. He thought probably, that he should not have done it, had he known it. He repented him of it, although with a repentance unto death. He had more human feeling than the Chief Priests, although he had now done that dreadful sin, for which it "had been better for him, that he had not been born." Perhaps Antichrist only, as he is described, shall have no human feeling; types of Antichrist there have been already, for whom people have felt compassion, whom the world has even admired[a]. We dare not wholly hate any but Satan. Of any one we must hope that by God's grace they might be converted, as of ourselves we must stand in awe, lest we be lost. It is something in the very worst that they are men and not devils; it is to us every thing that God still bears with them. The intensest evil then on earth is not yet what it shall be. It is softened still. One cannot think, of how great value one faintest spark of God's grace may be. It may be, we know, kindled by the Breath of God, His Holy Spirit, into a fire which shall melt the whole heart, burn away the sin of the whole man, change a vessel of destruction into a vessel of glory, one, the sport of and almost the companion of devils, into the fellow-citizen of Angels, the beloved of God, the image of his Redeemer, the partaker of His glory, his (aweful as is the majesty of His gift) yet through his Redeemer's Blood, his Redeemer's coheir in bliss. We know from what corruption and dishonour and loathsomeness, one, the

[a] as Bonaparte.

faintest spark of life, preserves the body. Leprous though it may be, and full of putrifying sores, it cannot wholly decay, while any life is in it. It may remain with scarcely an office or token of life, but it cannot yet decay. The worm had not entire power of Herod's body, even after God had stricken him, until he died. Yet the foulest decay of the body is but a slight image of the foulness of sin; for what is bodily life compared to the life of the soul, since this is the Presence of God? What an unutterable depth of mystery of love must there be in the very slightest remains of the Holy Presence of God! What an unutterable difference must there be between one whom God yet loves, and one from whom, as having finally rejected Him, God has for ever withdrawn Himself; between one who may yet love God eternally, and one who shall hate Him eternally; one whom God may yet love infinitely, as He doth all His redeemed, or whom He shall, fearful as it is to utter, hate infinitely!

But since in the very worst which we can conceive here on earth, sin is not what it shall be; if we cannot read of those, whom from Holy Scripture we know to be in hell (as Cain or Balaam) without some feeling of pity for them such as they once were, some longing that they had yielded themselves to the mercy and love of God; since even in them sin had not and could not have grown to the uttermost, but its nature was still kept in check; must we not, my brethren, stand in awe of any sin in ourselves? No one can know what any sin may grow to in this life in himself, if unchecked by God's grace; none can imagine what, if he dies unforgiven, it would be in hell. No one can tell what the amount of the evil in himself would be, if the grace of God were suddenly withdrawn from him. I mean not, what he might grow to, if left on his trial, (for this, of course, might be any amount of evil,) but if that evil were in him, separate from what of good the Presence of God's Good Spirit keeps alive in him. We can form no thought of entire darkness, while any light remains. I do not say this, as though we ought to fear lest God should leave us suddenly. When His grace is forfeited, it dies out mostly, slowly. But I mean that it should shew us the exceeding evil of any single sin in us, that, as we know not in this life what is the full evil of the actual sin of those who are all but most deeply lost, still less can we our own. This only we know, that one single spot of sin would mar Heaven. Had it been less than an infinite evil, it had not been atoned for at an infinite Price, as Scripture speaks, "the Blood of God." By the sin of one man, death entered into the world. On one sin, His coming was promised, Who being God should, as Man, die, and by His Death destroy death. Would we know the nature of one sin in us, we must read it in the Death of the Son of God, Who atoned for the sins of the whole world; but all the sins He atoned for were in their germ contained in one single sin; we must read it in the miserable depths of hell, which one sin opened to the whole human race.

Could you be at ease, brethren, with asps playing around you, and hiding themselves and nestling in your bosom? Could you "eat, drink, and be merry," knowing that there was death in the cup, even though a lingering poison? Yet what is this, compared to the dreadful, aweful, mystery of having that within us, which, if it lives, will "kill both body and soul in hell?" What aweful mystery like that, that the redeemed of Christ, whom He purchased for Himself with Himself, to whom He gives Himself, should have that within them, as a part of them, twined into their very souls, infecting their actions, swaying their thoughts and words, with which they cannot enter into Heaven where nothing unholy shall enter, which may for ever sever them from Him! What a pitiable thing to have that which allies (it is too aweful to say "us")—which allies the sinner to Satan; to have something in him, which unites him to God Blessed for ever, something about him which is of Satan, who is cursed for ever! Yet such is every secret sin. Every sin, in its degree, blinds us to itself. We cannot tell what or how deep it is, while we are subject to it. Rebel against it, bid it defiance in God's Name, be in earnest to subdue it, and thou wilt know the power it has over thee, thine own weakness, and if thou in earnest pray for it, the might of God's grace.

Gird we ourselves, then, the more earnestly, my brethren, to that noble warfare, wherein the noble army of saints made perfect have followed the Captain of their salvation and of ours. You came not here to gaze, but to joy with and over a penitent, and in a work which God gave him to do; you came not to be gladdened only at God's acceptance of this temple made with hands, but yourselves to grow the more into that living temple made without hands, whereof the Lamb is the light and joy. Let us not part, my brethren, never again all to meet together, except at the Judgement-seat of Christ, with mere gladness of heart or general purpose of serving God; but seek we out, if we have not yet done it, our besetting sin; if we have turned to God in earnest, gaze we by His Light upon our remaining darkness, that we may be wholly light in Him. There is a blessed harmony of graces, as well as an evil bond, link to link, of sin. There is even a blessed connection of sin with sin, to the uprooting of all our sin, as well as a destructive banding of sin to sin, to the more miserable enthralling of the whole soul. One sin, wilfully or secretly indulged in, binds the whole soul. As well might we assay to walk with one limb chained by a single fetter, as hope to walk Heavenwards with one single admitted sin. But as one wilful sin holds fast, so one resolute purpose, in God's strength, to break one sin, sets in the end, if he perseveres, the whole man free. In the devoted city, abandoned of God, "the satyr cried to his fellow," and "the vultures were gathered every one to his mate," i. e. each thought and deed of sin called to some other to make its dreadful abode there. Affright one unclean bird, in that dark ruin of thy soul, where they have been allowed to harbour together, thou mayest well be troubled with the din, but the whole brood is disturbed; follow on, and they will take their flight, and leave thy soul bright, serene, and clear. For so good is God, one stedfast purpose by His grace to do His will more heartily, in any one thing, draws down more grace, the very Presence of the Holy Comforter: and "where" He is "Guide, no ill can come." A new light shall shine in thy prison, where by one sin thy soul is bound and sleeping, and He shall touch thee on thy side, and bid thee "rise up quickly," and the chains shall fall off from thy hands, and He shall bid thee "gird thyself, and bind on thy sandals," that the dust of earthliness cleave not to thee, and "cast about thee thy garment," the new robe of His Righteousness, which He shall give thee, and bid thee, "follow Me," and thou shalt follow Him, often doubting whether it be true, or whether thou see a vision, and the iron gate which encloses thee, shall, of its own accord, open unto thee, and thou shalt "know of a surety that God hath sent His angel, and delivered thee out of the hand of" the Evil one, "and all the expectation of" those who sought thy life.

Only be earnest; and now, especially, if you are approaching to receive the pledges of your Saviour's love, pray Him by that love (it is a most blessed practice) to give you with Himself that grace you think you most need, and resolve by His grace to answer to His grace, in rooting out every fibre of the one opposed sin. Thou couldest not endure to live for ever with thy sin, in Heaven itself; set thyself in earnest to track out one of these, the deadly foes of thy soul, and God will drive them out by little and little, until not sin, but Himself, shall reign over thee, here in the beginning and foretaste, hereafter in everlasting bliss, to which He, of His infinite mercy, bring us all, Who, with the Father and the Holy Ghost, liveth and reigneth, One God, world without end.

O Lord, raise up (we pray thee) Thy power, and come among us, and with great might succour us;

that whereas, through our sins and wickedness, we are sore let and hindered in running the race that is set before us, Thy bountiful grace and mercy may speedily help and deliver us; through the satisfaction of Thy Son our Lord, to Whom with Thee and the Holy Ghost be honour and glory, world without end. Amen.

SERMON III.

THE SINNER'S DEATH [a].

(Friday Afternoon; Vigil of All Saints.)

PHIL. iii. 18, 19 [b].

"The enemies of the Cross of Christ. Whose end is destruction."

WE turn our minds for a while to sad and fearful things, that we may rejoice and be comforted the more safely, and that perchance, through the mercy of our Lord, we may bring some to be comforted with us, who must first be more sad before they can be rightly comforted. I do not mean only those who are altogether 'enemies of the Cross of Christ,' but those also who have never thought seriously enough of the misery of being so, and who, through 'minding earthly things,' are in danger of being drawn away by the Wicked one till they become so.

Let us think awhile then of the end of an unchristian life, that we may be the more earnest to prepare ourselves for a very different end, that we may be the more thankful for all means of so preparing ourselves, and the more diligent in using

[a] [Rev. C. Marriott.] [b] From the Epistle of the week.

them; and that we may do what we can to bring others to think wisely in time. It is but madness to take the present hour by itself, and leave the end out of our thoughts, save only in one way—when we leave the end to God. This we may do in faith, if we do His will for the present; but if we take the present time for doing our own will, it is only daring His vengeance to say 'we leave the end to Him.' 'In well doing' we may commit our souls to Him as to a Faithful Creator; but, in carelessness and self-pleasing, it is but presumption to expect that He will provide for us.

Let us look, then, at the end of a sinner's way, that we may learn to look more anxiously and seriously at our own ways. Let us look at him as finishing his life here, without having taken care in due time to secure his interest in the Cross of Christ. Let each one think of himself, as one whose lot may be or might have been such, that he may fear, and the more surely escape it.

Death comes about in many ways, but it is one thing. From that moment, whether it finds us in the midst of life or on a sick bed, prepared or unprepared, all our life in this world is *past*. All our interests, all our pleasures in this world are over. We are gone, and its course passes on without us; coldly, for the most part, and forgetfully; and if not, its remembrances are here, and we are far off, in another state of being. I speak not now of souls united by communion in Christ; how great may be their privilege in one another, we know not; but of those which are joined together by mere natural and worldly affection, relations, connections of business and social life, where all has been of this world. The dying man may keep up a kind of illusion to the last, and feel that they are still his own, and be eager about his designs for them and amongst them. But when he dies, all this is at an end for him. His eyes may be blinded to this truth to the last. The eyes of survivors may be blinded to it by the continuance (for a little while) of the effects of his labour. But so it is; he is gone; and it is no more for him. He is gone; and a new world opens upon him. "The soul returns to God Who gave it." Is it prepared to meet Him as its Judge? The body goes to the common dust, till it be raised again for judgement. Has it been kept pure and undefiled, as the Temple of the Holy Ghost? If sin has been committed in it, has it been again brought under and chastised and purified? These are now the questions that concern the departed, and which must be answered *now*, as the case *now* stands.

Holy Scripture leads us to think that the departed soul is aware of other spirits that are near it, angels, devils, souls of men, and that it finds its lot among these, according to the state in which it departs. A dreary lot for those who have not shared the communion of saints here! What shall they do then, who while on earth made no "friends to receive them into everlasting habitations?" Who had their good things in this life, and lived for it, and make no acquaintance, that they might know again for good in the world to come, but joined hands with Mammon and Belial, disguised under gain and pleasure, and now are in their grasp, and cannot shake them off? Who in all their ways turned their back on Him, in

Whose presence alone ' is the fulness of joy for evermore.' To Whom shall they turn for help, when they find Satan, who once had to flatter, now sure of them, and able to pour out on them his spite against their Creator; to the increase of his own damnation and confusion, but not the less to their misery? Who would not tremble to think that in that aweful hour the prince of evil should 'find any thing' in him, even though he were not to fall into his hands ? Who would not long at such a time to have his conscience clear, and his lot among the saints without question, contest, or drawback? And even on this side the grave, only think of the man, who has not made himself ready, drawing near to his end. Suppose him lying on the bed of sickness—let each one suppose himself in that case—not with all possible comfort and calmness, and the consolations of religion already taken to him, but as he has been, when in greatest sickness before, when he did not expect to die, with much pain, weakness, and wandering of thought; when at last, from some sign never seen before, some slight word, some tone or look of the physician, the heavy countenance of a friend, or the skance eye of a concealed enemy, he comes to the conviction that death is not far off.

If his thoughts are of earth, what a blank is here ! How crushing and confounding is the thought of becoming as though he had not been, being blotted from the world, of all its interests and enjoyments no thought left but, 'this shall never be mine again !' and then the cold tomb, and perchance the pageant of a funeral, in which the deceased shall take no part.

If his thoughts pass on with friends and kindred, still comes in the fearful jar, 'all I seem to foresee may be or may not be, but I shall not see it, and it will come to an end too.'

And suppose him even to dream upon these things to the end, and to be comforted in them, what then? Still there is a further end. He that would be wise must look to it.

So then let the sick man turn his thoughts now at last to the world to come. What will those thoughts be? True, there is hope for him yet; but why more than in all his past life, when Wisdom called and he would not answer? There is hope yet; but there is something to be done, to lay hold on that hope at all; and much to be done, to make it clearly and perfectly his own; and what can he do now? I do not say, he cannot do it; but is this the time, that any man in his senses would choose for doing the most important work of his life? Let pass all the gains he might have laid up in store for heaven, all the fruit of good works, in which he might have been rich against the day of account, and not one of which should have lost its reward. One can hardly think of degrees of more or less, while the great question is not yet decided, is he to be saved at all? What are now his opportunities? One *perhaps* he has, upon which men reckon far too much—the knowledge, that his end is approaching. I say *perhaps* he has it, for the common practice is to keep it from the dying man as much as possible. The physician says, it may aggravate his sickness, and break down his spirits, and take away one chance of recovery, to tell him of his real state; and not only so, but many have it not, even when they have been warned. The thought is uncomfortable to them; nay more, dreadful, intolerable, and they cling to any hope of recovery, and bind their thoughts on that, rather than on what ought to have been the work of their whole life. But this knowledge, which, he has perhaps trusted, would set all right with him, and make him all at once a dutiful child of God, what comes of it? We know but too well by experience, that it is not to be reckoned upon for doing all. Satan is at the dying man's right hand, if he has been there all his life, and he has his way of dealing with him at this hour no less craftily than before. One weapon he has especially for this time, a fearful, crushing weapon, Despair. He calls up past sins in all their number and blackness, he turns mock-monitor, and says when and how often the wretched man ought to have listened to the voice of God, and says that now it is of no use, the time is over. This may not be true; but if his lie is believed but for a few short hours, it serves his purpose. He puts in hard thoughts of God, and notions that, if it had been so, and if it had been so, it had been better. Any thing to turn the bewildered mind from laying hold on its last remaining hope, any thing to keep out a thought that has in it a gleam of Divine Love! And such sometimes is the end even in the sight and hearing of men. Bitter regrets, without a better choice. Miserable exclamations of despair, and a soul shut up in its own hardness, that refuses to hear the voice that invites to prayer, and gnashes its teeth upon its own anticipated doom. But forget not, that the real awefulness of death is not here. There may be those who shew it beforehand in despair; but there are other kinds of hardness, that lead to the same end hereafter. Hardly more fearful to the Christian minister is the very blasphemy of despair, than the much more common, dull, and immoveable calm of the death-bed. He does not wonder at it, but trembles. It is the summing up of a life of false peace. It is but too well in character with all that he has seen before. It is not worse than what went before, but it is not better; and all his hope before was, that it might one day be better. The time of hope draws fast to a close, but no light shines from above. There is no sign of the conscience being enlightened or cleansed, or of the love of God, or even the fear of Him, being awakened. The man perhaps expresses a trust in God's mercy, but is no whit more earnest in seeking that mercy, than he was before. This is but the peace of blindness, that sees not perils even close at hand.

More hopeful to the common eye is the death of those, who at last think with much feeling of the mercy of God in Christ, and say much in condemnation of their past life, and declare their trust to be only in Him. And indeed it is well that their thoughts are so far seriously turned to Him at last; but still this is not enough to assure us, that all is well. Many times has the sick man said and felt all this, and then recovered, and gone back to his sins. A soul that is gone far astray from God has more to do than to *feel;* it has a great submission of the will to make, without which feelings are but as the morning cloud that passes away. The man who has, in the face of Gospel-light, in spite of continual warnings, or in wilful keeping out of the way of them, taken himself for his own, and given himself to this world, has more to do than merely to *feel*, that this has been a bad choice. He has to make the contrary choice, and give himself up to it. Feeling may be the means of moving him to do so, but it is not the perfect act. The man who is burdened with heavy guilt may feel deep remorse one hour, and the next hour drown his misery in intoxication. His remorse is not penitence, though it might lead to penitence. Another man might be led by the same terrors of conscience to open his grief to the minister of God, and to seek relief in exercises of penitence. And so even on the bed of sickness, fearful as it is to think of, it is not uncommon for a man, deliberately to smother the voice of conscience with such opiates or distractions as are at hand. So too, even there, is there another course for the penitent, who obeys that last call of the grace he had slighted before. Even then might such an one, through the powerful grace and tender mercy of God, be led to confess his sin without reserves or excuses, "every night" to "wash his bed, and water his couch with his tears;" to grieve for and hate what he had been, because God hated it, and so to begin to be of one mind with God; to love only the bitterness of sorrow for his past unholy joy, and Him Who, he trusted, had given Him his sorrow, and had died for him, that He might not die the sinner's death; to take every pang of his sickness patiently, and pray that, in union with the sufferings of his Redeemer, it might be sanctified to his soul's health; to repair, as he could, the ill he had done to others; to conform his will, now at the last, since he had no more, with strong desire, wholly to the Will of God;

to give himself up to God for time and for eternity, in earnest striving after obedience, in the hope of His mercy. So different may be the acts of *will*, in which the same feeling issues.

Now, to make sure that he is really performing such an act, a man must collect all his powers, and be thoroughly himself. It will not do for some of his inclinations afterwards to come in and say, 'we were not considered.' God and the immortal soul treat for Eternity.

And this it is not easy to do at any time. Were it easy, men would not put it off till the last. Their folly is great, both ways; both, in that they think it matters little when the change is made; and in that they think it will be easier then. The world still hangs about the dying man. He has his friends to take leave of, perhaps his affairs to settle, and many things that claim shares of the little time he has left. The flesh is still with him, and cries out for ease amidst pain and weakness. It would sleep awhile, and attend to religion, when rested. It wakes weaker than before, or a little refreshed and able to take some relief, in amusement or the sight of a friend, to which the hour is given, and then comes weakness and drowsiness again. Such is the course of nature then, so that even were not Satan at hand to throw in his temptations, there is enough to hinder any serious work being done, in those few precarious days that end our sojourn here.

The only security for the mind being serious and ready for a great work then, would be its having actually accomplished such a work before. What has been made familiar to it before, is likely to be easy then, to dwell on the memory, and to fill the intervals allowed by pain and weakness. Happy for the soul, if good thoughts and words have been thus laid up in store for the trying hour! Otherwise, it is listless, and knows not what it has to do, just as it used to be. Old habits go on, and there is less and less strength to throw them off. The man dies unchanged. And if he dies unchanged from the state of a fallen Christian, it were better for him never to have been born.

O that men would be wise in time, and not let death creep on them unawares, but die to the world before it comes near them! The things that death will open to them are always about them, and always true. Death, come when it will, is the same thing, the passage from this state into another, in which we shall actually perceive what we now only know by faith, and in which all that we now see will be at an end.

Death is a solemn thing to all. Our life here is cut off, because it has been defiled with sin. But the new life, which is to carry us through death, and to triumph over it, is given us here. If we are fallen from this, death seals our destruction, and makes sure our lot amongst the enemies of Him Whose Cross we have dishonoured. But let him who is in that state remember that he is already in that depth of misery, and has to escape from it. "He knoweth not," says Holy Scripture, of him who is ensnared by the "foolish woman," the enemy of true holy Wisdom, whether in the lusts of the flesh, or of the carnal mind, or of the perverse will, "he knoweth not that the dead are there, and that her guests *are* in the depths of hell[a]." Death can but fix him, where he is. It will not be a change of his state, but an opening of it. He is a friend of the world and an enemy of God now. Death is not needed to make him so, but it is needed to shew him what is his everlasting portion.

There is all the same reason now, that there will be at the hour of death, for making sure the great work of recovering the new life. And the willing and active submission of the days of strength and health is much surer to be real and effectual, than the trembling interrupted efforts of a death-bed. Now, a man has time to think how he has fallen; what have been his chief sins; what are still his chief temptations; to confess and renounce his sins, and the things that are likely to be occasions of sin; to open his mind clearly and freely in all this to the minister of God, and to receive not only his absolution, but his directions for self-chastisement and self-government; to make trial of himself, and ensure his own sincerity; to strengthen himself afresh on any side, where he has not at first been guarded enough; to seek the healing of wounds that escaped his first search; to go on to higher graces.

How different is this steady and thorough execution of his great work from all that can be expected of a death-bed! How different will be his state at last, who has gained all this beforehand!

But let every one who sets about such a work set about it with death in his view, and do it now as he would do it, if he believed that death would cut it short, and fix it at what he is now attempting.

[a] Prov. ix. 18.

It is not done, if there is a sin left which he means to repent of at some future time, but neglects now. It is not done, if he makes reserves in his submission, or is careless in searching out his faults. By our Baptism we are already dead to this world, and if we have begun to live to it again, this life must die. We must treat it, as though we were passing out of this world altogether, only with the firmness of a man in the full vigour of his powers.

We can carry nothing with us when we die; no more should we attempt to carry any worldly affection with us, when we return to God and strive to recover the new life. Then only can we be sure, that we are really submitting ourselves to Him, when we give up willingly, with life before us, all those hindrances to His service, which we shall have to give up, willing or unwilling, when we die. The dying man can scarce know, whether he is ready to surrender them or not; he feels them going from him, and knows they must go; he has scarce the opportunity of an act of the will to give them up. All the time of life, that should have been given to God, is gone. There is scarce time even to bewail the misspending of it. He must go into the presence of his Judge, at best scarce knowing whether he is prepared or not.

The Day of the Lord cometh as a thief in the night. Hear therefore and obey the word which Christ said unto all,—" Watch."

† One only study need we in our whole life, to "learn to die." All before looks on to this hour; all after it, the never-ending "afterwards" of eternity,

hangs upon it. That one moment contains eternity. As all the growth and decay and restorations of nature, our sleep and our waking, do but prepare for the death of the body, so every action, motion, thought, word, deed, consent of will, balancing of the soul, defeat, strife in God's strength, victory, fainting and falling, stumbling, rising again, carelessness, wilfulness, joy, sorrow, suffering, prayer, Sacrament; every moment in the manifold, shifting, fleeting variety of human life, looks to this one hour, and tends to decide it. It gathers into one the whole past. All that is past may influence it. Not a wound, which the soul has ever received, but may, except for God's grace, re-open then. Not a thought of sin admitted once, but may, except for His mercy, assault the soul then. Not a careless habit, but may, unless He strengthen the soul, weaken it. Not a thought of vanity, but may draw down the soul to self; no care, but may distract it; no unloving thought, but may chill it, when, with its whole force and strength of unwavering love and trust, it should hold fast to God.

It is a perilous hour at best. The body is weakened; the soul often partaking of its weariness; and Satan puts forth then all his strength and malice and subtlety, because he "hath but a short time," and his prey, if he escape him then, escapes for ever. "The snare is broken, and we are delivered." He is allowed often to assail even the good then, to put forth his hand upon them, although He, Who made them His own by dying for them, withholds him, that he touch not their life. An aweful image is it of what may go on with the soul then, that, as our Blessed Lord reveals, that unholy, miserable being, dared to approach then [a] to Him, His Judge, not discerning His Divine Holiness in "the likeness of our sinful flesh." "The prince of this world cometh, and hath nothing in Me." Nothing had he in Him, "in Whom," says a father [b], "dwelt the fulness of the Godhead bodily, from Whom virtue went forth and healed all, in Whom was the Substance of virtue, the richness of Wisdom, and Knowledge, and Righteousness. For he skilleth not to see, save what is his own, he knoweth not to find, save what is his own; what are the things of Christ, he skilleth not to recognise." And therefore, the more, woe to us, in whom he may so often find so much which has been his own, his own ways, his own thoughts, his own words, his own pride, his own bad passions, his own wages, for which the sinner hired himself unto him, through whom he has insulted God, and trampled on His image! Woe to us, if we have not by deep and heart-searching penitence turned to Him Who blotteth out our misdeeds; so that the Evil one should no more find in us what is his own, since God has effaced it by His pardoning grace. Woe to us at our best estate, but that He, in Whom the Evil one "had nothing," has, at so dear a Price, paid our ransom, in whom he had so much.

Yet was he allowed to vent "the whole phrenzy of his unwearied malice" even on the blessed martyrs, whose toils we this day commemorate, as to-morrow, with the rest of the redeemed and perfected, their rest. They who witnessed their sufferings, felt, in the superhuman malice of their maddened

---

[a] See S. Bern. Serm. 7. in Ps. Qui habitat. § 2.
[b] Abridged from S. Ambr. de fug. sæc. c. 4. § 23.

torturers, the presence of fiercer hate, than man at his worst was capable of, as well as the consolations of Christ. And so too in peaceful deathbeds, he has been even seen [c]. Even by the death of holy children in our own day, his presence has been almost felt; it has been seen how in a long protracted struggle, hour after hour, in death, he seemed to put forth his skill to injure the sacrifice which he was allowed to dispute; and then at last, came serene triumph and victory and the sight of the Unseen.

But so systematic his assaults, that the wisdom to repel them, has become the subject of rule [d]. Sometimes he assaults the faith, sometimes hope; inexhaustible in his dreadful cunning, he shifts the attack; he will take ways the very opposite, will seek to turn the weapons, which the faithful soul has used against him, back upon itself. When it meets thoughts of vain-glory with humility, he tempts to despair; when it meets his suggestions of despondency with the thought of God's loving mercy, he tempts to self-complacency. He will turn quick round, and, but for God's mercy, almost thrust a person through, before he is aware. Our Lord compares the evil spirits, as other Scripture does the

[c] See e. g. vit. S. Martin.; and on the other hand, an awful struggle of one converted through prayer at the last hour, in S. Greg. in Ev. Hom. 19. and 38 fin. So also have in our own day and Church, the Angels been seen, who were appointed to "carry" the soul into "Abraham's bosom" and their wings heard.

[d] See e. g. "The Spiritual Combat," c. 58—62. "When we come to die, the great enemy of our souls will attack us with all his stratagems. It is good therefore to be prepared. If he attacks your faith, say with S. Paul, (2 Tim. i. 12.) "I know in Whom &c." "I believe in God &c." Bp. Wilson Sacra Privata, Sat. Med. Prep. for death.

blessed Angels, to lightning; they, like lightning to do God's will, seen at once in East and West; he "like lightning," which "falls from heaven," fallen to earth, and here only with great wrath to destroy; an Angel's wisdom changed into a devil's cunning; yet with Angel-powers still, even as one must suppose that in Hell every power will remain which God has given, all but love. Even here we see what dreadful skill bad men at last acquire in wickedness; and now Satan has an Angel's intelligence with his own hate and all the experience of six thousand years of men's manifold sin. He knows too well the souls which he influences, to which he is often so very near, within men's very bodies. And if he be permitted so to deal with the pure and hallowed, what, when he has a whole course of sin to appeal to! If he have such power to try God's servants, what power must he not have over the ungodly and sinner, who has, through his whole life, given him the mastery over himself, and would now, in weakness and distraction and pain, dispossess the strong man, to whom by each separate sin, in Scripture words, he "sold himself!"

Our past sins, even when forgiven, are not dead, but asleep. They are as dragons, the offspring of the dragon, the head bruised, so long as the Cross of Christ lies heavy upon them, but ready to start up again in their deadly life, to devour, if it be but removed. And Satan is often permitted to use them; in his purpose, to destroy; in that of God, to try the soul anew, and give it the victory, wherein it had been defeated, that it may please Him wherein it had displeased Him[e]. But where is searching trial, in that degree is there peril. And Satan avails himself of every thing, to the utmost that he is permitted. He clouds the mind, and then tempts it to despair because it is clouded; he will make even the confession of sin to God a snare, by tempting the soul to consent to past remembered sins: the act of expressing forgiveness, he will make an occasion of renewed angry thought; he will use feverishness or weariness and weakness of mind, to infuse thoughts connected with past sin or wayward and hard thoughts of God, or fantastic and unholy images, so that the mind shall not

[e] "We should know too, that mostly, whom he [Satan] has taken captive, on these he presses heavier sins, when he knows them to be approaching to the close of this present life; and as he thinks that he shall now complete the temptation, he heaps up upon them the greater weight of iniquities.—Whom he took captive by depraved beginnings, he makes worse at the end, that the sooner his temptations are to cease, the more mightily may they be fulfilled. For since he is eager to make their punishment equal to his own, the more ardently does he strive before death to aggravate every sin. Yet often doth that Behemoth possess the heart, through sin subjected to itself, and still doth the Grace of God cast him forth, and the hand of Mercy casts out, whom the captive will brought in to itself. And when he is driven forth from the heart, he essays to fix in it the more envenomed stings of iniquities, that the mind, assaulted by him, may feel those waves of temptation, which, even when possessed by him, it perceived not. Which is clearly set forth in the Gospel, when the unclean spirit is commanded by the Lord to depart from the child. See, he tore it not, when he had hold of it; for then does he more painfully rack the thoughts of the heart, when, constrained by the power of God, he is nigh to depart. Whom, as a dumb spirit, he had possessed, him he quitted with cries; because mostly, when he possesses, he inflicts fewer temptations; when he is driven forth from the heart, he harasses it with bitterer assaults." S. Greg. Mor. l. 32. c. 19. § 30.

know whether they are its own, or shall seem to itself incapable of thinking a holy thought; he will use past impatience to make the soul impatient under its present sickness, or at least betray it into momentary acts of impatience, or to solace itself in pain with some memory of past pleasure of sense. "I know," said a statesman of our own, when tempted to one single sin, "I know that Satan is very busy at death-beds; I would not have this deed upon my conscience at mine." "Blessed soul," says a holy man [f], "which shall then through the shield of truth so turn back the darts of temptations, that, allowing nothing envenomed to fasten into it, it shall not be ashamed, when it shall speak with its enemies in the gate. In me, deadly one, thou shalt find nothing [g]. Blessed, whom the shield of truth so encompasseth, as to guard his going out and entering in; his going out, namely, from this life, and his entering in into that to come, so that the enemy should neither from behind nor before make any assault upon him."

Were there not very special danger at death-beds, the Church would not so pray, "in the hour of death and in the day of Judgement, Good Lord, deliver us." We have probably been startled, at some time, by the intense and almost agonized earnestness of that prayer in our Burial-Service, "Spare us, Lord

[f] S. Bernard. l. c.
[g] "It is said, that on this he [S. Martin] saw the evil spirit at his side; and he addressed him in words expressive of his assurance, that his Lord's merits were fully imparted to him, and his soul perfected. 'Beast of blood,' he exclaimed, 'why standest thou here? Deadly one, thou shalt find nothing in me; Abraham's bosom is receiving me.' With these words he died." Church of the Fathers, c. 20. p. 397.

most holy, O God most mighty, O holy and merciful Saviour, Thou most worthy Judge eternal, suffer us not, at our last hour, for any pains of death, to fall from Thee." We had hoped that there was so little danger that, if we had not fallen from God entirely before, we could then! The piercing cry of that deep prayer amazed us. And well it might! But it should teach us, that there is a deeper peril in every hour of our mysterious being, than we can think of. How should there not be, in that intense mystery of the soul being formed for God, and capable of hating Him?

But if the whole Church have need of this prayer, —and it is a prayer which the whole Church offers, which we have all, one by one, offered, when the awfulness of death, and what follows upon death, was most penetratingly impressed upon our souls by the very Hand of God Himself, when He wounded our souls most deeply through the loss of those who were nearest to us or were as our own souls, and He opened our hearts through the very sorrow which pierced them,—how much more they, in whom sin is or has been strong, and grace weak! It is, in all cases, the memory or dread of past sin, which wrings forth this prayer; "Thou knowest, Lord," it begins, "the secrets of our hearts." It is the bitter consciousness of lurking sin, which makes the soul so dread its power. Yet in that the prayer is that we fall not from God, it belongs still more to those who have not deeply fallen, or who have by God's grace arisen, rather than to those who, having fallen, still lie prostrate. It speaks of the peril in any death, apart from all the thickening perils of a sinner's death.

But if there be peril then, lest even the righteous fall from God, what must be the state of those who having fallen, have not yet with true and hearty repentance returned! Who can tell the miserable dangers of an unexamined, uncleansed, conscience then? It is difficult (as they who have tried, have known) to disentangle it, after long neglect, even in life. Sin gathers upon sin, until penitents often scarce know what to repent of, which to bring before God; they reel to and fro, and stagger like a drunken man, as they are faced on every side by some fresh sin, seeking rest and finding none, driven backwards and forwards by frightful sights of past shocking sin, and seeing in each the blackness of the wrath of God. They despair at beginning, because they hope not to see the end. This, again, is Satan's wile; for if they would begin, counting them all, one by one, before their Saviour's Feet, He would enable them to discharge them all before Him; He Who carried our sorrows, would willingly let us, nay, invites us to cast our loathsome burthen before His Feet; His mild Eye looks pityingly on that, from which we ourselves turn with loathing; even as some kind physician turns not away from the loathsome corruption, from which his piercing wound has discharged the body. Our sins defile not His Holy Presence, which unholiness cannot reach.

But if there be this difficulty in life, what in death? How will not Satan justly say, "I redeemed thee not; I never became man for thee; I shed not my blood for thee; I hung not for love of thee in agony upon the Cross; I bore not for thee the wrath of God; I gave thee not Sacraments, promised thee not my love nor everlasting bliss; yet me thou hast chosen in life, mine shalt thou be in death."

Brethren, if we would not have the misery of a sinner's death, one only remedy there is, to meditate on death, prepare for death now, do what you do, or, at least, pray so to do, as you would at the hour of death. Imagine thyself stretched on the bed of death, its sweats bursting from thee, its faintness encompassing thee, its terrors appalling thee, and thy Lord alone to comfort thee, all the world vanished from thee, and no thought now before thee, except thyself and Him, before Whom thou art in a few moments to appear; set this before thee, gaze at it, master it, if thou canst, and act now, as thou wouldest then. If thou wouldest then choose hurtful lust or excess, misuse any beauty God gives thee, profane thyself, God's holy temple, seek men's applause, use careless speech, detract from a neighbour, lie, covet, defraud, gather up riches neglecting Christ's poor, spend on vanities, what might be placed in God's treasury, then do it now: if thou wouldest then flee from these, as thou wouldest from Hell itself, flee now, while thou hast strength to flee. "That act," it has been said, "is well done, which is done as though it were the last in life." "That is a fervent prayer, which is made, as though it were the last cry for mercy thou couldest utter; that is a holy action, which is done as if it were forthwith to be judged; that is a devout Communion, which is received, as though it were to sustain thee in the valley of the shadow of death; those are good alms which are given, as though into His Hands, Who shall at the great Day own them." Accustom thyself through life to act as in the sight of death, as having to die; learn to do thy actions, as a dying man; be this thy rule, to do them now as thou wouldest thou hadst done them then, and He with Whom thou hast sought to be through life, shall be thy Shepherd then; with each peril He shall be with thee; "I," He saith, "will be with thee in trouble;" the deeper the peril, the nearer His Presence; if He allow thee to enter with fear into the valley of the shadow of death, yet shall His Blessed Presence temper thy fears; He shall make thy very fears a blessing to thee, in that, as a child, thou shalt press closer to His wounded Side. What thou hast ever healthfully feared, thou shalt not fear to thy hurt then; Whom thou hast ever sought to love, yea to Whom thou hast sorrowfully owned, "Lord, too late have I loved Thee," thou shalt love eternally, where with the Father and the Holy Ghost He liveth.

O merciful God, the Father of our Lord Jesus Christ, Who is the Resurrection and the Life; in Whom whosoever believeth shall live, though he die: and whosoever liveth, and believeth in Him, shall not die eternally; we meekly beseech Thee, O Father, to raise us from the death of sin unto the life of righteousness; that, when we shall depart this life, we may rest in Him; and that, at the general resurrection in the last day, we may be found acceptable in Thy sight; and receive that blessing, which Thy well-beloved Son shall then pronounce to all that love and fear Thee, saying, Come, ye blessed children of My Father, receive the kingdom prepared for you from the beginning of the world: Grant this, we beseech Thee, O merciful Father, through Jesus Christ, our Mediator and Redeemer. Amen.

SERMON IV.

GOD'S MERCIFUL VISITATIONS BEFORE JUDGEMENT[a].

Wednesday Afternoon, Oct. 29.

1 KINGS xvii. 18.

"And she said unto Elijah, What have I to do with thee, O thou man of God? art thou come unto me to call my sin to remembrance, and to slay my son?"

HERE we have the heathen widow of Sarepta acknowledging some great principles, which lie at the root of all true religion, yet which many Christians in effect deny: the contrariety between God and sin: the searching power of His visitations, and the way in which His judgements find us out.

The Prophet Elijah, one whose intercession had such awful power with God, that, as an ancient Saint has observed, God speaks as if He could not send rain upon the earth, until Elijah had prayed that it might come:—this wonderful person had come to a poor widow's house, and being there most charitably received, had brought with him God's especial blessing: so that the widow and her only son were fed many days, as it may seem, three whole years, by miracle, in answer to his prayer. At the end of

[a] [Rev. John Keble.]

God's merciful visitations before Judgement. 71

that time the boy falls sick and dies; and presently the mother begins to have other thoughts of her inmate Elijah, and the effect of his abiding there, from any which she had had before. As if a veil should suddenly draw up, or light burst into a darkened room, and manifest to a man some glorious or fearful presence, of which he was till then unconscious, or only half conscious: and at the same time shew to him all the foul corners of the room, the spots and blemishes and impurities by which he was surrounded: it would fill him with awe and terror, with confusion and amazement. Such is the searching effect of God's visitations upon hearts, tender and open to notice them.

So it was with the widow of Sarepta: her thoughts flew back in a moment to the sins, perhaps the forgotten sins, of years gone by. Evil which she thought she had repented of and throughly put away, began anew to vex and haunt her. Like a bitter taste in a feverish mouth, so the remembrance of her past life troubled her, and would not let her rest; she felt how utterly inadequate had been all her past repentance, all her good works, and how much darker and more intolerable her sins, than she had ever yet imagined; and then came the thought, "All this I have done, these evil motions I have encouraged, these checks of conscience I have disregarded, these poor, mean, undevout ways I have had, and have pleased myself in them; and all the while God was so near me: nay, now for three whole years His especial messenger has been dwelling in my house. No wonder, if a sore judgement come upon me; no wonder, if so awful a presence do in an especial manner recall my sins both to God's remembrance and to my own: causing them to be, in God's sight, far worse than they otherwise would have been, and at last, by this severe visitation, giving them, even in my own sight, something like their true and horrible shape." Somewhat in this way we may understand the widow's cry, "Art thou come to call my sins to remembrance?"

And whereas she adds, "to slay my son," we may observe upon this, how God's afflictions always find us out, as it has been said, in the very tenderest part. As a wise and considerate father, who knows how to soothe and how to chastise, takes care never to chastise but in earnest, but so aims and tempers his blows, that each one shall tell, and produce its effect: such are the visitations of His Almighty Providence. "God shall wound the head of His enemies, and the hairy scalp of such an one as goeth on still in his wickedness." He knows what is nearest men's hearts; how to touch them as the apple of an eye. How often do afflicted persons find cause to complain with holy Job, "The thing which I greatly feared is come upon me, and that which I was afraid of is come unto me!" The very loss or care which they most dreaded and most anxiously prayed against, that is it which overtakes them. The whole of life is changed by one blow. And they are made to acknowledge God's searching power and presence, not only by the depth and force of the calamities which He sends, but also by the keen and subtle way, in which they are adapted to each particular case: every one having that special trouble allotted to him, which his Maker knows to be most critically suited to his condition. Thus the widow of Sarepta loses her only son: Jacob is tried by separation from Joseph, the favourite child of his old age: Moses had one darling object, on which all his hopes and imaginations were fixed, the entering into the Land of Canaan, and that one object was denied him: David, whose heart overflowed with family affection, lost one son after another by miserable and shameful deaths; and even to the day of his death the sword never departed from his house. Thus God's judgements have ever made themselves known, in general by awakening the thought, what a thing it is to sin in His Presence; in particular, by pointing, in one or other of their circumstances, to, the very sins which especially need to be repented of.

So we should expect, on looking to Holy Scripture: and such we find to be the case, as with fear and trembling we endeavour to trace the order of Divine Providence, in our own and our brethren's experience. However carefully persons may have been trained in the fear of God and in the conviction of His hatred of sin, they are but too certain, if left to themselves, to have those wholesome impressions deadened within them. In the ordinary state of men's health and spirits, they are sanguine, impatient of prudential and serious thought, unwilling, for various reasons, to meditate deeply on the awful side of God's Truth. They too easily sin and repent, and persuade themselves of their being but where they had been. Their evil thoughts, words, and actions pass over them too lightly: they do not make themselves felt as a sore burthen, too heavy for them to bear.

And besides this, too many of us, for the last two or three generations especially, have blinded themselves, or have been not unwillingly blinded, concerning the doctrine itself, of sin bringing punishment. Granting that in itself it is so, yet to the believing Christian, they think, it is not so. The virtue of the blessed Cross in their estimation is, that their punishment is already borne for them, and whatever affliction befals, they look upon as a mere trial of faith, to make their crown brighter; they do not consider it, as falling on them for their sins: they do not welcome it, and humble themselves to receive it, as part of the healing though bitter process, by which Almighty God intends to save their souls at the last. In short, their notion of a Redeemer is, One Who has suffered to exempt them from all punishment, not One, by the communication of Whose merits their punishments and troubles obtain a healing power.

For reasons like these, even well-disposed persons do not in general represent God to themselves as "a God of judgement," a God angry with sinners. But when it is their own turn to suffer, when He lays His hand on them in earnest, the case is presently altered. To-day, perhaps, you are tolerably easy in the remembrance of your past transgressions: you are rather sorry for them, but they do not very much trouble you: you see no reason, notwithstanding those sins, why you may not do well enough. And this, either from sanguine animal spirits, and a natural flow of cheerful thoughts, or because you have been taught that, if you are in a state of justification, it is no better than a sort of unfaithfulness and distrust of Almighty God, to be vexing and punishing yourself for sins past.

Thus it is with you to-day: but what if before this time to-morrow, Almighty God should strike you down, or any one whom you dearly love, with a sore sickness? What if you should be watching by him in pain, or mourning over his untimely death? more especially if your conscience smite you for some past undutifulness towards him. What if you should have to bethink yourself, "I might and ought to have warned him, and out of sloth I let the matter pass:" or, still worse, "I should have set him a Christian example, but my conduct has but helped to encourage him in sin?" What if you have positively used him ill? What if he were near and dear to you, and you have reason to think that your wickedness drew down the judgement upon you, as it were, through him, and so you are in a measure answerable for his pain? How will the sins then return to your memory, which you have allowed yourself to forget, foolishly imagining that God would forget them too! How will you wish and pray for but one hour, wherein to practise real charity towards his soul; to make up in some measure for the sin and neglect and unkindness of time past! What if you must think that one, brought by God within your influence, might have had a higher place in everlasting glory, had you been faithful to your trust?

Or suppose the pain and danger your own: what will be your thoughts, if God spare your understanding, of your own past life? Surely you will then make, in your conscience at least, a heartier and a fuller confession than ever you have done yet. You will mean what you say, when you call yourself a miserable sinner: mean it more earnestly than at any time before. You will wonder at your own blindness and folly, first in doing such things, then in caring for them so little, after you had done them. You will loathe yourself in your own sight for all the evils you have committed. O blessed and kindly pains, desirable loathing, sickness not unto death, but unto life! when by feelings such as these it seems good to the Allmerciful God to improve penitence, before imperfect though sincere, and to prepare His unworthy children for His nearer Presence in the other world!

Yet, be these throes of penitence never so surely pledges of mercy, we are still to regard them as pledges of judgement too. All the miseries of this life, however sanctified, however mitigated by the exceeding grace of God, are yet to us in some sense tokens and signs of the wrath to come: even as its innocent joys and solaces are tokens and assays of heavenly delight. The sickness and languor of the body, we know by the Psalms, represent to us, in figure and mystery, the far more miserable sickness and languor of the soul: its functions disordered, its inward senses clouded; all its appetites and aversions depraved by sin. The death of the outward man, the separation for a time of soul and body, what is it but a faint shadow of the horrible second death, the eternal separation of both soul and body from God? The reproach and reviling of bad and spiteful persons is as a kind of distant echo of the evil spirits, accusers of the brethren, exulting over them that are lost: the grave and sorrowful censure of the good may give us some notion how the Angels will look and speak, when in the last day they will be forced to depart finally from any of the charges, as unable to do them any more good for ever. In like manner, Scripture gives reason to believe that all other miseries of this life, thirst, hunger, cold, restlessness, and most especially burning heat and gnawing pain, and whatever feelings of desolation, despair, and anguish, do at any time overwhelm the heart, each one has its counterpart in that future world of misery. And by whatsoever temporal calamity it may please God to try us, while He graciously permits and invites us, on the other hand, to soothe and sanctify it, by bringing it to receive virtue of the Cross of Christ, so on the other hand we do according to His will, by using ourselves, in such visitations, to tremble at the thought of there being a time and place, where the whole misery and unutterably more will be present, but no Cross to heal or assuage it.

So again, those who watch the turns of a sickness, still more he who experiences it, seem, in a very aweful way, to be taught in Whose Hands they are, how entirely He knows their frame, which way they may most effectually be comforted or tormented. It is a matter very earnestly set forth in some parts of the book of Deuteronomy. God threatens His own people, that as they were nearer to Him than others, so, if they offended, His plagues would touch them more nearly: according to the rule laid down in one of the Prophets: "You only have I known of all the families of the earth, therefore I will punish you for all your iniquities." Agreeably to which, after the Lord had enumerated one after another all the worst calamities, and had threatened all to the wilful and froward Israelites, thus He closes the dreadful list: "Also every sickness and every plague, which is not written in the book of this law, them will the Lord bring upon thee, until thou be destroyed." He opens all the treasure-house of His wrath: we seem to look down an endless avenue of miseries, each one more piercing and thrilling, each striking deeper home, than the last. We are made to feel, what the punishment of the ungodly must be, how infinite Power and heartsearching Knowledge do indeed combine to inflict it.

Then consider, in addition to all this, that the Person so threatening is our Father, the Father of our Lord Jesus Christ; our Father by Redemption and Regeneration, as well as by His first creation of us. All men may perceive, what a pang it is to a tender and affectionate parent, when he is obliged to chastise a son severely: and we are the more entirely certain, how deeply he must hate and abhor the faults which he so corrects. Nor is it the Father alone Who threatens, but according to the incomprehensible union of the Three Persons in the One adorable Godhead, the Son also, the Incarnate Son, He speaks the words of terror also. His Incarnation, Cross and Passion, as they cause Him mysteriously to know our frame and be touched with a feeling of our infirmities, so we may believe that in some equally mysterious manner they qualify Him to pour out vengeance at the last. "God hath given Him," we read, "authority to execute judgement, because He is the Son of Man." And Scripture speaks very emphatically of "the wrath of the Lamb," as something over and above the wrath of God, sitting on

His Throne. As though the saving Cross, if rejected, would crush a person with intolerable weight.

Could we once give our minds in earnest to this thought, it might help us more than we can well imagine to understand God's intense hatred of sin. He hates it so eternally, so essentially, that even that deep yearning love of His, which drew Him down from Heaven to take our nature upon Him, and submit Himself to all the miseries of man; His Agony and Bloody Sweat, His Cross and Passion, His Precious Death and Burial, all in a manner is over-mastered and comes to nothing, when we go on in impenitence. There is no wrath like the wrath of the Lamb: even as there is no sin, like the sin against the Holy Ghost the Comforter. No expectation of man's heart so fearful, as that of beholding the sign of the Son of Man, the saving Cross, in the firmament, and feeling that to him it brings no salvation, but judgement.

These are indeed distressing and alarming thoughts: yet, on consideration, who could wish it otherwise? The question has been well asked[b], "Would we be deceived in our calculation of the anger of the Almighty against sin? Would we wish to think that it is not exceeding sinful? Is there not something within, which sooner or later must bring us to the Psalmist's reflection, Surely Thou wilt slay the wicked, O God?" A person may indeed, by continued deliberate sinning, bring his heart and mind into such a condition, that he may wish there were no punishment for sin. But this is in fact wishing there were no God. If we turn with horror from

[b] Miller's Bampton Lect. Sermons, p. 156.

such a thought, if we could not wish God to be less Pure, less Holy, less Perfect, in a word, less God, even if we were thereby safe from perishing, let us also turn, with glad submission of heart, towards Him and His fatherly chastisements, patiently conforming ourselves to His eternal law, that, sooner or later, those who have sinned must suffer: and thankfully remembering, that as He knows how to wound, He is also able to heal. The depth of His wounds are the depth of His love, in reaching the depth of our sins. The punishments in His left Hand are a token of the rewards in His right. Hell itself is the counterpart of Heaven. If you cling to the last part of His final sentence, "The righteous shall pass into life eternal," you must humbly and tremblingly receive the first part also, "The wicked shall go away into everlasting punishment."

Instead therefore of blindly and foolishly wishing that things could be ordered otherwise, let us endeavour with all our hearts to conform ourselves to His righteous and everlasting decrees. As we discipline children and brute creatures to expect pain after transgression, so let us discipline our own childish minds. We have sinned, alas! grossly, wilfully sinned: let us make up our minds to expect punishment. When it comes, let us thankfully submit ourselves to it: too happy, if it visit us in time, and so give us hope that we may be spared in eternity. If God's judgements seem slow to come: if, by His unmerited indulgence, health and ease, quiet and abundance, comfort and affection, dwell around our homes: let us fear, knowing our own unworthiness, how it may be with us hereafter: let us dread exceedingly the sentence of the rich man, to have his "good things in his lifetime:" let us pray that it be not said of us as of the Pharisees, "They have their reward."

And more than this: if we be wise, we shall judge ourselves in time, not waiting for Him to judge us. We shall prevent His afflictions by afflicting ourselves. Hear the great teacher of our Western Church[b]. "If thou beginnest to judge thyself, to be displeased with thyself, God will come to have mercy upon thee. If thou willest to punish thyself, He will spare. He who performeth penitence well, is his own chastener. He must be severe to himself, that God may be merciful to him." And again[c], "God hateth sin. If thou too hatest in thyself what God also hateth, thou art thus far united in some sort by thy will to God, in that thou hatest that in thyself which God also hateth. Exercise severity on thyself, that God may intercede for thee, and not condemn thee. For sin is certainly to be punished. This is due to sin, punishment, condemnation. Sin is to be punished, either by thee or by Him. If it is punished by thee, then it will be punished without thee; but if it is not punished by thee, it will be punished with thee." The more God spares us, the more it concerns us to suspect, and chasten, and deal rudely with ourselves. Fasting is more especially the duty of those, who are in a condition to fare sumptuously every day. But even the poorest of you, my brethren, though his daily meals be fasts, may yet find ways of denying himself. If you take your hard lot willingly, and humbly offer it up as a

[b] S. Aug. Serm. 278. § 10.   [c] Serm. 29. fin.

sacrifice to God in union with His All-Holy and meritorious Sufferings: this will no doubt be in His sight a Fast, an acceptable day unto the Lord, though in your actual meal you make no difference. Or if not in meals, in ten thousand other ways, which an earnest and dutiful mind will discover for itself, the work may be carried on, of sober and religious penitence. In dress, in diversions, in employment, in waiting on others, in ordering our own ways when alone, the good and gracious Providence of God will always supply to a willing and dutiful mind ways of self-denial, little in themselves, but altogether most effectual in promoting our spiritual life: just as each breath we draw is but for a moment, yet, by breathing, life and its functions are preserved.

Blessed for evermore be our gracious God and Father, Who hath provided us so amply, whichever way we turn, with what we most need: occasions of self-denial and of drawing near to Him: means of chastising ourselves, and preventing His judgement. And, O my brethren, great and heavy is the burthen which we go on heaping for ourselves against the Last Day, so long as we neglect such ever-present tokens of the watchful help of our Divine Lord, such special helps to perfection in His service.

I thought it good to set before you these few plain remarks, on the certainty of punishment, though it be with forgiveness, after sin: now at such a time as this, when the Almighty is, we trust, visiting this place, and drawing nearer to it, as in other ways, so also by the consecration of this Church to His Son's honour. Because if any one thing is more certain than another in the order of God's Providence, it is this: that the nearer He comes, the more severely must we expect to answer for what we do amiss. Times therefore of special favour are times of special jeopardy also; they call for intenser watchfulness, deeper humility, more unwearied warfare against our appetites and passions. May He give us grace so to take them! May it please Him, this day, to touch our hearts with true earnest longing after true inward penitence, whereby being effectually joined to our Lord, and made partakers of His Cross, we may find and gather "the peaceable fruit of righteousness!"

And be not too much cast down, nor blame yourself too sharply, if when you have besought God to admit you to penitence, and He has heard the prayer, and begins to chasten, you find the Cross heavy and uneasy, and naturally pray and strive to have it taken off again. You must not at once condemn yourself hereupon, as if your repentance were altogether unreal. No doubt there have been saints who, in eager love towards our Saviour and in anxious fear of themselves, have welcomed all kinds of penal suffering, have refused to be relieved, when, humanly speaking, they might have been. But the more usual process (and it is not an unhealthy one) is this: God touches the sinner's heart with anguish and fear, and he prays for a portion in the Cross; and when he is taken at his word, and the Cross is held out to him, nature shrinks back, and he prays again that it may be withdrawn, or greatly tempered to his hold: but neither prayer is wrong, neither unblessed, if resignation go along with both; if the first be accompanied with a wise and humble petition, to be "always prepared for what His providence may bring forth," the other humbly laid at His Feet, with a hearty endeavour to have no will but His [d].

Whoever shall walk by these rules, humbly and simply, as he began with the widow of Sarepta to own God's Presence, calling his sin to remembrance, so shall he end, with her, in full and entire faith: receiving back his blessings in this world or in another; and owning, from his own joyful experience, that the word of the Lord in the mouth of His saints is Truth.

Grant, we beseech Thee, Almighty God, that we, who for our evil deeds do worthily deserve to be punished, by the comfort of Thy grace may mercifully be relieved; through our Lord and Saviour Jesus Christ. Amen.

[d] "In the day of my trouble I sought the Lord." Who art thou, who so dost? In that day of thy trouble, see what thou seekest. If a prison causes thy trouble, thou seekest to go forth from prison; if a fever, thou seekest health; if hunger, thou seekest satiety; if losses, gain; if exile, thou seekest the country of thy mortal life. And why should I recount all, or when could I recount all? Wouldest thou pass onwards? In the day of thy trouble seek God; not any other thing through God, but out of thy trouble seek God, that to this end God may remove the trouble, that free from anxiety thou mayest cleave to God." S. Aug. in Ps. 76. § 3.

SERMON V.

THE LAST JUDGEMENT[a].

(Thursday Morning, Oct. 30.)

REV. xxii. 12.

"And, behold, I come quickly, and My reward is with Me, to give to every man according as his work shall be."

FROM THENCE HE SHALL COME TO JUDGE THE QUICK AND THE DEAD. One would think it impossible for any one, however careless and hard of heart, to hear and believe this Article of the Creed, and remain unmoved and indifferent to it. A man may be told of God the Father Almighty, and may go away and think no more of it: it is no wonder; God is out of sight, and the man is swallowed up by the things of sense. He may be told of the infinite love of the Father and the Son, as shewn in the humiliation and Incarnation of Jesus Christ; and it may fall dead on his ear: and no wonder; he is selfish and sensual, and cannot understand what disinterested love means. The Cross of Christ may be lifted up in his sight, and he may behold and see, and not understand how it can be any thing to him. He may read of our Lord rising from the dead and ascending into Heaven

[a] [Rev. John Keble.]

and sitting on the Right Hand of God, and it may seem to him no more than if he were told of any other good man departed. For why? He sees things going on according to the ways of this world, and has no faith to perceive the Arm of the Almighty Saviour, ordering all things in heaven and in earth to the good of them that love Him.

So far one may go in the Creed, and not so very much wonder at people's indifference: but when we come to the article of Judgement, when we are reminded that "this same Jesus, which is gone away from us into heaven, shall so come in like manner as we have seen Him go:" that we shall be all there, every one of us, forced to look towards Him, though we be never so unwilling, and to feel that His heart-searching Eye is fixed upon us: that the very secrets of our hearts shall there be laid open, and the things which now make us shudder, whenever we do but inwardly recollect them, shall be exposed before men and Angels; that the books shall be opened, and the quick and dead shall be judged out of those things which are written in the books, according to their works; and that, after all this, there will be no change, no repentance, nothing for each one of us but everlasting fire or everlasting glory, according as our work shall be: surely these things, one should think, *must* come home to the heart and mind of every one who does believe them possible.

And not only must they touch us deeply themselves, but they must also bring home to us all the former articles of the Belief, which else might fail to make impression on us. For thus we come to perceive the awefulness of the trust, which God the

Father, our Creator, has laid upon us; we understand that nothing is our own, but that we shall give account of all to Him. Meditating on the two resurrections, the one to life, the other to damnation, we understand a little of that Infinite Love of God, which caused His Son to be made Man, and to suffer so extremely for us, that He might save us from the one, and prepare us for the other. Looking forward to that Day when every eye shall see Him, we shall learn to tremble under His outstretched arm, and to own Him as our King, and obey His voice, though as yet we see Him not.

Thus it is, that men would reason with themselves when they heard of a judgement to come, were it not that sin, and the world, and the devil, have a blinding, deadening power, of which the best of us know too much by sad experience, to make even the sharpest and most prudent dull and stupid as to the things of Eternity. God grant, that it be not so always with us; with us, I say, who are here present: for we are the very persons concerned in these fearful things: we ourselves, and not another for us, shall behold that Day, and stand before the Judge, and hear our sentence, and go away to our place. God grant, that when we hear or speak or recollect these things, we may do it seriously and in earnest, and not so as to make our burthen heavier in that Day! God grant, that we may meditate very often, day by day and many times a day, on the Coming of the Son of Man, and that every such meditation may not only bring us to the foot of our Saviour's Cross, but also cause us to take up our own cross, humbly and heartily, before it be too late!

If our thoughts and purposes be like these, we may, with good hope of a blessing, proceed to consider some of the particulars contained in those words of unspeakable warning, "I come quickly, and My reward is with Me."

Such sayings imply that the Government of our Lord must be for the present a government out of sight. His rewards do not prevent Him: they come with Him. He will, as His own parables teach, bear, we know not how long, with the tares growing in His field, the bad fish in His net, the wild grapes in His vineyard: but bye and bye He will come from thence: He will cause the clouds to roll away, and will make bare that holy Arm, which now governs all things, Itself unseen: He will come and set all things right: the crooked shall be made straight and the rough places plain: the righteous shall no longer be as the wicked; He will no more endure in His kingdom any thing that offends, nor them that work iniquity.

Who it is that shall do this, and when, and how, and by what rule, the great Judgement will take place, our Lord Himself tells us in few words, so far as was necessary for us to know, here in the conclusion of His last Revelation of Himself to His beloved disciple S. John. In few words here and elsewhere, and more at large in many of His parables, He has given us with His own Divine lips full warning of a Judgement to come. "Behold, I come quickly, and My reward is with Me, to give to every man according as his work shall be." "Behold"—the word sounds as if He had said, "If you ever take notice of anything, I charge you, take notice of this." It is like His own warning added to many of His parables, "Whoso hath ears to hear, let him hear."

"I come quickly;" I, and no other; I, the Son of Man, the Incarnate Word. The Scriptures throughout, and especially the discourses of our Lord, invite our particular attention to this circumstance. "The Father," He saith, "judgeth no man, but hath committed all judgement unto the Son; He hath given Him authority to execute judgement, because He is the Son of Man." Because of His Incarnation, and because He endured the Cross, therefore He and no other shall come to be our Judge.

This is probably the reason, why in almost all places, wherein our Lord foretels the Day of Judgement, He uses the title, Son of Man. "The Son of Man shall come in the glory of His Father with His Angels, and then shall He judge every man according to His works." "Whosoever shall be ashamed of Me and of My words, of him also shall the Son of Man be ashamed, when He cometh in the glory of His Father." "The Son of Man shall send His Angels, and they shall gather out of His kingdom all things that offend, and shall cast them into the furnace of fire." And just before His condemnation by the Chief Priests: in aweful forewarning, how they who judged unrighteous judgement, should stand before their Judge. "Ye shall see the Son of Man sitting on the Right-hand of power, and coming in the clouds of heaven."

Now this circumstance, that He Who shall come to be our Judge is not only the King of Glory, the Everlasting Son of the Father, but also the Same Who took on Him to deliver man, and neither abhorred the Virgin's womb, nor drew back from the sharpness of death—this circumstance, I say, is at once most aweful and most encouraging, to such as will consider it dutifully and in earnest.

It is most aweful, for it brings the truth home to our very senses. Our very eyes shall discern on the Throne the Body of our Lord Jesus Christ, as plainly as He was discerned in the cradle at Bethlehem, in His daily walk among men, and on the Cross at Calvary: His murderers will look on Him Whom they have pierced; and the thoughtless ones, who now care not for their Saviour, because He is out of sight, will then be assured by that kind of witness, which alone they regard,—the witness of their senses, that *He is*, that He is close to them, that they are in His hand to be punished or rewarded for ever.

Besides, Scripture speaks of the wrath of the Lamb as of something inexpressibly dreadful, over and above the wrath of God. The enemies of Christ shall call on the mountains and on the rocks, saying, "Fall on us, and hide us from the face of Him that sitteth upon the Throne, and from the wrath of the Lamb; for the great day of His wrath is come, and who shall be able to stand?" And indeed, according to our human feelings, who does not acknowledge in his heart, how deep and bitter the remorse is, when we know that the person whom we have at any time displeased, and under whose rod we are smarting is a Father or fatherly Benefactor? How much more, when the impenitent shall feel that it is his Saviour with Whom he has dealt so ungraciously, and that even from Him he may never more look for compassion or forbearance!

On the other hand, to those who seek mercy in penitence, no thought surely can be so consoling and encouraging, as the thought of its being the Son of Man, their crucified Saviour, and no other, Who will come to be their Judge. To them every one of the kind words, gracious looks, and most merciful and bountiful actions of our Lord, performed while He was here on earth, and written for our comfort in the holy Gospels, becomes a sort of token, or pledge, or sacrament, of His perfect absolution and blessing, to be pronounced at the last Day. We hear Him saying to the paralytic, "Son, be of good cheer, thy sins be forgiven thee;" to the woman who touched the hem of His garment, "Daughter, be of good comfort, thy faith hath made thee whole; go in peace, and be whole of thy plague;" to the blind men, "According to your faith be it unto you;" to the mother of the lunatic child, "O woman, great is thy faith; be it unto thee even as thou wilt." Again, we observe Him turning and looking on S. Peter, with that mild and yet reproving eye which at once won him back to Himself: we watch Him, as He went about doing good: we mark especially His unspeakable condescension after He had risen from the dead, as before, calling His disciples brethren, saluting them with, "Peace be unto you," graciously asking them, "Why are ye troubled, and why do thoughts arise in your hearts?" and promising to be with them always, even to the end of the world: and every one of these instances of His heavenly goodness is to the dutiful and considerate heart a pledge of that gracious blessing, uniting in itself all mercy, forgiveness, and acceptance, "Come, ye blessed of My Father, receive the Kingdom, prepared for you from the foundation of the world." He can be touched with a feeling of our infirmities, for He was in all points tempted like as we are. Therefore even from the Throne of Judgement we may imagine His Rays, if I may so speak, coming softened and tempered to us: and we may take comfort, as S. John did in his vision, beholding in the midst of God's glory, otherwise not to be approached or endured, the likeness of this Holy Lamb, slain from the foundation of the world. So much mercy is conveyed to us by the heavenly intimation, so often repeated, that it is the Son of Man Who will come to be our Judge; and that even on the throne of glory and of Judgement He will still remember mankind as brethren: "Inasmuch as ye have done it, or not done it, unto one of the least of these My brethren, ye have done it, or not done it, unto Me."

In the next place the text tells us, what also we are assured of in many parts of Holy Scripture, that this great Day will soon be here: "Behold, I come quickly:" quickly, that is, in God's account, with Whom a thousand years is as one day, and one day as a thousand years; and quickly too, as it will one day seem, in the accounts of the children of men: for when once that Day is past, and we look back on it from eternity, no doubt all on this side of it will appear to us nothing, yea, less than nothing, and vanity. Of which we may form some slight judgement, by considering how differently we feel, even now, concerning time past and time to come. Forty years, for instance, seems a long time to look forward to; but what is it to look back on? A short unsatisfactory dream.

Our Lord therefore might be truly said to come quickly, though He should be as many thousand years in coming as He has yet been hundreds; and to the greater part He will seem to have come the more quickly, because He will find them unprepared. "Of that day and that hour knoweth no man, no, not the Angels which are in heaven;" not even the Son knew it, so as to reveal it to His brethren; it was a secret, as it were, in the Bosom of Godhead.

This is the circumstance regarding our Lord's coming, so earnestly dwelt on in the parable of the Ten virgins. Then, when the Son of Man comes, the kingdom of heaven, the Church of the living God, will have in it, as it had all along, a mixture of persons good and bad, wise and foolish, pure and corrupt. As though, of the Virgins appointed beforehand to wait on the Bridegroom at a marriage feast, some should come prepared with oil to trim their lamps, some in their idleness or wantonness forget it altogether; even so some Christians will be found provided with spiritual oil, a treasure of good works wrought by the grace of the Holy Ghost; others, destitute of that heavenly treasure, and therefore of all true heavenly hope. But all in the parable, wise and foolish too, all, we read, slumbered and slept. Which sounds as if our Lord intended to warn us, as His prophet had done long before, "The vision is yet for an appointed time: though it tarry, wait for it." It will be long ere that day come, and Christians in general, even the best of them, will be tempted to count the Lord "slack concerning His promise." Thus it will come to pass, that, to wise and foolish alike, the arrival of the Bridegroom will be unexpected. There will be a cry made at midnight. He will come as a thief in the night; and well will it be for those who have still their lamps burning, who have not forfeited the treasure of baptismal grace, who will be in a condition with trembling hope to go forth and meet their Saviour, relying on no merits of their own, but on His manifold and great mercies. They shall go in with our Lord to the marriage feast, and presently the door will be shut; there will be no room for any more; and any vain hopes they have cherished will be met with the fearful word, "Verily I say unto you,.I know you not."

Such is the drift and purpose of the parable of the Ten virgins; it answers to those warnings in the book of Revelations, "Behold, I come quickly," "I come as a thief:" and the shutting of the door on those who were unprepared fearfully reminds us of the great gulph in the account of the rich man and Lazarus: it shews how unchangeable is the Judge's doom, once fixed; it cries aloud, "Watch, for you know not the day nor the hour," after which repentance will be impossible.

As the parable of the Virgins urges so earnestly the danger of being caught unready at Christ's coming, so the next parable to it, that of the Talents, puts before us the absolute certainty of every one's being called to account. It is the same lesson as those words of the text, "My reward is with Me, to give to every one according as his work shall be." My reward, that is, Christ's reward; eternal life and death committed to Him, according to the counsel of the Father, to be dispensed to whom He will.

And observe, the blessing as well as the curse to be dispensed at the last day is called a *reward;* that is, although it is altogether a free gift, the least measure of it infinitely surpassing the highest deserts of man, if he could deserve any thing of God, yet it will be distributed to each person in the manner of a reward. God's blessings, the blessings of heaven, every one of them infinite and eternal, will admit however of comparison one with another, and the greater measure will be assigned to those who have done more, according to their opportunities. As we see in the like parable in S. Luke; he whose pound had gained ten pounds was ruler over ten cities, and he whose gain was five pounds only over five cities: the rewards were, all of them, out of all proportion to the services done, but in themselves they differed by a measure depending entirely on the amount of those services.

Christ's rewards therefore will be unequal, answering to the goodness and holiness, the practical goodness, of those who shall be found meet to receive them, and His punishments will differ in like manner. For He has told us of some who shall be beaten with many stripes, and some with few. Even the same transgression is, in His sight, more or less excusable, as it was done in knowledge or in ignorance of our great Lord and Master's will.

But after all, the main point in this parable of the Talents is, to make us understand that there is none of us all, whom God will not call to account; no one so poor, so weak, so ignorant and helpless, but the secrets of his heart, his idle words, his profane and careless doings, will be made manifest. Every one will be tried, and for every thing: and not only for what we have done, but also for what we have left undone. For the unprofitable servant was cast into outer darkness, not for making a bad use, but no use, of his talent; for hiding it in the earth, as if it were not worth improving. It was but one talent, and therefore, in a wilful mood, he went on, as though he might safely neglect it altogether. Let the poor, the hardworking, the uneducated, mark this; for they are apt, in their want of many outward advantages, to excuse themselves strangely for their neglect of what little they have. Let them remember the poor widow and her two mites, and the high praise she received from Christ our Saviour. Let them remember the reward promised even to a cup of cold water given to a Christian for Christ's sake. Let them encourage themselves with the thought of the good centurion, who, compared with one of God's own people, had surely but one talent, but for his devout use of that one obtained from our Lord more praise, than the Israelites themselves with their ten talents. "Verily I say unto you, I have not found so great faith, no not in Israel."

I wish this thought was more considered than it is; that we are *all*, *every one* of us, to appear, or be made manifest, before the judgement-seat of Christ. The poor aged helpless person must appear, to give account of his poverty, age, and helplessness, whether he have improved them rightly, as opportunities of great patience, sweetness of mind and behaviour, command of temper, submission to the will of God. Those who are sick and in pain must appear, to give an account of their pain and sickness, whether they have made the most of it, as an opportunity for obtaining something like a martyr's crown. Those who are weak and slow of understanding, or incurably ignorant from want of education, they too must appear, to give an account how they have acted on what little knowledge they had: whether they have kept the plain rules of honesty and truth; whether they have been temperate, chaste, and sober; whether they have kept their tongue from swearing and other bad words; whether they have been kind, and have done to others as they would wish to have done to themselves; whether they have tried to say their prayers heartily in the Name of Jesus Christ crucified. Those who died in childhood, they also must appear, as many as had begun to be at all aware of the difference between right and wrong; and must give an account, how far they have resisted or obeyed the warnings of their conscience; rather I should say, the motions of that good Spirit, which entered into them at Baptism to be the Guide of their life. Servants must give an account, how far they have profited by opportunities given them in strict and holy families; and in particular, whether they have not wilfully forfeited the grace which God there provided for them, by continual indulgence in what seemed to them little sins, such as pilfering in trifles, petty deceits, falsehoods, and concealments, and other liberties of the like kind; which are thought little of at the time, but will make a heavy burthen hereafter, as hindrances in the way of Christian perfection. And masters in their turn must give account, and a sad account it will be to many of them, of their too great easiness and carelessness about the souls of

H

their servants, of their suffering the law of God to be broken in order to save themselves trouble or inconvenience; and worse still, of the bad examples they have set, and stumbling-blocks put in the way of the little ones of Christ, committed to their charge as part of their household. They who have wealth, will have to give account of their wealth, as the poor of their poverty.

All evil or good is from God; all therefore is a talent, and we know that His most precious deepest gifts are sickness, sorrow, pain, bereavement, poverty, suffering, whatever, in a word, likens us to the Sufferings of our Lord. We shall have then to give account of things which people commonly call God's gifts, or of their absence; not only whether we bore patiently God's merciful chastisements, but whether they produced in us that amendment or penitence, or deepening of our souls, for which God sent them. We shall have to give account of our use of daily public worship, if bestowed upon us, and of the many blessed times when the Bread of Life was held out to us; and I know scarcely any thing which causes such a pang of deep unworthiness, as to see one who has lived the greater part of life, untaught perhaps concerning this sacred gift, devoutly using it when he came to know of it: and then to look back on all the grace, which one's own solemn existence, as in such wise a member of Christ that " He dwelleth in us and we in Him, He is one with us and we with Him," ought to have brought with it, and its little fruit and manifold waste and misuse. And for ourselves, my brethren, who have more than an Angel's office, even that of our Blessed Lord Himself, to seek out unweariedly His lost sheep, and as His instruments, His hands, voice, and feet, Who through us seeketh, through us speaketh, through us ministereth, to seek and to save that which was lost;—which of us had not rather be silent, lest that be true of us, "Out of thine own mouth will I———[b]?" Which of us can have any other hope, than that "mercy may triumph over judgement?" Which of us but must earnestly pray, " Enter not into judgement with Thy servant, O Lord; for in Thy sight shall no man living be justified!"

Not to be more particular at present, the serious, the anxious, the terrible thought is, Christ will give *to every one* according as his work shall be: the dead, *small and great*, shall stand before God: we must *all* appear before the judgement-seat of Christ, every one to receive in the eternal world according to the deeds done in the body, whether they be good or bad.

And we shall be judged according to *all* our works: not with respect to this or that thing only, as men now vainly flatter and judge themselves. A man's being kind to the poor will not then save him from the wrath to come, if he have neglected Jesus Christ and His holy religion: neither will his having done no one any harm be taken in exchange for his want of sobriety and chastity. There will be found in that day but One Only Ransom worthy to be taken in exchange for any sin: the Precious Blood, namely, of our Lord and Saviour Christ Jesus; and that ransom will be applied to none of us, except we have seriously applied ourselves here to the serving Him in

[b] In the delivery, the awful words were thus broken off. There was no power to speak them. [Ed.]

holiness, according to our baptismal promise, not in one part of our duty alone, but in all.

We are justified by faith: but "faith without works is dead, being alone." We see how the two are united in that parable of our Blessed Lord, which finishes the twenty-fifth chapter of S. Matthew, and which is especially remarkable, as being the *last* parable which He spoke, before He was betrayed to be crucified. "When the Son of Man shall have come in His glory, and all the holy Angels with Him, and all the nations shall be gathered before Him, and He shall have separated them, one from another, as a shepherd divideth his sheep from the goats: the sheep on the right and the goats on the left;" the one thing mentioned, according to which our places will be fixed in the eternal world, is our having or not having done works of charity to Jesus Christ our Saviour. Here are plainly both faith and works; works, such as feeding the hungry, clothing the naked, and the like: faith, in that all Christians, all who have learned the Gospel, understand that these things are to be done as to Jesus Christ, and in love and honour of His Name.

Here too is very plainly a most aweful warning, how very serious our doings on earth will be found in that Day to have been, far more serious than the most thoughtful of us ever imagined. For, as a good and wise writer[c] has said, concerning this part of S. Matthew's Gospel, "Neither the saints here know their own goodness, nor the rejected their own crimes." When Christ the Judge tells them, "You treated Me so and so," it seems strange to them, and

[c] Quesnel.

they both answer, "Lord, when saw we Thee, to be kind or unkind to Thee?" And He will tell them, "Inasmuch as ye did it, or did it not, to one of the least of these My brethren, ye did it, or did it not, to Me." Consider well, my Christian friends, what our Lord here teaches us all. He teaches us, that He is Himself present with us, in the persons of our of our brethren, to be well or ill treated. You are out on the road, perhaps, or you are sitting quietly at home, and you meet with some one, or some one comes to you, who needs your help, and you have the power to help him. You refuse perhaps to help him, for some selfish reason: perhaps you treat him with rudeness and scorn. He goes away, and you think no more of it. But see what our Lord here teaches, concerning you and that person. Your meeting with him will be remembered at the last Day, and you will find then, what you little thought of at the time, that it was Christ Himself Whom you were scorning and rejecting, Christ Who laid down His Life for you, and Who, at that and every other moment was giving you all that you had. He asked you for a very little out of His gifts back again: a little money, or time, or trouble, or may be only a kind word or look, and you refused it.

On the other hand, if you, from a sense of duty, put yourself out of the way, to do another person good in body or soul, though you might not distinctly consider it at the time, you will find at the last, that Christ was really there, that He reckons it as if you were doing good to Him: it is written in His Book and will in no wise lose its reward. Our Lord spake it about bodily charity only: but it holds true also with regard to works of purity also, and of that charity which regards people's souls. It seems a trifle, to all but earnest believers, to give way to bad thoughts, to take sinful liberties with the eye or hand: but what says the Scriptures? Your eyes and your hands are members of Christ; shall I then take Christ's Eye and Hand, (O horrible!) and make an unclean use of it? Indeed we shall never understand how grievous are our sins against purity, until we have learned to believe in deed, that we are members of Christ ourselves; nor against charity, until we believe that our brethren are so. The last Day will shew us what a depth of good or evil lay in all that we did willingly. It will shew us that nothing could be a trifle to us, where there was a right and a wrong.

Why then doubt we any longer? why do we not give ourselves up, once for all, to serve Him Who died for us, in all works of love to His members, and of purity in regard of ourselves, morning, noon, and night; this day, and every day of our lives offering to Him the sacrifice of righteousness, and putting our whole trust in Him: and that we may do so with a quiet mind, calling ourselves daily to a strict account, judging and punishing ourselves in time, that we may not be accused and condemned in that fearful judgement?

As you love your own souls, think on these things, for surely they are true, and the time is short. And may He by His Holy Spirit make good in us that prayer, which we offer to Him daily in His Church: "We believe that Thou shalt come to be our Judge. We therefore pray Thee, help Thy servants, whom

Thou hast redeemed with Thy precious Blood. Make them to be numbered with Thy Saints in glory everlasting."

Almighty God, give us grace that we may cast away the works of darkness, and put upon us the armour of light, now in the time of this mortal life, in which Thy Son Jesus Christ came to visit us in great humility; that in the last day, when He shall come again in His glorious Majesty to judge both the quick and dead, we may rise to the life immortal, through Him Who liveth and reigneth with Thee and the Holy Ghost, now and ever. Amen.

SERMON VI.

HELL [a].

(Thursday Afternoon, Oct. 30.)

S. MARK ix. 47, 48.

"If thine eye offend thee, pluck it out; it is better for thee to enter into the Kingdom of God with one eye, than having two eyes to be cast into hell-fire: where their worm dieth not, and the fire is not quenched."

AGAIN, my brethren, I have very solemn words to utter; it is a solemn, aweful, passage which I have read; and I cannot but fear, lest, unknown as I am to you, I may sadden some whom I would gladly cheer. Each solemn truth drives home more closely, and reaches our inmost selves. Healthful blessed pain is it, which reaches our deepest sores, touches to the quick some diseased part, that so, pouring out before our Lord in penitence every thing which clogs and chokes and stains our memories, we may await His healing touch, and our whole leprosy, in His time, vanish, and our very scars be effaced; yea even that deep loathsome treasure-house of memory, whose defilement so often remains our punishment, even

[a] [Rev. John Keble.]

for forgiven sin, be wholly cleansed. For such is God's love, even in this life, that, after deep penitence, He will bestow the privilege of the blessed, when He sees best, so that they can look back even on that dark mass of past sin, unstained by its pollution, with calm deep loving sorrow, like Magdalene at His Sacred Feet. Yet these solemn subjects must often be harrowing. How must it not, when we are sinners and these speak of what, but for Christ's mercy, were a sinner's doom? It oftens needs a physician's hand, such as our office is under the great Physician, to mitigate the pain, and pour in the oil of God's consolations, and shew how the very pains with which He visits us, are His mercy; how even past sin may be overruled through penitence to the ends of Almighty love. And since it could not but be seen that some, even when about to receive the pledges of their Saviour's love, had sorrow of some sort, they whom He has sent to comfort you with the comfort wherewith, we trust, He has comforted us, could not but long to be able to minister to their distress. I may then again remind you of the direction of our Church, that any who has grief should open it; and surely you must feel that to us there can be no more blessed office, than, under the guidance, we hope, of the Holy Ghost the Comforter, to comfort the mourner, and heal the broken in heart.

Bearing this in mind, we may endure, without overmuch fear and sorrow, to meditate on the alarming words of the text: "If thine eye offend thee, pluck it out; it is better for thee to enter into the Kingdom of God with one eye, than having two eyes to be cast into hell-fire: where their worm dieth not, and the fire is not quenched." Aweful words indeed, to come from the God of all mercy and goodness! from Him, Who poured out His soul unto death, the just for the unjust; from Him, Who when He knew no sin, was content to be made sin for us. You see how plainly, how positively, He speaks of everlasting death: it ought not then to be esteemed harsh and unkind, or unlike the sound of the mild and merciful Gospel, when His ministers do the same. Nay, it is plainly our duty to do so: we do not give Christ's message truly, except we tell you plainly and often, and suffer you not to forget, that hell-torments are prepared for those who obey not the Gospel, and that hell-torments will be everlasting. They are not indeed mentioned in the Belief: it finishes, as you know, with life everlasting, saying nothing of eternal misery: but the places of Scripture which affirm the one, do as plainly affirm the other: clearly it was the will of the Most High, that the one should be continually set against the other: that His Church should sound in the ears of His people life and death, blessing and cursing, that they might continually choose life. But because the Creed is the baptismal Creed; because, at the moment of first professing it, we are taken out of the kingdom of darkness and put into a state of salvation; because it is throughout a confession of faith, i. e. of trust and hope as well as belief, we may well understand that it was not so fitting for express mention of everlasting punishment to be made as one of its Articles. It is enough that it is clearly understood and signified by what is said of our Lord's coming to judge the quick and the dead; and in the other Creed, the Creed of S. Athanasius, it is taught in so many words: "As they that have done good shall go into life everlasting, so they that have done evil into everlasting fire."

Sore, indeed, it is, brethren, to speak on this very aweful subject, sore it is thus to speak, as it were, into the air, not knowing how deeply the sharp arrows of God's fearful message may pierce some heart already wounded. Yet we dare not withhold it. Yet let it not bring heavy desponding thoughts, (desponding thoughts are of Satan, not of God,) but pray we rather that we may thereby feel more deeply our own aweful being, and that these intense thoughts of Him and His dread Justice may, by His grace and mercy, help us to perfect holiness in his fear!

In that fear, then, let us now together meditate on the dark side of Eternity, the condition of those who shall be lost at the last day. Our Lord Himself has set us the example of such teaching: where, in order to make us *very* pure, *very* particular, *very* cautious of the souls of our brethren first and afterwards of our own, He tells us first that we had better have a millstone tied round our neck and be drowned in the depth of the sea than cause one of these little ones to sin: and afterwards, three times over, that if hand or foot or eye lead us into sin, we had better cut it off or pluck it out, we had better cast from us the dearest thing we have, than consent to that sin: we had better enter into life halt, or maimed, or one-eyed, than having two hands, feet, or eyes, be cast into hell fire, where their worm dieth not, and their fire is not quenched.

Our Saviour says it three times over: a symbol, perhaps, of that Holy Trinity, against Whom all sin is committed, and by Whom it is punished. It must therefore be a matter of the greatest consequence for every child of Adam to attend to. It is the true terror of the Lord, by which He would have us persuade men to regard the things which belong unto their peace. Let us consider with fear and trembling— it must be with fear and trembling if we consider them at all,—the chief points taught in the Bible concerning the future lot of the wicked. God grant that it may not be our own; that the warnings of our Redeemer may be no longer lost upon us, as hitherto too often they appear to have been!

Consider, first, those deep and grave words, "What shall it profit a man, if he gain the whole world, and lose his own soul? or what shall a man give in exchange for his soul?" He Who said this was the Creator of soul and body. We may *imagine* and *believe*, but He *knew* with perfect knowledge, what the soul is, and what is its worth, what it is to lose it, and how intolerable that loss. Our Lord knew all this, and by these few solemn words, " what shall a man give in exchange for his soul?" has given us to understand that though we cannot know it, we must believe it, and live by faith in it. Whether we will or no, we have souls; we may wish that we had not any, that we were like the brutes that perish; but it may not be: we have souls, and those souls may miscarry for ever. Our Maker and Judge has Himself assured us of it.

And what is it for a soul to be lost, and miscarry for ever? We cannot know but in part. How should we, seeing that the soul is something breathed into our nostrils by the Almighty Himself, and made especially after His own image: and no thought of ours can come up to the misery and sin of defiling and destroying that which comes to us so immediately from the Almighty. But our Lord has taught us, in the words of the text and elsewhere, to conceive something of what it is: as, that it is infinitely worse than the worst evils that can happen in this world, all of them put together. To have a millstone tied round one's neck and be cast into the depth, to lose a hand, a foot, or an eye, are frightful, hopeless, miserable things, things at which nature shudders; but they are nothing, compared to the punishments prepared for those who wilfully tempt others or suffer themselves to be tempted: for that will bring them into hell, "where their worm dieth not, and their fire is not quenched." So our Lord spoke, using words which His Spirit had before spoken by His holy Prophet Isaiah: for the very last words of Isaiah's prophecy speak of "the carcases of them who have transgressed against God, that their worm shall not die, neither shall their fire be quenched, and they shall be an abhorring to all flesh." When the Jews read or heard those words, they would naturally think of a certain valley near Jerusalem, called Tophet, or the valley of the son of Hinnom, in which, as is reported, the bodies of great criminals were cast out unburied, and where the idolaters of old time used to burn their children alive to their false gods. By the horrors of that place our Lord instructs us to form some notion of the condition of lost souls and bodies: only that the worms in Tophet died after a time, and the fire that was lit for sacrifice to Moloch went out: but this worm never dies, and this fire never shall be quenched.

Further, we are told that everlasting death will mainly consist in this: that the wicked will be separated for ever from the Presence of Him Who is the Life of our life, even Christ the Son of God. For this will be His word to those who shall be set on the left hand: "*Depart from Me*, ye cursed:" and again, to hypocrites, "I know you not whence ye are: *depart from Me*, ye that work iniquity:" and S. Paul says, He will appear "in flaming fire, taking vengeance on them who know not God, and who obey not the Gospel of our Lord Jesus Christ: who shall be punished with everlasting destruction *from the presence of the Lord*, and from the glory of His power." For as the light of God's countenance, which can only be seen in the Face of Jesus Christ, is the only joy and comfort and glory of His redeemed, so the final and entire withdrawing of that Light, the turning away of Christ's Face for ever, will be the very death of the soul.

And yet those miserable ones will not be so separated from the Presence of their Judge, but that they will feel His heavy Hand on them; they will be tormented with the feeling that their condition is without remedy, because it comes from Him, in Whom, if mercy could be at all, it would surely be found. They will perceive that the wrath, under which they are suffering, is the wrath of the Lamb, of Him Who loved them so well, that He took on Him their flesh, and was made Man to redeem them: and if even from Him they have nothing to expect, but a never-dying worm and an unquenched fire, what hope remains? There is none. God can no more cease from punishing them, than He can cease to be good and just.

This seems to be part of the meaning in those many parts of the prophetic Scriptures, in which the wicked are threatened with having "the cup of the Lord," the unmixed unassuaged cup of His indignation to drink; taking it out of His own Hand. Thus in the Psalms, "In the hand of the Lord there is a cup, and the wine is red; it is full mixed," that is, mixed, not with any thing to allay, but with that which shall make it more fiery and parching and intolerable; not with good and evil, but with different sorts of plagues and torments; "and He poureth out of the same. As for the dregs thereof, all the ungodly of the earth shall drink them and suck them out [b]." And in Isaiah, when Jerusalem was most sorely punished, we read that she had "taken from the Lord's hand the cup of His fury:" she had "drunken the dregs of the cup of trembling, and wrung them out." But these judgements upon guilty

[b] "They shall suck them out, shall drink them:" such is the order in the original, as though, when they should have squeezed out the very dregs, the bitterest, strongest, most delirious portion, there should yet remain more to drink. So should they never cease to drink them. "They shall drink," He says again, "and be moved and be maddened," i.e. as the blessed shall be out of themselves for joy through the rich fulness of the House of God, and be bedewed and overstreamed for ever with the infinite sweetness of the torrent of pleasure which shall flow forth from God, so shall these be ever out of themselves from misery, restless, unbearable to themselves, yet ever receiving anew that portion, which they have chosen, through which they shall be unable to endure themselves.

nations are as nothing, compared with the sentence pronounced in the Book of Revelations, on those who shall finally be found, not on Christ's side but on Antichrist's. They are images, earnests, forerunners of it; faint gleams of the hidden fire of the horrible pit; shadows of it, as all things in the world, joy or suffering, are but the very faintest tokens of the unutterable joy or woe. As eye hath not seen, nor ear heard, nor heart of man conceived, the good things which God hath prepared for them that love Him; so neither, of the misery of those who shall be found to have hated Him does this world afford any sufficient measure. "The same shall drink of the wine of the wrath of God, which is poured out without mixture into the cup of His indignation, and he shall be tormented with fire and brimstone in the presence of the Holy Angels and in the presence of the Lamb[c]." The drinking of the wine of God's wrath unmixed seems to mean that they will have an eternal, unmitigated sense, that God is angry with them, that they have never any thing to expect from His mercy. And this is enhanced by the circumstance with which the verse ends. Their torments will be endured "in the presence of the Holy Angels, and in the Presence of the Lamb." The passage seems, in a certain way, to answer to the merciful assurance in S. Luke's Gospel, about the pardon of penitent sinners. "The Son of Man came to seek and to save them,", and "there is joy in Heaven over them:" the direct contrary to which is the threat just mentioned, against those who are finally impenitent: the blessed spirits, nay the Son of God Himself, will look on and be consenting to their misery:

[c] Rev. xiv. 10.

there will be no thought in Heaven of relieving them. And this again the Prophet Isaiah had particularly mentioned. Those who come up to worship at Jerusalem, that is, as appears, the glorified members of the Church, "shall go forth and look on the carcases of them who have transgressed against Me." This is a great mystery, that good and charitable spirits should look without pain, and without seeking to change it, on the eternal misery of any one: but it must not be doubted, for it is the plain word of God; and so far we may conceive, that the nearer any glorified spirit is brought to the Father of all spirits, the more exactly will he learn to look at things with the same sort of eye, that God does Himself, and so may look, calmly and with satisfaction, on things which are now too fearful to think of, although the faith of Christ even force us to believe them.

As the punishments of the world to come are thus without hope, because they are in the presence of the holy Angels and of the Lamb: so are they without intermission, without rest or stay. "The smoke of their torment ascendeth up for ever and ever, and they have no rest day nor night." As the blessed "rest not day nor night" in Heaven, praising God and saying, "Holy, Holy, Holy, Lord God Almighty:" so neither do the accursed in Hell find any rest: the smoke of that furnace goeth up, like the smoke of Sodom or Babylon, or of the land of Edom when visited by God's wrath; and since it is kindled, as Isaiah writes, by "the breath of the Lord, like a stream of brimstone," it seems that it can no more go out, than that Breath can cease: it will go up therefore for ever, since for ever and ever God is just, to punish those who reject or abuse His mercy. There is no rest, no intermission, no sleeping and waking again, no relief through very weariness and inability to suffer more, such as occasionally comes in to assuage in some measure the most violent pains of this life, whether of soul or of body.

And worst of all, there is no end. The most grievous sufferings of this life must at least cease when death comes: but no such death comes after the grave. To those whose sins have separated them from Jesus Christ, it will be a worse death, a living death for ever: the pains of death, without the unconsciousness that follows.

Now, this of all doctrines is the most startling to weak human nature, and of course most astounding and unpalatable to wilful sinners. Yet we cannot doubt it; we know it by Christ's own word: He Himself says plainly, of those who shall be set on the left hand, "These shall go away into everlasting punishment;" even as of those on the right hand He adds, "But the righteous into life eternal." If the punishment of the one be not properly everlasting, then neither will the reward of the other. Either both alike will endure death, or both alike will be kept in being for ever.

Again, see the token which God has given, in His many fearful judgements on guilty nations and persons here, that He will surely visit, when and as He has said He will. "He is not a man that He should lie, nor the son of man, that He should repent," out of favour or pity. "Hath He said, and shall He not do it? or hath He spoken, and shall He not make it good?" The smoke and ashes of the land about Sodom is even now a witness to this. He said He would destroy Sodom and Gomorrha, and the neighbour cities thereof, and He did destroy them, although, for the intercession of Abraham, He would have spared Sodom, had only ten righteous been found there. The signs and tokens of the Flood, wherever they are found, are another witness of the same truth. God said beforehand, He would bring on a flood of waters, and would destroy the earth which He had made. The wicked would not believe this, because for a time they saw all things going on, as they had gone on before. But in its time it really came to pass. "They did eat, they drank, they bought, they sold, they planted, they builded: until the day came that Noe entered into the ark, and the flood came and destroyed them all." Again, the very Angels in Heaven, "who kept not their first estate, but left their own habitation," whenever and however that happened: did God relent towards them? He did not relent. Great and glorious as they had been, and among the chief of the works of God's hands, they are now "reserved in everlasting chains under darkness until the judgement of the great day." They are, among spirits, appointed for the same kind of pattern of God's severe unchangeable justice, as Sodom and Gomorrha and the cities about them are here: who "giving themselves over to fornication and going after strange flesh, are set forth for an example, suffering the vengeance of eternal fire." To them might be added the many instances of mighty cities, such as Tyre, Nineveh, Babylon, and above all, God's own highly favoured city Jerusalem, prophesied against and overthrown accordingly.

These, and all the rest of God's sore judgements in the world, are so many reasons why we must believe that the most awful Prophecy of eternal misery will also find its accomplishment. He waits long, but it must not be counted slackness; it is not that He has forgotten, or that the Church has mistaken Him: but He is "long-suffering to us-ward, not willing that any should perish, but that all should come to repentance." God forbid that any of us should turn His great mercy into an occasion of falling, by doubting whether He will strike at last, because He stays so long. Let us rather humbly endeavour, in His true faith and fear, to treasure up in our minds some of those serious warnings which may best help us to avoid these dreadful things: for He only knows how near to them we may have been, how near we may be at this very moment.

Observe then, first, that it is not only positive sin, on which this intolerable sentence will fall, but also wilful neglect of duty; leaving undone those things which we knew in our hearts ought to have been done. "[b] The cowardly, and unbelieving and the abominable, and murderers, and whoremongers, and sorcerers, and idolaters, and all liars, shall have their part in that lake which burneth with fire and brimstone: which is the second death;" this is fearful enough, and it is sad to think, how many of those whom Christ has called to Himself are included in this dreadful list. Some of us have perhaps, in childhood, been ourselves startled and roused out of a sinful state,

[b] Rev. xxi. 8.

on seeing how what is thought and spoken of so lightly, as a lie, what with many comes first to the very lips, if we be not on our guard, which often, as men think, does no harm to any, is, by our loving Lord Himself, placed among the most dreadful sins, which shall condemn to the second death. So awefully strange does it seem, that people have gone about to invent some other meaning for it, as if it could not be, that what seems to have so little effect here, could bring down such fearful hopeless ruin hereafter. And yet He Who would by His own Blood redeem us from death says, "All liars shall have their portion in the lake of fire," which is the second Death. What again, alas! so common as religious cowardice? How many of us, in childhood, or youth, or to this very hour, have shrunk from avowing the truth, when perhaps we should have been jeered at! The fear of the world has destroyed, it may be, as many as its love. How many religious practices have been given up, how much sin consented to, how much, if not committed, even feigned, out of cowardly fear of the sinful world's dispraise! "I was ashamed amongst my equals," says a penitent [c] of old "of a less shamelessness." And yet it is our Redeeming Lord, Who counts the "cowardly" with "the abominable and murderers." He has said, "Whosoever shall be ashamed of Me and of My words, of him shall the Son of Man be ashamed, when He shall come in His own glory and in His Father's and of the holy Angels."

But it becomes still more alarming, when we call to mind our Lord's express declaration, that He will

[c] See S. Aug. Conf. ii. 7.

say to those who have but neglected to wait on Him, "Depart from Me, ye cursed, into everlasting fire." And if this seem hard and unaccountable to some of us, as no doubt it does to many men, (for even at that day, our Lord tells us, those who are condemned will not at first be able to comprehend their own guilt:) let us say to ourselves, Who are we, that we should reply against God? He has told us plainly what He will do: let us take His gracious warning, however different it may sound from the judgements of men, and from our own too partial and corrupt imaginations. Surely the remembrance of our own childhood ought to teach us, what poor judges we are of the guilt of our own doings, or the measure of punishment we may be bringing on ourselves. How often did we find, as children, that what we made light of was, in the eyes of our parents and elders, a very great and inexcusable offence, and that we really had to suffer for it, when we perhaps had believed they had been only trying to frighten us! And so, depend upon it, it will prove in regard of God's threatenings.

Again, think of the direct punishments of sin, which sin of itself brings, even apart from the Lord's chastening Hand. What bitter fruits has one sin had, how has it pursued the sinner through his whole life, what moral decay has it wrought! Mostly, perhaps, they who have been entangled in a course of sin, knew not the nature of that their first sin, knew of it only as something wrong, not how sinful. And long after, when they have sickened at the foul hideous stream, which issued from it, they have seen that it was all contained in that one sin. The whole misery of life which has haunted the sinner, has often followed on one childish sin, of which at the time he made little account. One sin, scarcely known to be sin, has multiplied into years of deadly, grievous, corroding, daily sin.

How often again do those who break the law of the land, reckon on being let off easily, and find too late that the law was quite in earnest: that they must lie in prison, or leave their country, sometimes perhaps even lose their lives, for what seemed to them a very pardonable offence! By all such things, as they happen, God is silently teaching us to expect at the last day something very different from what our corrupt hearts would fain promise us. We shall then find too late, if we have not considered it before, that neglect of prayer, neglect of the Church, neglect of Sacraments, not preparing ourselves according to God's will, is in fact preparing ourselves to be servants and companions of the devil.

Again, we shall find what some are most unwilling to believe, that want of faith, not submitting ourselves to the Gospel and the Church, will forfeit God's blessing as well as what we call immorality. This S. Paul especially warns us of, when he says that Christ "shall be revealed in flaming fire, taking vengeance of them who know not God, and obey not the Gospel of our Lord Jesus Christ." It will not be safe therefore for any one to say, "he does his duty to his neighbour, he is an honest sober man, and what could he be more, if he was ever so regular in Church services?" Nay, but God, Who is the Giver of salvation, tells you, that it cannot be had on these terms only. You must turn to Him with your whole heart; you must learn to delight in His presence, and in the place where His honour dwelleth: more especially you must seek communion with Him through the Body and Blood of His Blessed Son. Without the love of God, as shewn by fruits such as these, in vain do we reckon upon the love we seem to bear our neighbour.

Let me prevail on you to consider this also, that true faith and obedience are so necessary, that no strength of temptation can excuse us from it. What temptation could be stronger than the saving of a right hand or a right eye? Yet we see this is not enough to acquit a person before the Judge for any wilful breach of His Law. He tells us this, Who died for us; and if we will not take Him at His word, how can we expect to be saved by His Blood?

And if this be true of all, more especially does it concern us, who have so many talents and advantages for coming near our Lord and Saviour, who are born within reach of the full benefit of His Church, His Word, His Sacraments. For there is one word more to be spoken, and that perhaps the most aweful of all. There are degrees in punishment, as well as in glory everlasting. "Unto whom much is given, of him shall much be required." "[d] And that servant, which knew his Lord's will, and prepared not himself, neither did according to His will, shall be beaten with many stripes."

Surely we do well now and then to pause and think seriously of these aweful things. In our eager pursuit of worldly objects, we are very liable to be carried away, and to forget entirely the great peril

[d] S. Luke xii. 47.

we are in, of losing ourselves, both soul and body, for ever. Like young persons in the heat and spirit of some chase, or some interesting game, who rush by the most dangerous places without once thinking of their danger. But as it is better and safer for them to be warned, so should we count it very considerate in Christ and His Church, to speak so plainly as they do to us concerning the place of everlasting torment. When we hear of God's threatenings, the enemy would tempt us to disregard what is said, under the notion that He is very merciful, and all will come right at last. And truly He is unspeakably merciful, else who could abide His Presence? Yet He will have us know and remember, that there is a place where He is, but where His Mercy will never come: there are persons whom He keeps in being, bad Angels and reprobate souls departed, who will know Him for ever and ever by His wrath alone. And this place is not so very far from us: we might at any moment cast ourselves into it; we know not how near to it our wilful backslidings may before now have brought us. And though we know not, among our acquaintance on earth, who will come to that dismal end, yet some among them, we must needs fear, will be of the number: we are sure it will be so with all who care not to avoid it.

Meditate then, I beseech you, sometimes, upon that fearful place: terrible as the thought is, yet turn not your mind away from it. Think what it must be in the last Day, to have that Face which is the Light of the world turned for you into darkness and horror: and try to have the two last words, "Come, ye blessed of My Father," and "Depart from Me, ye cursed," for ever ringing in your ears, that walking in humble fear and love, you may make sure of the one, and for ever be safe from the other.

"In the midst of life we are in death: of whom may we seek for succour, but of Thee, O Lord, Who for our sins art justly displeased? Yet, O Lord God most holy, O Lord most mighty, O holy and most merciful Saviour, deliver us not into the bitter pains of eternal death. Thou knowest, Lord, the secrets of our hearts; shut not Thy merciful ears to our prayer; but spare us, Lord most holy, O God most mighty, O holy and most merciful Saviour, Thou most worthy Judge eternal, suffer us not, at our last hour, for any pains of death, to fall from Thee."

SERMON VII.

LOVE OF CHRIST FOR PENITENTS[a].

(Wednesday Evening, Oct. 29.)

S. LUKE xv. 1, 2.

"*Then drew near unto Him all the publicans and sinners for to hear Him. And the Pharisees and Scribes murmured, saying, This Man receiveth sinners and eateth with them.*"

OUR Blessed Lord came to give us all the wishes of our hearts, although not in our way. He "the Desire of all nations" came to fulfil all they had ever sought, all the longings of the weary, aching, heart of man; yea more than all; for He came to give that which it hath "not entered into the heart of man to conceive." But His Wisdom must choose the way, in which His Love should bestow it. He would have given it us in our own, if He could. But our eyes were weak and sore, and could not without pain behold Him, our True Sun, until they were healed; our hearts were filled with vanities, and could not contain both Him and His creatures; they were corrupt, and until He cleansed them, all which should be poured into them must be spoiled. So

[a] [Rev. W. U. Richards.]

then He must come in a way in which we looked not for Him. He came to give us, in the end, infinitely more than all our restless hearts craved for; but when healed, not in our sickness; in heaven not on earth; or on earth in hope and in earnest, not as yet in its fulness. He came to replace the shadows by His own Substance; to give us what our heart really longed for, while it was busying itself with earthly things; something which it could love above all things, and whose full love it should have for itself; something which should abide with it, which should fill it, which it should never be weary of loving; beauty which should never fade, riches which should never flee away, pleasure which should never pall, life which should not decay, joy which should be for ever new, love which should raise us up to that we love. All which we could long for, He came to give, yea Himself to be; our true Life, our true Riches, the true Light which lighteneth our eyes, the Torrent of Pleasure, the Richness of the House of God. He came that we might love Him in His Humanity, that so we might behold and love Him hereafter in His unchangeable Wisdom and Majesty and Truth. But He came to give all in a new way. He would give riches, but to the poor in spirit; life, but through death; deadness to the world through His Death, that we might live to Him in the life eternal; He would exalt us, but by teaching us to abase ourselves; He would make us first, when we had of Him learnt to be last; through sorrow, He would give us true joy; through shame, everlasting glory; having nothing, to possess all things, by possessing Himself, in Whom are all things.

But these things, although blessed when learned, were hard to learn. And so our Good Lord began in Himself that new life, which through His grace His members were to live. In the Manhood which He took, He began that new creation, which was to be carried on in those redeemed by His Blood. He received in His Manhood without measure the Spirit, Which, as God, He gave, that through His Human Nature, It might, according to their measure, flow over to all the members of His mystical body.

He came to change powerfully all our earthly thoughts, and so He first reversed all things in Himself. All which the world honoured, its greatness and its glory, its dignity and majesty, He put from Him, that we might learn from Him to be lowly of heart. He came to found a kingdom which should not pass away, but His Crown was woven of the thorns of our sins; the sceptre which He bare upon His shoulder, was the Cross; that so He might make us too kings, when crucified with Him, lords, through grace, of our own wills, and coheirs of His everlasting kingdom. He was born Christ the King, but at "Bethlehem, the least of the cities of Judah," and was there an outcast amongst the beasts of the field. He lived and grew up at despised Nazareth, the reputed son of a poor mechanic. He came into the world to save the world, and yet remained unknown for full thirty years of His short life. And when He did manifest Himself, the proof of Him and of His ministry was such as man had never before seen, and which the world could not comprehend. For as He came to purify our dregs, to re-form to Himself, out of our mass of corruption and decay, those who should be heirs with Him in glory, so would He shew at once the might of His grace and the depth of His love, by stooping, as the Great Physician, to the very lowest of our miseries. What should feel itself too lost for His love, when publicans and harlots were among the first, who were admitted into the kingdom of heaven; and He vouchsafed to be called " the Friend of publicans and sinners?" What sickness should be thought too great for the Heavenly Physician, when " the sick" were they whom He came to heal, although, He became, thereby, with them, Himself "the scorn of man and the outcast of the people?"

And herein was manifested the difference between man's wisdom and the Wisdom of God, yea Him, Who came among us, being the Wisdom of God and the Power of God. Man's wisdom, when it would effect any thing, must use the best materials it could; it must, to gain disciples, teach the wise and the learned, at least the better and honester part of mankind. Philosophy of old turned herself to those who sought wisdom: for the wisdom of man has no constraining power over the heart of man; she sent away from her those who had not yet gained the mastery over their passions, as unfit hearers for her school [b]. Not so the Uncreated and Creating Wisdom, Who Himself created all things, and Whose " Word," whereby He created them, "was with power," in Whose Hands are all the hearts which He hath made; in His Hands to fashion them, and in His Heart to love them. His

---

[b] Arist. Eth. Nic. i. 3. "The young man is no fit hearer; for being inclined to follow his passions, he will hear to no purpose, since the end is not knowledge but practice."

special mission was to preach the Gospel to the poor, to seek and to save that which was lost, to call not the righteous but sinners to repentance. And so we find that one of the chief reproaches, which the Pharisees and Doctors of the law cast upon Him, was, "This Man receiveth sinners, and eateth with them." Contrary to their practice, who thought themselves defiled even by the touch or company of sinners, He was ever to be found with the poor, the wretched, and the outcast. As He feared not and disdained not the touch of the leper, so He shrank not from the lips of the far more unclean, those who were infected by the leprosy of sin. Thus when they beheld Him sitting at meat with many publicans and sinners in the house of S. Matthew, they said unto His disciples, "Why eateth your Master with publicans and sinners?" And again, when He sat at meat in Simon's house, and the woman of the city, of whom the Gospel record is that she was a sinner, came behind Him weeping, and washed His feet with her tears, and wiped them with the hairs of her head, and kissed His feet, and anointed them with the ointment, the Pharisee, we read, spake within himself, "This Man, if He were a Prophet, would have known, who and what manner of woman this is that toucheth Him; for she is a sinner."

We see then, my brethren, what men thought of these things; and because they were offended at our Blessed Lord, we learn at once, how very different their manner of life and sense of what was right was from His. They loved to be with the righteous and self-satisfied, but He with the humble and heavy-laden sinner. They sought to be with the rich and great ones of this world; He, with the poor, the sick, and the needy. They loved to have many salutations in the market-place, and were found in the highest rooms at feasts; but He in solitary places or humble dwellings, where He would be most likely to meet with those, who, feeling themselves to be wretched and miserable and poor and blind and naked, had withdrawn from the notice of men to weep and to mourn. And while all others loved to be with the many and the great, He, to seek and to save the lost and penitent whom the world despised, and never to leave off seeking till He found them.

This then I say was the characteristic of our Blessed Lord's ministry, this was the difference of His temper and man's—of the Son of Man Who came to save that which was lost, and of men whom He came to redeem. It was His reproach; the reproach indeed of them that hated Him, but the joy of them that loved Him. Hear Him in the synagogue at Nazareth. "He found the place where it was written, The Spirit of the Lord is upon Me, because He hath anointed Me to preach the Gospel to the poor. He hath sent Me to heal the broken-hearted, to preach deliverance to the captives, and recovery of sight to the blind, to set at liberty them that are bruised, to preach the acceptable year of the Lord." Bruised and broken Himself, and emphatically The Man of Sorrows, if there be any whom He especially loves and seeks, and for whom He has reserved His tenderest and sweetest consolations, it is the broken in heart, the heavy-laden, who feel their sins to be a burden, intolerable, too heavy for them to bear. For it is to those who mourn, that He is the Comforter, to those who labour and are heavy-laden, that He giveth rest, to those who are sick, that He is the Physician and giveth medicine to heal their sickness; in a word, He is the Saviour of sinners, the Justifier of the unjust.

It was then not only to justify His own conduct, but much more, we may be quite sure, for the encouragement of these poor publicans and sinners who thronged around Him to hear the words of love and mercy, that our Blessed Lord deigned to answer the murmurs of the Scribes and Pharisees by three parables, which you heard in the second Lesson of this morning's service. Holy Scripture is throughout one record of human sorrow, the fruit of human sin, and of God's love in healing and recovering us. And these parables bring these truths before us in a most striking manner. The *first* is that of the shepherd, who, leaving the ninety-nine sheep in the wilderness, goes after that which had strayed from the fold, and never leaves off seeking for it, till he finds it. The *second*, of the woman, who having ten pieces of silver, if she lose one piece, lighteth the candle and searcheth diligently until she finds it. The *third*, of the prodigal son, who having received his portion of his father's goods, leaves his home, and in a far country wastes his all in riotous living; and then finding there nothing but strangeness and cruelty and unkindness among his new associates, he at last comes to himself, recollects the happy home which he had left, and resolves at once to return to his Father, Who receives him with the open arms of love and forgiveness. And who, brethren, is this Shepherd, but He Who laid down His life for

His sheep? or who this woman, but the Church, so often thus described in Holy Scripture? and God the Father is the father in the parable of the prodigal son. All three are represented as seeking, recovering, reconciling lost souls. Christ the Good Shepherd, Who hath brought us on His shoulders back to our lost home, toiling under the weight of our sins, and His garments stained with the taint of our impurity. The Church, who lights the candle and sweeps the house, while she searches for the lost piece of money bearing the image of Him Who created us. The Father Who receives and restores us to the place, which by our manifold sins and rebellions we have forfeited. Each has but one object. The weary sheep is brought back again to the fold, the lost piece of money is found, and the repentant son retraces his erring steps, and is restored to favour.

Again. Our blessed Lord in these parables seems to point out especially three things: why God pardons us, and why He loves us, and why, when He came in the flesh, He conversed and sought with so much earnestness to save sinners. He first represents the simplicity and weakness of man, who is betrayed by a cunning adversary; he strays from the fold like a simple sheep; as the Prophet says, "[b]We all like sheep have gone astray, we have turned every man to his own way;" first deceived, before we deceive others, and seduced to our own destruction. In the piece of money which was lost, bearing the king's image and superscription, we behold another motive of God's great love and compassion towards those who were created in His own image,

[b] Is. liii. 6.

the work of His own hands, bearing His Name, on whom, both within and without, in body and in soul, had been traced a likeness of Himself, marking them out as His own. And in the third, our necessity and poverty are set forth in the returning prodigal, who was perishing with hunger. For when men are in misery and so learn to feel their afflictions, then it is that God chiefly manifests Himself to them as the God of love and mercy, even anticipating their return, as the father in the parable, for " when the son was yet a great way off, his father saw him, and had compassion on him, and ran, and fell on his neck, and kissed him."

Our Blessed Lord then, in answering the murmurs of the Pharisees, sets before us the strong claim which sinners, however sunk in iniquity, had upon His love. He could not but love them and be merciful unto them, even when their fellow-men had cast them off: because they were His members, His own flesh and blood; because, in the very worst estate of a sinner, there is so much to lament over and to pity; so great the loss of his own good, so much blindness to his own happiness, so much real wretchedness, so much barter of that which is inestimable for the mere husks and garbage of the world, his own precious, glorious, immortal soul, pawned, as it were, to the devil, for a grovelling short-lived pleasure, which after all in the very enjoyment of it makes him only the more wretched! At the very sight then of the wretchedness and misery of fallen man, our Lord could not but have compassion on him. And the greater the loss, the more intense the pity and compassion which He feels. Thus it is, O most wondrous love! though man strays as far as he will, that he never can stray beyond the reach of God's mercy or of Christ's desire to save him: though he wander like a sheep in the wilderness, and leaves the fold, yet, rather than that he should be entirely lost, our Lord searches diligently, early and late, until He find it. Nay, He speaks of that loss as His own personal loss. "What man of you," says He, "having an hundred sheep, if he lose one of them, doth not leave the ninety-nine in the wilderness, and go after that which is lost, until he find it?" And when through its manifold wanderings it is faint and weary, as men are wont, who have trodden in the paths of sin, have worn themselves out with their own folly, wishing, yet having no heart, no courage, to return, He layeth it on His shoulders like the good shepherd, and carries it back to the flock rejoicing; not grudging His own toil and suffering, Himself afflicted in all our afflictions, and joying in our redemption, making His Sufferings our glory and joy, and our redemption the satisfaction of His Soul [c], although all the gain was ours, all the suffering and the love His. And when He cometh home, (and that home which He left for us was heaven,) He calleth together His friends and His neighbours, saying unto them, "Rejoice with Me, for I have found My sheep which was lost." And who are these friends and neighbours, but the Angels and the hosts of heaven? They rejoice because He does, and His joy is the joy of them all. They rejoice, because one more is added to their number, because of him who is brought back to God's fold, the repentant

[c] Is. liii. 11.

sinner, who has washed away his sins by penitential tears. There is greater joy over that one penitent, than over ninety-nine just persons which need no repentance, greater joy over one fallen man brought back to God's bosom, than over Angels themselves who have never fallen; not, because God loves the pure and innocent less, but because for sinful men Christ has undergone greater labour and suffering. And so the joy is greater, because that Blood which He shed is not all shed in vain, because He came to seek and to save that which was lost; and, behold! that lost is found!

"[d]Come unto Me," saith Christ, "all ye that labour and are heavy laden, and I will give you rest." O, brethren, "no word of comfort," writes S. Augustine, "such as this in all the wisest systems of philosophy. In the writings of the sages of old you will find many clever things acutely said, many things to warm the surface of the heart, but no where will you find such as this." Here then, O Christian, is thy Hope; if thou art sick, here is thy Physician; if thou art thirsty, here is thy Fountain; if thou needest help, here is thy Strength; if thou fearest death, here is thy Life; if thou desirest heaven, here is thy Way; if thou art sorrowful, here is thy Joy. It may be thou hast forsaken thy Father's house, and squandered away His goods, and the talents which He entrusted to thy keeping; thou hast, it may be, given to the world thy heart, thy affections, thy time, thy zeal, thy service. And how has the world requited thee? Did it not send thee to live amongst its offscourings and impurities? But now perchance thou art sick

[d] S. Matt. xi. 28.

at heart, and loathest the world; thou rememberest the happy days of thy home, the time when thou wast innocent and light-hearted, and so thou longest to retrace thy steps. Well! there is hope for thee. But by the path of penitence must thou come back: by confession of thy sins must thou be restored to favour: like the son in the parable, thou must confess to thy Father, and say unto Him, " Father, I have sinned against heaven and before Thee, and am no more worthy to be called Thy son." He feared the loss of sonship, and he was restored to his dignity; he dreaded reproach, and he was received with rejoicings; he was afraid of punishment, and his father fell on his neck and kissed him. And what this father was in the parable, such is our Father which is in heaven. Even so, brethren; not disdaining the name of Father from the lips of us His disobedient, wayward, and polluted children, not withholding His fatherly affection even from him who had forsaken his home, who had given his all to the world, and who was brought at first to repentance by no higher or nobler motive than the sense of his own extreme wretchedness.

Now a little consideration will shew us, how it is just this peculiar characteristic of our Blessed Lord's ministry, which is so full of loveliness and attraction to all true mourning penitents. For when they feel their wickednesses to be like a sore burden too heavy for them to bear, and by them are brought into so great trouble and misery that they go mourning all the day long; when at such moments nothing in the world appears to them of any consequence, compared with the hopes of forgiveness, then it is surely that one should especially dwell upon the unfathomable, inexhaustible, indefatigable love of Christ, "lest they should be swallowed up with overmuch sorrow." For great fear there is, lest some penitents, being overwhelmed by the enormity of their guilt, should only realize the Lord to be to them a God of justice, and not a merciful and forgiving Father. And this, we know, is a very favourite device of Satan, to destroy the sinner's confidence in the mercy of God. He would, for example, unfold to the penitent the severity of God's judgements, and then do his utmost to persuade him, that there is no message of forgiveness for him; that God, provoked with his repeated rebellions, has abandoned him and left him to eat of the fruit of his own way. And thus, while on the one hand Satan bids him take to himself, as his very own, every menace and judgement in God's holy and righteous law against impenitent sinners, so, on the other hand, he would try to put doubt and distrust into his mind, if perchance the words of love and mercy fall upon his ears. He suggests despairing thoughts, which, if they get possession of the mind, at once prevent him from applying God's message of forgiveness to himself. Such an one would willingly return to God, but Satan keeps him back. Ever-mindful and calling to his recollection the sins of infirmity into which he may daily fall, or perchance the sins of his youth, which are of a graver character; clever too in finding out new sins for himself and over-nice in his refinement of them, he exaggerates to himself every fault, that he either has or thinks he has committed. He forgets the mercy which pardons, and only remembers the justice which punishes. God seems to him only terrible, just, and righteous, one that will by no means spare the guilty. And if, since he sees it to be his only hope, he does return from whence he strayed, it is to live in his Father's house not as a child with a kind and forgiving father, but rather as a slave with a severe and angry master. He may walk with faithfulness in the ordinances of the Church and in the commandments of God, but then it is with pain and heaviness. Night and day, with tears of penitence and contrition, he tries to wipe out the foul blots of sin which he has contracted on his Baptismal robe, once so clean, so pure; still he gains no relief; he gets no rest; he forgets that suffering is the necessary consequence of sin, and takes it as a token of God's anger. And so, not being instantaneously relieved, he is disheartened. He forgets that suffer we must for our sins either here or hereafter[e]; and so thinking that God, so far as he is concerned, has shut up His lovingkindness in displeasure, he is unable to realize to himself the mercy and love of God. Now this is, I am persuaded, no imaginary case. It is one to be particularly guarded against in these days, when God is calling so many, in a voice, against which they cannot shut their ears, to awake from their sleep of death and to repent, and if they would be saved in the Day of the Lord, for the future to be more watchful, and to strengthen the things which remain, that are ready to die. You will remember,

[e] Bp. Wilson Sacra Priv. Tuesd. Even. Suffering. "Punishment is due to sin. We must be punished here or hereafter; it is the cause of all afflictions, and designed by our Gracious Father to bring us to repentance."

that in the case of the Corinthian who had grievously sinned, S. Paul, fearing these sad consequences, bids the Church receive him back again upon his repentance, he bids them confirm their love towards him, to forgive him and to comfort him, "lest perhaps," he adds, "such an one should be swallowed up with overmuch sorrow, and Satan thereby get an advantage of us; for we are not ignorant of his devices." Now let such an one, as I have before described, be told of Christ's exceeding love for all true penitents, that He rejects none that come to Him in faith and penitence, and then what a change takes place! Equally alive, as before, to his numberless sins and unworthiness, yet now he becomes full of love and thankfulness to God in graciously extending to him the message of peace and forgiveness; his love increases his confidence, and his confidence nourishes his love. He knows that God's mercy is greater than his ingratitude, that, though terrible in wrath, His wrath is not proof against an humble and contrite heart, that His power is chiefly manifested "in shewing mercy and pity;" he brings to his recollection the penitent and returning prodigal, such as he is pourtrayed in the Gospel, either in the person of the prodigal son, or in that of S. Mary Magdalene. True it is, that with confusion of face he draws nigh to the throne of grace, because he knows, how great and holy and just and good the Lord God of hosts is; and himself withal, how wretched and miserable and poor and blind and naked; yet this confusion does not keep him back, his fear yields to his love, because he is assured that God retaineth not His anger for ever, but that He delighteth in mercy: and so, conscious that he has much forgiven him, he loves much; and mourning much, he is greatly comforted.

To such of you then, my brethren, whose hearts have been pricked by the sting of conscience, and so aroused to a sense of your own exceeding sinfulness, if you be truly penitent, to you is this message of love and mercy sent. It may be, that you feel your sins to be a burden too heavy for you to bear; still do not despair: this very feeling of wretchedness is from God; and all distrust of His mercy to penitents is of the devil. We have an express assurance that "if we confess our sins, He is faithful and just to forgive us our sins, and to cleanse us from all unrighteousness." And so, when the prodigal had resolved to arise and go to his father and confess his sin, his father is represented to us, as already looking out for him and hastening to meet him. Indeed, so very ready is our Heavenly Father to watch the very first returns, however feeble, of confession and repentance, that even when the wicked Ahab humbled himself and shewed signs of humiliation, God spared him the judgements in his day. I do not say, that penitents can all at once regain that peace of mind, which would have been their privilege, had they never grievously fallen; or indeed that they will be quite sure to regain it this side of the grave. God graciously forgives them, and suffering is now a token not of anger but of love, it is the merciful Physician's hand pressing out their wound, probing it, it may be, to the quick, that He may afterwards close it and bind it up for ever, and soften it with the blessed Anointing of His Holy Spirit. Such need not only not despair, they have every thing to hope for; if they will but take patiently whatever God may see fit to lay upon them, and so walk with fidelity and thankfulness in the way of God's commandments. Their condition is a blessed one, though not so blessed as if they had never strayed, and their hope (and is not that a blessed one?) is in the God, "Who so loved the world that He gave His only-begotten Son, to the end that all who believe in Him should not perish, but have everlasting life." If then, brethren, you are, any of you, sensible of God's loving-kindness toward you, if you have a good hope that your sins, though many, have been forgiven you; if He has, of His infinite mercy, snatched you, as it were, as a brand out of the fire, what reason is there for you to give for the future the greater diligence to make your calling and election sure! Oh! let the recollection of the past only quicken you to walk the more zealously and circumspectly in the way of His commandments; to be more watchful hereafter over your whole self, thoughts, words, and actions; striving to please Him in all things, Who hath so lovingly sought and found you, being confident of this very thing, that He, which hath begun the good work in you, and given you the desire to live to Him, will, if you will but continue faithful to Him, perform it until the Day of Jesus Christ.

O! may we not cry out, "What is there in man, O Lord, that Thou art so mindful of him, or the son of man, that Thou so regardest him?" What is there so attractive and engaging in the polluted souls of sinners, that for one soul only Thou couldest leave Thy ninety-nine sheep in the wilderness, and go after that one sheep which was lost, and never give over searching for it, till Thou hadst found it? That for more than thirty years Thou wentest up and down upon the earth, traversing hither and thither, condescending to the most menial offices and enduring every hardship, and all the while doing good and healing those that were oppressed of the devil? All night on the chilly mountains in prayer, all day in the scorching plain, preaching to the multitudes that flocked around Thee, that the kingdom of God was at hand! Houseless, for Thou hadst not where to lay Thy Head, lest the sinner should pass by unseen by Thee; sleepless, lest he should escape Thy vigilance! "O! what is man, O Lord, that Thou wert so mindful of him, or the son of man that Thou dost so lovingly visit him?" And not content with this, Thou hast left behind Thee on earth Thy Church, to carry on Thine own work; Thou hast willed to join on our poor love with Thine own Almighty love, and to pour out the riches of Thy grace and message of reconciliation through us earthen vessels, and to seek and to save, through sinful man, those whom Thou hast purchased with Thine own Blood. But, alas! how have we shepherds under the Great Shepherd fulfilled the trust committed to us? Where has been in us that which was our Lord's peculiar characteristic, an intense, untiring zeal for lost souls? Oh! to our shame be it spoken, what little account do we take of them, for whom He suffered so much; of those thousands of poor perishing souls, who are famishing for want of the Bread of Life at our very doors, and whose blood will hereafter be required at our hands! And yet one would fain hope, that God is rousing us to walk more after the mind and example of Christ, and so more faithfully to reflect His image. It is surely something, that we are but coming to own and confess our past crying sins of indifference and apathy. Our Church indeed is now many ages in arrears; but has she not already set herself to the work, which has been accumulating upon her hands? The blessed occasion, upon which we are met, is, we may trust, such an instance of God's forgiving love; for He has mercy in store, when He stirs the hearts of penitents. Gladdening is it to the Holy Angels, gladdening to the Church, gladdening too and an encouragement to us to do the like, that one who wishes to be known only among his fellow men as a penitent, has, at all the cost he could, built this Church to the praise of his Redeemer, Who, he hopes, has not only sought, but found him; and for love of Him, he hath done what he could for the poorest of his brethren. O wondrous and most affecting mercy of our God, which not only accepts the love of the penitent, but turns that penitential love into an occasion of His own glory and the saving of others' souls. His gifts of nature and of grace must have been wasted by this penitent once, the callings and re-callings of His Spirit; His own Image, more or less, injured in him. And now with what favour and lovingkindness hath He not overwhelmed him! "ᶠWho am I," says holy David, "and what is my people, that we should be able to offer so willingly after this sort? For all things come of Thee, and of Thine own have we given Thee." But now to have received not only his sin-stained self, and, as we trust, to have cleansed him; but to have ac-

---

ᶠ 1 Chron. xxix. 14.

cepted a sinner's gift; that He, Whose are all things, should have received and hallowed those fragments which He enabled him to bring; that He, the Good Shepherd, should have thus admitted this once stray sheep, to help to gather into His fold those yet astray; that one, no more worthy to be called His son, should by His love be employed to bring back other sons to the Bosom of their Father, and add to the joys of Heaven; of a truth, "O God, the broken and contrite heart dost Thou not despise."

But one thought more, religious seasons like the present, which is of more than usual solemnity, bring with them their responsibilities; and their use is to put us all on the examination of our own hearts and lives. They remind us that life is short, and this world is vain, that here we are pilgrims, and heaven is our home. And the shortness of time, the vanity of the world, the price of the immortal soul, and, as the foundation of all spiritual advancement, the consciousness of sin and our own unworthiness, these are the great and solemn truths, which the world would have us forget, but which the Church seeks to reclaim. We are nearer death this year than we were last, to-day than yesterday; life too, at the longest, is but short, and we are not certain even of to-morrow; and besides this, sure I am, that in proportion as each one knows himself, he must acknowledge, and that too from the bottom of his heart, that it is of God's infinite mercy only, that he has been hitherto spared, and not long since been in hell. Every one knows, as none else but God can know, the plague of his heart; the sins and offences of his youth; the deep lodgment of corruption, which like

Love of Christ for penitents.

a well of poison, is continually issuing forth and diffusing its noxious streams around, tainting, alas! with sin all that Christians and even Saints think and say and do. Indeed this is what even the holiest feel in themselves, and the more, in proportion as they are the holier. My brethren, may God work this knowledge in all of us, whoever we may be, and whatever our state! For this knowledge is at the root of all humiliation, and humiliation lies at the root of penitence, and penitence is the very condition of acceptance. We must all seek to become penitents; to attain to the spirit of the prodigal, who confessed himself unworthy of the least of God's blessings. And if we will but henceforth walk in this spirit of penitence, O what may we not do, for others as well as for ourselves, towards gaining an entrance into that holy place, into which nothing that is unclean shall enter! We have more than usual tokens of God's Providence on every side, fresh proofs day by day of His exceeding love and mercy; and though there be a threatening of the clouds, still all will but issue in brighter sunshine, as it ever does to the Elect, if we will but cast ourselves on Him, and seek to be worthier of His mercies, more accessible to His guidance, and more obedient to His Will. Oh! be assured, that Christians are never farther from spiritual exaltation than when they are elated with thoughts of self; and never so ripe for the consolations of Christ, as when they are brought very low, whether by God's merciful chastisements, or by their own willing self-abasement. "[g] For thus saith the High and Lofty One that inhabiteth eternity, Whose Name is

[g] Is. lvii. 15.

Holy; I dwell in the high and holy place, with him also that is of a contrite and humble spirit, to revive the spirit of the humble, and to revive the heart of the contrite ones."

Almighty and everlasting God, Who hatest nothing that Thou hast made, and dost forgive the sins of all them that are penitent; Create and make in us new and contrite hearts, that we worthily lamenting our sins, and acknowledging our wretchedness, may obtain of Thee, the God of all mercy, perfect remission and forgiveness; through Jesus Christ our Lord. Amen.

SERMON VIII.

TEMPER OF THE RETURNING PRODIGAL[a].

(Monday after the Consecration, Nov. 3.)

S. LUKE xv. 18, 19.

"*I will arise and go to my Father, and will say unto Him, Father, I have sinned against Heaven, and before Thee, and am no more worthy to be called Thy son.*"

BY placing these sentences at the commencement of her daily Service, our Church seems to teach us, that we may well be returning to God every day of our lives with this confession and prayer of the penitent prodigal. As the Lord's Prayer, wherein we ask for forgiveness, is suitable to every hour of life, and to all conditions of men, and therefore seems a pledge to us, that as we all need pardon, so may we all obtain it: so in like manner this penitent prayer, thus put into our mouths, seems to intimate, that we may always feel ourselves in the condition of this poor prodigal, and may always be accepted as such. He who for the first time is becoming deeply sensible of his sins, will feelingly understand, how it comes home

[a] [Rev. I. Williams.]

to his own case; and he who has grown to fuller stature in the practice of holiness, will become more and more sensible of the holiness of God, and therefore more conscious of his own sinfulness; and will feel that no prayer better expresses his self-abasement, as he draws nearer to the Presence of God. So wonderful and so manifold is the healing application of God's Word to the necessities of us all.

But that we may not render the mercies of God an occasion of sin, let us consider what the true purport of this parable is. All these things in Holy Scripture imply a thorough repentance. What is here represented is the thorough conversion of a sinner in itself; it holds out no encouragement to one that falls back. I mean not, that there is not recovery, even from very serious relapses; relapses are very dangerous; their very great peril in serious bodily illness, is a type of what they are to the soul; still, blessed be God, there is recovery, though all who have ministered in such cases, know their anxiety and sorrowful peril; every relapse increases the anxiety; yet where God still continues the grace to struggle, there is hope yet. Still the case of such is not contained here; when this prayer is used, it implies growth and progress in grace. But now if true repentance is very rare, then the case to which this parable will apply in its depth and fulness must be very rare also. There are few to whom it will properly belong with all its consolations, although there are perhaps none who do not hear it again and again, and take it home to themselves with self-assurances of pardon. But although it may be pleasant to us to hear of the unbounded mercies of our Heavenly

Father being open to us all, yet we have no right to feel comfort in them as if they were our own, unless we are sincerely putting ourselves into that condition, to which those mercies are promised.

Let us consider the account in the parable. The prodigal son returned to his Father's house once and for all; he returned in great contrition and lowliness, and there continued. Those who would daily take to themselves the parable of the returning prodigal, because they are daily sorry for their sins, and as often return to them again, will find nothing to encourage or comfort them in this parable. To be like them, and to correspond with their state, the prodigal son must be every day acting over again his return, which would be but a mockery of repentance, instead of that affecting scene which the parable presents to us.

Certainly there never was any thing written so affecting as this parable, and the more so, because, being given us by the Holy Spirit, we know that it is infinitely true respecting the return of a sinner to Almighty God, and of that wonderful depth of Divine love with which he is received. And no doubt far more affecting than this parable and the literal history it contains, is every case in real life to which this parable does truly apply, and which it is intended to represent.

There is, in such a case, deep and bitter distress, such as was that of the penitent David, when he expressed his exceeding grief in the fifty-first Psalm; and of the king Manasseh, when he bewailed himself in prison; and of king Hezekiah, when he turned his face to the wall and wept sore; and of holy Job, in his lamentations of himself; and of Daniel, in his memorable confession. Such was the state of mind in S. Peter, when he went out and wept bitterly; and of Mary Magdalene, when she wiped Christ's Feet with her tears, and wiped them with the hairs of her head.

And as in these cases there were circumstances of bereavement; the loss of his child to David, Manasseh's prison, Hezekiah's sickness, Daniel in captivity, S. Peter in the night of desolation, the Magdalene in ill report and contempt: so likewise are instances of such repentance generally accompanied with outward circumstances corresponding to it, and in some measure, by God's gracious Providence, bringing it about. "There arose," it says in the parable, "a mighty famine in that land, and he began to be in want." The failure of outward supports and succours, of health, or of friends, or of money and condition in the world, on which the soul has been used to lean, are often found to go before so great a change, when the soul begins to be in want, to feel her own hunger and nakedness; that hunger of the soul, which God Alone can supply; and that her nakedness, which Christ Alone can cover. Difficult as repentance is at all times, it is far more difficult when the world looks favourably on us, and its objects are in our heart; so that our Lord speaks of such conditions, as being states in which it is impossible to be saved; impossible, although not with God, yet, with men: and in various ways He mentions such with warning, with woe pronounced upon them, and in His parables for these conditions He takes His examples of men that are lost; because sinners are not likely to come to the temper of the poor prodigal, till there arises around them a mighty famine, and they feel themselves to be in want. And for this reason we know of no cases of repentance without fasting and mortification; for as "the body never thrives," as a holy Bishop [b] has said, "but at the cost of the soul," so the soul never thrives more than when the body suffers; the spirit is never strong, but when the flesh is subdued, and the body, as S. Paul says, "kept under."

But the distress which is occasioned by the loss of worldly consolations is not repentance, nor is it even the beginning of repentance, although by God's mercy it often precedes it. All this had now happened, he had spent all, a mighty famine arose, he had begun to be in want; he had looked around on every side for succour; and no man gave unto him. Nothing could man give to satisfy the cravings of an immortal spirit; and the dregs of sin, the husks of the swine, the degrading vanities of worldly men, could not heal a wounded soul. It is then that, according to those expressive words, "he came to himself," and thought with longing desire of his Father's house; and how he himself was perishing with hunger.

And now his repentance begins in self-abasement. All his hope in returning is to be as an hired servant. He looks not to take even the lowest place at his Father's table, but to be, (O mysterious resemblance to the Son of Man!) to be "as he that serveth." And now his journey homeward is the whole progress of his repentance. Already, on commencing his return, he had carefully resolved on what he should

[b] Bp. Wilson, Sacr. Priv. Wedn. Medit.

say; "I will arise," he adds, "and will go unto my Father, and will say unto Him." These words of humiliation were the prayers that filled his heart at every step of his journey thither. The expectation of such a gracious acceptance never crossed his mind; he went on in humble hope, but with no assurance of pardon: if he had presumed and calculated on all this beforehand, he would have been of a far different spirit; on the contrary, hungry and thirsty his soul fainted in him; he thought of what he was in truth, unworthy to be called a son, and he knew that he was indeed poor and naked and miserable; not fit to take care of himself any more. Thus was his whole journey made up of that affecting prayer for mercy, while he scarce ventured to hope that even that would be accepted: and of course he had thus proceeded far on that journey, before he beheld the gracious advances of his Father. The penitent who has gone into a far country, must make some considerable progress on his way towards Heaven, before he must expect to meet with the full consolations of religion. If he has been unchaste, he must make some decided progress in purity of heart, before he can expect to see God: if he has been dishonest, he must not only have made restitution, but be ready to do far more, before Christ will meet him with the gracious words which He spake to Zaccheus. If he has been proud and vain in times past, he must come to the temper of this self-abasing prodigal, "going on his way weeping and bearing good seed," as the Psalmist expresses it.

All this must be done in our returning to our Father's house, in which we were placed at our Baptism, and from which we have wandered far away; we must arise, when brought to ourselves, with the prayer of the poor Publican, that is, with the temper of mind and with all such lowly duties as that prayer expresses. It is indeed the yearning of our Heavenly Father, and the bowels of His Fatherly compassions towards us, which move us to the first beginnings of repentance; His watchful Eye is with us during all our wanderings; His careful Providence guides every thing that constrains us towards Him. But all this is as it were unknown to the sinner, until he has made some progress back along that path, by which he has gone astray. Then he beholds Him, hastening indeed towards him and coming to meet him, in His foreknowledge seeing him afar off, in His mercy preventing him, with His peace embracing him, that he may not be overwhelmed, as S. Paul says in a like case, with over-much sorrow. He must not presume, I say, on this acceptance, until he has gone far on his way towards his Father's house, by improving in all Christian graces. Otherwise he will be found at the last, sitting at the marriage feast without the marriage robe, with which the Father clothes the true returning penitent; and the bridal ring, which is the seal of His covenant. Such was the case with that incestuous Corinthian, whom S. Paul put out of the Church. The holy Apostle wrote with indignant remonstrance at such an one being received among them without repentance; and it was only after signs of a great sorrow and entire change, that he would have them confirm their love towards him, that he might not be swallowed up by Satan's devices with too great despondency.

And thus, in better days, the meaning of all this was shewn by the Church itself, when it required confession of sin and a painful repentance, before sinners were reconciled to the Church. After some crimes men were never again admitted to the Holy Communion in some Churches[c]; in other Churches only on their death-bed; for other sins they were not admitted, till after undergoing a certain number of years in privation and sadness; and when at last received into the Church, it was with such signs[d] of joy and welcome as were calculated to express the penitent's return to his Father's house, to set forth, as it were, his Father seeing him afar off, and running to meet him, and falling on his neck and kissing him. But now men seem to apply all this to themselves on the very morning after a night which they have spent in intemperance, and are sick and ashamed of it, and again return to their sin, and the next day or the next Sunday again take to themselves all this hearty reception of the penitent prodigal. And what is the effect of all this? Of course such hardening of the heart, that if at any time they should be brought to a true sense of their condition, this very parable itself can afford them no substantial consolation, because they have so often mocked themselves with it.

We may depend upon it, that we shall never have any substantial comfort in religion, unless we deal very severely with ourselves. That easy way which men in general have of speaking of the Gospel and its great mercies, as it does not lead them to any great holiness of life, so it will not be any true support to

[c] See Bingham, b. 18. c. 4.   [d] Bingham, 18. 2. and 19. 2. Morinus de sacr. Pœnit. l. ix. c. 30. from the Gregorian Sacramentary. [Ed.]

them in the day of trial. After all, the way of mortification and of the Cross will be found at last to be the only way of true comfort : it is the only way that has the promise, "blessed are they that mourn, for they shall be comforted ;" and doubtless the more they mourn, the more shall they be comforted of God.

In short, it is as much as our eternal salvation is worth, that we do not take up half-truths; unreal imperfect views, on this subject of repentance ; such as can have no safe warranty in the general bearing of Holy Scripture, and cannot be rested on by our conscience in the Day of terror. God's words, such as in this parable, as they reach far and wide, so they go deep into the soul. Nothing but a repentance broad and deep and long can make room in the heart for the Cross of Christ, in its breadth and depth and length and height. What is needed is reality ; the Spirit of God, if I may with reverence so express it, "searching the heart with candles ;"—the Spirit of God interceding therein with unutterable groans ; the Spirit of God reviving all the dead branches, and shewing fruit and life thereon ; and then the Spirit of God comforting with the Anointing of the Holy One, in those that are by mortification made like unto the Great Anointed One.

But now such a repentance, as it is of all things in the world that which is most needed, so it is of all things in the world the most difficult to meet with. Nay, in religion itself it is easy to find all things else but this; and yet all things else are but shadows without it. And this is allowed by the unconscious confession of all; it is that which is not afar off, but "in thy heart and on thy mouth ;" it ever rises to the lips of us all. Doubts in religion and divisions in religion, and controversies and disputes, and scruples in religion, and fine feelings, and peaceful assurances, and even much external shew of labour and busy works so as to swallow up, it may be, all our time; these it is not difficult to find; but thorough repentance; daily humbling, daily loving, daily praying, daily fasting, self-judging, self-correcting, self-renouncing, self-hating repentance; there may be many goodly pearls, but this is the jewel of great price; the heavenly Householder may " bring out of His treasures things new and old," but this is that "treasure hid in a field," which he would give all that he has to purchase: this is the one thing that is needed, to give us eyes to see and hearts to love God and man, in Him Who is God and Man, Christ Jesus.

What a mockery to suppose the heart-broken returning prodigal to be taken up with catching at straws blown about by the wind, while the night is drawing on, and his father's house is afar off, and he knows not what acceptance he shall find, and no where else but the bottomless pit to turn to. No! Let the Jew be of the temper of the elder brother; be assured that the Christian must ever bear about him no other temper than that of the poor prodigal. But if even in religion itself this thorough repentance be so rare, that all things else are to be met with but this alone; what shall we say of the world at large where religion is little thought of and little known; among those who know not what divisions are in religion, because the whole subject of religion is afar off, and it is all one to them; except it be that for the natural instinct of evil, the world is ever glad to join against that shape of religion, in which there prevails for a time a deeper call to repentance? Nay, to him who looks at all deeply and reflects on human things, it will be seen that all, who themselves long not to be deeply penitent, will join to persecute, wherever the "Man of Sorrows" is seen in true repentance.

But let us look around: where is this repentance? Many know not what godly sorrow is at all, nor intend ever to know, but keep it far from them. Others indeed know what sorrow for sin is, but it is only a superficial sorrow without change of life, and when they are spoken to of repentance, they have nothing to think of but this sorrow which they have occasionally entertained: whereas such sorrow at the very best is but the first step toward repentance; for repentance signifies an altered heart; and change of heart cannot be without change of life. A tree is known to be alive by its putting forth leaves, and without those leaves its life cannot be sustained: a new heart can only be known by new works; and without these it cannot itself be kept alive. How then can mere sorrow, of itself, be taken for the whole of repentance?

In others again there has been a repentance bitter and long, such as has broken by God's grace the bonds of sin, and brought about a serious amendment for many years; yet if the period of trial should be prolonged, it often happens that circumstances will again shew that the undying worm, which had once gained admission, is but asleep and hidden for a while, and not cast out altogether. His former self is still strong within the sinner, and when he ceases to press forward for a time, the old serpent whom he thought he had left behind is fast gaining ground upon him; and he has not the strength he once had to resist him. The love of evil finds that in his thoughts on which it may feed, and live, and grow: the root of the old sin spreads forth its branches again within the heart, on which the undying worm may feed. Here then the repentance has been imperfect; the wounds of the soul have been too easily healed: how can a sinner safely meet death with no greater change than this?

Now let me ask, where shall we find a Christian state in these days, that is not contained in one of these three classes, either an imperfect kind of repentance, or a mere shadow of repentance, or none at all? And therefore, I say, there is nothing in the world so uncommon as a true and entire repentance. Whether we have to deal with mankind as ministers of Christ, or become acquainted with them in the many various intercourses of life, our own experience must surely bear witness to this, that whatever sins men have fallen into, there is nothing so rare as a living repentance, extending to all the heart and conduct.

And this corresponds altogether with the view which Holy Scripture gives us of mankind; especially throughout the Prophets; for the Prophets had to deal with men as they are, and to express to them the sense which God Himself entertained of their condition. And therein we find throughout calls to repentance, connected with every thing that could move men's love and fear, in numberless expressions of the great tenderness and compassions of Almighty God, together with His hatred of sin and His heavy judgements. These calls to repentance are repeated again and again in every manner; and yet, like the calls of conscience itself and of His Holy Spirit pleading silently with every man, they are repeated more and more loud, as if there were almost none that answered; as if, from one generation to another, they were repeated in vain: the invitations and the warnings of God were equally unheeded; or if regarded for a time, their repentance was but as the morning cloud which passeth away. If we open the books of the Prophets, we shall find in almost every page that this is the case: "thou shalt speak, but they will not hearken unto thee." "I hearkened and heard, they spake not aright: no man repented e." All their expostulations may for the most part be shortly contained in this expression of the last Prophet, "Return unto Me, and I will return unto you, saith the Lord of hosts. But ye said, Wherein shall we return f?" And every one must be to himself sadly conscious, that the same spirit lies under all our Lord's mournful appeals to us in the Gospels, blended with the same unwearied loving-kindness of God towards us.

In this respect Holy Scripture is very wonderful; that whereas the view which a thoughtful Christian cannot but entertain of the world, as he sees it around him, is very different from that which is usually taken, yet he finds that it exactly corresponds with that view of things which is taken in the Bible. Holy Scripture holds up to his eyes, as it were in a glass,

e Jer. vii. 27. viii. 6.   f Mal. iii. 7.

both his own heart and also the world around him; holds it up to his view, as it is in God's sight.

Would to God that we might consider these things not as spoken as a matter of course in Sermons, but as they are, most concerning truths. If Holy Scripture and experience teach us with the still small voice of God, that this thorough repentance is so difficult and rare, and if our own heart pleads within us that this is borne out by our own case, and if such a repentance is the only thing in the world to be cared for, the only thing on which we can trust; then let us cast aside all unrealities and shadows, and labour above all things to obtain of God this repentance, and in the first place a healthful sorrow, which although it be not repentance, yet is the first step towards it, and, without which sorrow going before, there can be no true repentance.

He that has lived to sin in any way, must die to sin in the same degree, before he can live unto God; and there can be no dying to sin without pain.

Blessed is he who, after having fallen from the high state of adoption, lives in bitterness and humiliation all his days, and feels himself indeed " wretched and miserable and poor and blind and naked," if only, at the end of his journey, he may be welcomed as the returning prodigal to his Father's house, be received at the Marriage Supper of the Lamb that was slain, and be clothed on that Day with the robe of His Righteousness.

† Yet must we not be disappointed, if, at first, we feel not the penitence we would. Deep penitence is an exceeding gift of God. Its sharpest pang

comes perhaps at the sinner's first conversion, when, doubting about past and present, the love of God and his own salvation, he finds himself "in want." Yet is its first state often a confused sense of "want" in itself, rather than a deep loving sorrow towards its Redeemer and its God. And well is it for the soul, if it feel even this "want." It is the earnest of all beside, since He Who is more ready to give than we to desire, requires but our longing, that He may fill us. But yet, for the time, far other is that first desolation of want from that ardent longing of the holier soul, which knows by experience the sweetness of what it "wants," and wants and longs the more, because it, in some measure, has. Far other the fervent desire of the soul, which is athirst for the living God, and the more He satisfieth her by His consolations in the way, so much the more thirsteth to appear before the Presence of God; far other such "hunger and thirst after" the Lord, our Righteousness, from that first state of the soul, when, in real destitution and want, she saith, "I perish for hunger." Far different to be drawn forth to what the soul knoweth, and to faint because it knoweth not its God. Far other the humiliation of one really restored to the full privileges of sonship, who yet, feeling that he loveth not God enough, would be as the lowest and last of those who serve Him, and that first dearth and famine of the soul, which too truly feels that it has been serving itself or divers lusts or passions or vanities, even while, perhaps, it thought it was serving God. The unwatched, unexamined, soul is, on its awakening, a stranger to itself as well as to God. It scarcely ever, perhaps, held converse with itself, entered into itself, enquired about itself, "searched out its spirit," knew itself or about itself: perhaps its very employment has been, by the din and distraction of this world, to deafen itself to itself, to close its inner ears against itself, to bring into itself other things which might smother its own clamours against itself, to go abroad out of itself amid things outward as well as away from its God; to flee itself, lest, within it, it should hear the Voice and see the law of God; to bribe, dissipate, lose, forget, deceive, itself; to put a mask over the hideous self it was, day by day, becoming, if by any means it might escape the pain of seeing its true form and hearing its own reproaches. And too well did it succeed. One's self is often the most painful sight one can behold in God's creation; for it is one's own undoing of God's gracious work. No wonder that they who are strangers to God, long to be strangers to themselves, or that, longing, they at last attain it. No wonder that obeying not His holy law without them, they would turn away their eyes from reading that same law written in their heart, which condemns them[g]. And therefore the first call of God, is to bring thyself back into thine own heart[h], whence thou hadst been an exile. To "recall" the soul's "ways to remembrance," is the first step in "turning the feet to God's testimonies;" to "commune with thine own heart," the first step towards "offering" it "a sacrifice of righteousness" on God's altar: to "come to himself" the prodigal's first step towards returning to his Father's home[h]. The very voice of

---

[g] See S. Aug. in Ps. 57. init.

[h] Is. xlvi. 8. "redite ad cor, prævaricatores." Vulg. taking שוב intrans. as 1 Kings viii. 47. Ezek. xviii. 30.

Nature herself teaches us that the sinner is estranged from himself; for the very name which she gives for any repentance of ill, is "he came to himself[1]." But in itself what findeth it except its sins, its sore "wants?" What finds it, but a "waste of the substance" it had of God? All it had had of God; all it had taken into its own keeping; all it had wasted in that consumption and decay of the soul, sin. All gifts of God, how are they defiled, all graces gone; all, understanding, memory, wit, speech, imagination, knowledge, will, turned aside from their right use, debased, weakened, corrupted, enslaved; all senses, avenues to let in sin into that fearful sink, into which all evil flowed, the heart of man: all turned to nothing; the inward light of the soul darkened; the understanding dulled; the affections chilled; the perception of good confused; the will weakened; the taste depraved; the memory emptied of God and of holy thoughts, and haunted with the spectres of its sins; too often, a very charnel-house of corruption or of vanities. Oh what a sad waste and nothingness is a sinner's self! And therefore once anew it must go forth out of itself, not, as before, to the world, but unto God; it must empty itself, "pour out its heart before Him," take with it all its heavy, weary, load, and lay it down at the Feet of Christ.

Yet, even thus, will it not always, at first, find full relief. It cannot as yet, as it would, either hate itself or love God. Both are as yet too much strangers to it. Its true hate and love must grow together. It knows as yet but the surface of its own misery;

[1] redit ad se: εἰς ἑαυτοὺς ἐρχόμενοι. Heathen ap. Westst. ad loc. Mali ubique sunt, præterquam secum. Senec.

it knows only afar off its Father's mercy. In the abyss of its own misery, it will learn hereafter the abyss of God's mercy; in the depth of His mercy it will see, reflected, its own former misery. But deep contrition comes slowly with deepening grace. The soul, until it is restored to fuller grace, cannot see the real nature of its sins. As it is restored to the light of the Divine Presence, and the light of His countenance shines into the soul, then it sees more, what it has been, and by what foulness surrounded. At first, but a glimmering light is shed within it, and it sees confused hideous shapes around it, but it has been so much accustomed to them, it feels them so very near itself, that, while it loathes them, it seems unable to loathe them as it would. It sees nothing clearly, sees only "men, as trees, walking," having but just been freed from the blindness, which had gathered around it through its sins. It has but as yet, perhaps, a trembling hope of the love of God, that God can love it. And yet it is God's overwhelming love, which kindles love. "We love Him, because He first loved us." The first faintest thought, that He has indeed sought us out and found us, that this longing to retrace our steps to our Father's house is His secret drawing, that His Precious Blood-shedding, though so long and so often wasted by us, is still of avail to us, does kindle a new light in the soul. The first purpose to return to Him seems, by His mercy, a bright, pure, spot within the soul, amid all which around sickens and affrights us. But depth of penitence is in proportion to the depth of our love, and the fulness of Divine grace. At first we have but a faint penitence and a faint love. Our sins are so much a part of our whole selves, that we scarce know how to endure the abhorrence of ourselves. For we must love ourselves, even while we hate what we have made ourselves. And we have perhaps so deeply sinned, that our whole self seems the very self we hate. I mean, sin has too often penetrated the sinner so through and through, has so marred all his acts and so stained himself, that he hardly sees what in his whole self he can love, except that inmost self, the soul which God gave, and in Baptism renewed after His own image, once so bright and pure, now so stained that he scarce knows how to hope that it may yet again be purified. And so that very natural love of self, without which we cannot be, seems almost at strife with that hatred of defilement or of sin, so worked into himself.

But we must not be impatient, even in penitence. We must not think that we can win it or any degree of it, for ourselves. What we have, is His gift. Any further degrees of it must be His gift too. Be we, only, diligent by His grace to bring forth such fruits of repentance as He may enable us, and for the rest, pray we Him and await His time. It may be that it is a part of our restoration, that we should feel our weakness and our misery, by neither being able to repent nor to love as we would. What could so teach us the misery of our fall, as that we cannot, when we would, arise? We felt not our darkness when we sat almost wholly in it, and it blinded our eyes and, the pure light of day not having been poured in, we knew not our darkness. And so God often keeps souls (perhaps most often) for a while in the horrible pit, wherein they sunk themselves, giving them hope of deliverance, in that He sheds a ray of His blessed light within it, yet not bringing them out, at once, into the full radiance of His light. There while they survey by that light the loathsome forms of sins which they had gathered around, while their noise and din terrifies them, and they seem allowed almost to crawl over them and again to defile them, and their whole inmost self seems one decayed mass, and the worm of evil thoughts, if not of evil habits, seems to creep in and out at its will amid the corruption of the body of this death, until they "say unto corruption, Thou art my father, to the worm, My mother and my sister," they learn a deeper knowledge of their loathsomeness, and a deeper hatred of them. "God cleanses," it has been said [k], "many souls, as silver is cleansed, by what seemeth to defile it." But while the soul is thus wearied and confused and sickened with the presence of its sins, it is gaining real repentance, although it scarcely perceives it, or not at all. More will it gain, the longer that heavenly light shines, and the more it prays that it may shine upon it. It is in our Father's Countenance, in grave though forgiving sorrow over our sins, that we see their real depth. It is the adoring study of His thorn-crowned Head.

Think you not that the restored prodigal, as he lived in his Father's house, again admitted to behold His Face, and hear His tones of love, and brought nigh to His holy Presence, must have felt much more where he had been, how miserable his exchange, how loathsome their unholy company with whom he had

[k] Surin.

squandered his Father's earliest gift, than when he first arose trembling and in wretchedness from among them, shaking them off from him, hoping to be re-admitted to be a servant in the house where he was once a son? Think you not he must have felt more his past sickening and shameful nakedness, when his Father clad him anew with the best robe of holiness and righteousness? or the filthiness of the swine-husks, when his Father gave him that rich and costly Food, which had been offered in Sacrifice for him? Think you not, that in the blessed nearness he must have felt far more than before the misery of having been once "in a far country," himself estranged from his Father, and receiving from Him no tokens of His love, no heavenly visitations, no consolations of His Spirit, no grace to revive his soul? or that, in the happy freedom in which he walked up and down under his Father's Eye, he must have loathed far more the wretched servitude, in which, "an exile from home and a citizen of the world," he was yet bound to the unsatisfying service, from which he could not at once free himself[1]? Must he not, when his ears were filled with the heavenly melody of his Father's palace, have hated more the revelry of that riotous living in which he had wasted his substance? And, when he knew again the bliss of his happy home, must he not have shrunk far more from every thought akin to those which once drew him from it, than when he had but that faint memory of the abundance in which they lived, who yet lived in his Father's house as servants?

O then, my brethren, in whatsoever state we may

---

[1] This seems implied in the passive ἐκολλήθη.

be, let us neither despond that we shall not one day see our Father's Face, nor in any glance of that blissful Face and in the Sacraments, which, it may be, we might dare hardly claim, forget what we have been. Wherever we are, we still need deeper penitence and love. Of ourselves, we cannot gain them. Pray we Him continually, Who Alone can give them. Hold we fast to Him, Who holdeth us; forget we not in the robe wherewith He hath anew clothed us, our own inward wretchedness, nor in the Blessed Food wherewith He hath revived our souls, to what penury we once brought ourselves. But pray we Him, that that holy robe may so clothe our whole souls and enfold our whole selves, that it may remove our inward shame, and virtue go forth from it and enter into our inmost hearts and heal them; pray we, that each fresh Sacrament He offers, may be to us a food of incorruption, restoring our decays, efface or more deeply remove some inwrought stain of sin, and fit us, by Angels' Food, for an Angel's life; pray we Him daily to give us perseverance to the end, that we leave not again His Blessed Presence, and ourselves beware of all which would anew seduce us; and He will Himself lead us through the valley of the shadow of death, to those more blissful halls, the mansions of our Father, where, pure from all spot of sin, we may be able to look back on our past sins without defilement and without pain, only overwhelmed by the exceeding love of our Redeeming God and Father, Who, when we were afar off, drew us back by His secret calling and inspiration[m], found us when we in ourselves were for ever lost, gave us life, when we by our sins were dead.

[m] See S. Aug. in Ps. 77. § 24.

Now unto Him Who loved us and washed us from our sins in His own Blood, and hath made us kings and priests unto God and His Father, be with the Father and the Holy Ghost &c.

O most mighty God, and merciful Father, Who hast compassion upon all men, and hatest nothing that Thou hast made; Who wouldest not the death of a sinner, but that he should rather turn from his sin, and be saved; Mercifully forgive us our trespasses; receive and comfort us, who are grieved and wearied with the burden of our sins. Thy property is always to have mercy; to Thee only it appertaineth to forgive sins. Spare us therefore, good Lord, spare Thy people, whom Thou hast redeemed; enter not into judgement with Thy servants, who are vile earth and miserable sinners; but so turn Thine anger from us, who meekly acknowledge our vileness, and truly repent us of our faults, and so make haste to help us in this world, that we may ever live with Thee in the world to come; through Jesus Christ our Lord. Amen.

SERMON IX.

VIRTUE OF THE CROSS THROUGH LOVE[a].

(Friday Morning, Vigil of All Saints.)

GAL. vi 14.

"But God forbid that I should glory, save in the Cross of our Lord Jesus Christ, by Whom the world is crucified unto me and I unto the world."

WHATEVER differences of opinion may exist respecting the use of the Holy Cross, and the advisableness of having it to meet the eye at every turn, all surely will agree in this, that our very perfection and salvation consists in having it ever impressed upon the heart, and upon all that we say and do and think; if not as a sign on the hand or as a frontlet between the eyes, if not literally on the posts of our house and on our gates, yet that in going out and coming in, in sitting in the house and walking by the way, in lying down and rising up, we should ever bear about in the body the sense of Christ crucified.

But is the Cross all of humiliation and pain? No, surely. It speaks indeed of shame and sorrow, but of these as lost and overwhelmed with love unspeakable. The Cross sets before us the truth of our condition, the truth as it is in God; but not the truth only, for that we could not endure to contemplate,

[a] [Rev. Isaac Williams.]

but the truth united with love. It is that blissful and inseparable union which God Himself has joined, and which man must never, either in his practice or his teaching, rend asunder. It is in this mystery of godliness that mercy and truth are met together; and righteousness and peace have sealed their covenant with the kiss of charity.

It is not for truth then that we ask with the heathen judge, but for the Truth as it is in Christ crucified. And this our Blessed Saviour ever set forth in the teaching of His Gospel; for although He ever spoke of bearing the Cross, yet it was of bearing it together with Him. As He had never spoken to man but from between His mercy-seat of old, so it was from the midst of works of mercy, nay, rather it was by works of mercy, that He taught and proclaimed His kingdom. If it were truth alone which were needed, this the devils were earnest to proclaim. For as they believe and tremble, so were they desirous, if one might so speak, to confess and preach Christ; and our Lord in casting them out exercised His Divine authority and power to prevent their doing this. "He suffered not the devils to speak," we read, "because they knew Him." It was the constant desire and effort of the evil spirits to make Him known. "I know Thee Who Thou art," said one, "the Holy One of God." "Art Thou come hither," cried another, "to torment us before the time?" Now what was this but to confess the Son of God, to acknowledge Him as the Eternal Judge; to make known among men His holiness; to shew that He was their enemy, and therefore the great Saviour of mankind? But yet He suffered them not.

He would not have the everlasting truths of His kingdom made known but from the midst of His healing miracles. When John the Baptist sent to Him for His own evidences of the Christ, His only answer was an appeal to His works of mercy. "Then Jesus answering said unto them, Go your way, and tell John what things ye have seen and heard; how that the blind see, the lame walk, the lepers are cleansed, the deaf hear." And when He sent forth the twelve Apostles as heralds of His kingdom, and afterwards the seventy disciples, the healing of men's bodies was to be the very seal and outward sign of their commission. Through these proofs of loving-kindness was the call to repentance and the Cross. "Into whatsoever city ye enter, heal the sick that are therein, and say unto them, The kingdom of God is come nigh unto you." Even as our very prayer for "daily bread" brings with it this world's goods and the pledge of that better Bread, even the Living Bread, Which came down from Heaven to be our Life. And when He Himself would remonstrate with His enemies of truth and of judgement, He first puts forth His compassionate Hand full of tenderness, and heals the wounded ear, that they might listen to His heavenly voice. And as Christ by His Cross constraining, so His martyrs by their deaths bear witness, His saints by their sufferings, S. Paul appeals by his bonds, S. Peter is by repentance made meet to "strengthen his brethren;" all speak from the Cross, by the Cross are made full of compassion, and by being made compassionate convert souls. Even unto the end His true prophets shall be known by their fruits, by fruits of love; and the good Samaritan, by his healing the bodies of men, shall be known to be He that poureth oil and wine into their wounded souls; and the Good Shepherd, that gives His life for the sheep, shall be known again on His coming from the grave, by carrying the lambs in His bosom. All the boasted seeking for truth is to be suspected, if it be not combined with a compassionate consideration for others. Satan may speak truth, may transform himself into an Angel of light; but habitual love he cannot counterfeit.

All the Gospel narratives are but the embodying of the unutterable love and humiliation of Christ crucified, embracing all, but embracing them in bleeding Arms, and Hands transfixed with pain. For such was His watching over all, praying whole nights and fasting, and seeking for all in thirst and wearisome travel; the birth-pangs of anguish indeed, but of love unspeakable. In like manner is all the Old Testament replete with Christ crucified; I speak not of the Cross in type and figure, but of God speaking to us in Christ, as if even from the foundation of the world bearing the Cross for us, and coming down from the throne of His glory to speak to us from the Cross. For God is Love; and God is only known among men by the Cross of Christ, and therefore the Cross is inseparable from love, and encompassed with the rainbow of His promise, with His love shining upon our tears; and in the Old Testament He appeals to us among burning thorns, as setting forth His thorny crown; and is typified by men suffering pain; and in His prophets He ever speaks as the "Man of sorrows and acquainted with grief;" because He bears our sicknesses in healing them, and carries our sorrows in relieving them. "In all their affliction He was afflicted, and the Angel of His Presence saved them.".........." He bare them and carried them all the days of old." The guiding rod of Moses was but His Cross; and the pillar of fire and the cloud but set forth His guardian care, that day and night ceased not to watch, "as an eagle fluttereth over her young, spreadeth abroad her wings, taketh them, beareth them on her wings." The expressions of His love are ever such as denote suffering compassion; for His compassions are truly, as the word imports, a suffering with us; putting on humanity and every tender relationship, in order that He may suffer in pleading and expostulating with us, "even as a father pitieth his own children; for He remembereth that we are but dust." "Can a mother forget her sucking child, that she should not have compassion on the son of her womb? Yea, they may forget, yet will not I forget thee." It is throughout that Father that waited long and sad, and hastened to meet the returning prodigal. "Is Ephraim My dear son? is he a pleasant child?—for since I spake against him, I do earnestly remember him still. Therefore My bowels are troubled for him." Thus was He amidst heavy judgements as it were stretching forth His Hands to them from His own Cross. And because the Cross so far exceeded all that man could know of compassionate love, more than once is it added, "as the heavens are higher than the earth, so are My ways than your ways, and My thoughts than your thoughts:" and the reason is given, because "His mercy is so great towards those that fear Him."

Now the Old Testament is in great measure an unfolding of God's natural providence as subservient and ministering to the kingdom of grace. In nature also is God ever speaking to us from the Cross, and inviting to the Cross, but ever covering that His Cross with unspeakable love. What does decay and death and sickness, and "the whole creation groaning and travailing in pain together," teach us but the Cross? But in decays of autumn and in setting suns, and in pains of all suffering creation, and in sick beds and death, the Cross is blended with loving-kindness, with gleams of beauty, and consolations, and peaceful hopes; and the darkness of night brings forth the unspeakable and hidden glories of the heavens that encircle us, and like love itself, when appearing most dark, embrace and enfold us most distinctly and lovingly. No calm and peace is so exquisite as that which is connected with sickness and affliction; so that the meanest flower after the sick room is, says the poet, as an "opening Paradise." For Gethsemane has become to us now in the place of Eden.

Thus would God teach us the mystery of the Cross, from the midst of love, and as it were self-humiliation; and, in bidding us bear our cross, goes before us in bearing His own for our sakes; teaching us thereby to follow Him, and thus to partake of His anointing, and of that "virtue which goeth forth from" Him. Thus by Himself, and by all His appointed messengers, filling up that which was behind of His Sufferings, and bearing about His miraculous charities. And surely there is no other method for us to teach the same. If not from the bonds of

S. Paul and from the midst of his many infirmities and afflictions, yet not from abundance and ease and honour, but in some way from the Cross; like holy David, and S. Peter, and S. Paul, himself by repentance and self-humiliation rendered compassionate, that so we may drink of that Divine love which bleeds for the souls of others.

And not thus only is it in doing good to others, but the mystery of the Cross hath passed into every duty; and as the fulfilment of every work of grace is called a bearing of the Cross; so does it also partake of the virtue of the tree of Life, of which "the leaves are for the healing of nations." Every duty is a denial of self, and therefore a bearing of the Cross. But be it so; for the same reason it is not painful; for, pain and shame though it be, yet these are made easy by love. The penitent thief found his bitter agonizing bed of death sweet and consolatory, because it had brought him near to Christ crucified; and painful martyrdoms and lingering sicknesses have become very tolerable for the same cause. And thus the very thorns which are set about our dwellings are good and for our good, because they were borne on the bleeding Brow of Christ. As Christ resigned Himself to drink of the bitter cup of Suffering for our sakes, so have we to drink of the same; and if it be with resignation and for His sake, that His Will may be done, then will it become sweet to us, because it is "the cup of salvation;" the Blood becomes Wine, and the Wine becomes Blood, fresh blood of true life poured into our veins.

And as the image of Christ crucified passes into all things that are His, like the sun in the heavens, infinitely multiplying itself in all things even the most insignificant, on which it looks, so does this great law pass into all Christian duties, even the smallest of daily occurrence. If painful, yet because they are painful, they are all the more connected with peace and hope. "If any man compel thee to go with him a mile, go with him twain:" here is love enduring hardship; and therefore it becomes marked with the Cross of Christ. Rise early to prayer, and it may be that it is an hour that has pain, but it has sweetness also, for it has the image of the Cross upon it, the pain of the reluctant flesh and sweetness of Divine love; it has the Cross upon it; and therefore as such, it goes forward and is stored in heaven. Fasting and alms are acceptable offerings, but not, unless they have the Cross stamped upon them; for without this they will not endure: nor become as the widow's mite in His treasury, in the balances of His sanctuary. This is the rendering unto God of the things that are His in this evil world; whatever bears the Image and superscription of our King as reigning below upon His Cross, these the Father treasures in the royal treasuries of His kingdom against the hour of our great need.

As we walk on the shore, and look forward on that vast ocean on which we are so soon to be launched, and are like children gathering pebbles on the beach, with our heads turned downward to the ground, let us look out for those only, which bear the mark of the Cross[b]. Even amid the trifling pursuits of this

[b] A friend of the writer's once said to him, "My little girl (she was ten years old) was gathering pebbles on the beach with other children; they were looking for a sort of agate found on the coast;

our daily life, we may find something of which to make a sacrifice, and to turn our thoughts to Christ crucified.

And not our duties only, but the efficacy of our prayers arises from some connection with our cross, as bearing the reflection of Christ's Cross, and therefore bringing down the dews of God's grace; shame of confession, deeper earnestness of fasting, Divine love wrought by almsgiving; these are the burning incense on which our prayers rise upwards; these are the grafts of the Cross, in love taking root downward, and upward in love bearing fruit. Nay, our very petitions themselves are steeped in the Blood of the Cross; for when we pray that God's Will be done as in heaven, what else do we ask but that the Cross be established in us according to the Divine pattern in the mount? and when we pray to be forgiven as we forgive, we ask to be admitted to embrace Christ crucified, bearing our own cross as the pledge.

but she had another end in view, she brought me this one marked with the Cross, and to find this had been her object." As a much younger child, her chief pleasure in any object of sight or in dress was to see (as so often may be seen) some form of the Cross. "Never perhaps," he often said, "was there an eye so quick and so glad to discern the Cross;" and the inward eye saw and owned the Cross as well as the outward. As the Cross had been gently laid upon her by her Heavenly Father during life, and had, as it ever does, borne her, while borne by her, so was it her stay in death. The Church of Holy Cross (as it was then called) is inseparably connected with the memory of this child. Of the plate given for the Altar, part was the fruit of her self-denial in life, part her gift in death. At her wish, it was enriched with the Cross, and the last thought connected with this earth, which interested her, the day before her departure, were the Crosses she loved, on the design, which then arrived, for the jewelled Chalice; on which her thin finger rested

One who is a sinner, and knows himself to be a sinner beyond all sinners, has this one thing still left him for the short remainder of his days, to sit at the foot of the Cross, to embrace the Cross, and to refuse to know any thing else in this corrupting world, because, in being willing to suffer pain and shame, he feels that pain and shame bring him near to the infinite love of God in Christ crucified: he loves the Cross, not because he loves pain and shame of themselves, but because they are so bound up with love: and in speaking of the Cross, he knows not how to distinguish or separate his own cross from that of Christ; for he feels his own to be Christ's Cross, and the Cross of Christ to be his: only this he knows, that to bear the cross himself gives him a single eye to gaze on Christ crucified, and leads him to dwell there with more intense affection, with the hope that, when Christ looks into the eye of his soul, He may see something of His own Image there pourtrayed: and that when he himself, after the death of sin, shall arise after His likeness, he may be satisfied: his hunger and thirst be at length filled with His Righteousness: his mourning make him meet to be comforted of the great Comforter, and as he comes to know the dark abysses of his own soul, he may be able to fathom the depth and breadth and length of Christ crucified.

We have occasion enough for sorrow, if we be thus minded, but our sorrows will be different from those of the world; we have enough to bewail and be sorry for, not in the cross we have to bear, but in the many things around us, that bear it not. We have enough to bewail in the worldly goods we enjoy, lest in them we have our reward. We are rich and live at ease, He was poor and had not where to lay His Head, excepting on that hard bed of death which we His creatures had provided for Him. We have a fair name with mankind, but His Name was cast out as evil, and no name could be found so opportune and suited to the Cross as that of Jesus of Nazareth. We are still on the look-out for a little more ease, but the only ease granted unto Him was in order to sharpen and protract His pains: on this side and that, we turn our restless longings; but every turn on the Cross was fresh infliction of anguish. We can scarce be induced to turn our eyes upward at all, except it be for sensible consolations and assurances of salvation and gleams of peace; but on His, when He looked heavenward, was the abiding cloud of His Father's wrath for our transgressions. We have, at least, some domestic joys around us; but He "trod the wine-press alone," and for this solitude of His anguish was made an alien unto His mother's children, and His acquaintance put far from Him, and He abhorred of them: we have loving friends with whom we share our sorrows; but His was that our bitterness of the heart, with which the stranger intermeddles not. We have soft worldly appliances for every annoyance; He, stripes oft renewed like our sins, till every part of His Body shewed the corruption of our entire souls; when His "whole head was sick and the whole heart faint," and "from the sole of the foot even unto the head there was no soundness in Him, but wounds and bruises and sores." But from speaking of our own consolations we wander to His griefs; for there we may see, that these our many worldly satisfactions are true matters for sorrow, because in them the Cross is not; they are a medium that reflects It not.

But yet if these are our sorrows, they are godly sorrows, and they also will bring us near unto Christ; and those He loves, He will by chastening bring more near unto Himself, that they may be hid under His healing robe, which was saturated with Blood: if we are ready in heart to go out of these things which allure us to take our rest here, and remembering that in them we "have here no continuing city, go forth unto Jesus without the camp bearing His reproach." The Jews looked into His cup of agonies which they brought Him, but would fain have Him drink it all, even the dregs of gall which they had infused; but to His own He gave each to see His own image in that cup made radiant with His own Blood, and invited them to draw near and taste of the same with Him: each, according to his measure of love; nearest of all, the Blessed Virgin-Mother, of whom it is written, as of none else, that the sword was in her soul: and the disciples, each according to his nearness; S. Peter, chief of all, to be all the while on the most bitter Cross of repentance, shedding tears, and placed thereon, from henceforth to preach from the same unto his death: and the beloved disciple and his honoured brother taken to be with Him and share His Agonies, and admitted to enter into the cloud. "They sought lofty things," says S. Augustine[b], "and knew not that through the lowly valley of death was the passage to them;" they spake to Him of the greatness which they longed for, even

---

[b] See e. g. Tr. 28. in Joh. § 5. Serm. 329. et alibi.

life with Him; He spake of the way, the cup of lowliness and of the Passion, and the baptism in His Blood. And thus at His Death hath He pledged His Church, and given to her also to drink of His cup; and after Death sent forth the Blood and Water from His Side, that we may, even unto the end, be baptized with His Baptism, and drink of His cup.

And where else hath the Church ever found her strength but in this? To us of these latter days she appeals not only by the Cross of Christ, but by the sufferings of martyrs surrounding that Cross, and the bonds and afflictions of Apostles, and the voluntary poverty and mortification of the saints. Thus does she bear witness and pass on the light unto the end. When the fire of her truth seems to wane, the blast of persecution kindles it; by no other pastoral staff has she been able to guide her sheep into the fold, nor to protect them, when there, from the devouring wolf, but the Cross of her Lord. This she bears before her, and in adversity more firmly grasps. Even in these latter days[c], if any have been allowed to teach the great truths of God, He has placed them for a while on the Cross, that they may teach from no other seat in His kingdom, and from no other throne give laws. Some shape of reproach or sorrow hath first imprinted on them His mark: He hath purged their lips with the fire of affliction from His altar, before they have been allowed to preach Christ crucified. Not only with regard to the angels of Churches is it true, that "as many as I love, I rebuke and chasten," but in every parish the same may be seen. When taken into the fellow-

[c] e.g. Bp. Wilson.

ship of His sufferings, and made compassionate by drinking of His Cup, it is given to men to speak effectually; and if His appointed herald bears not this his Master's sign, on some other in that place shall His mantle fall, whose silent example shall speak more than words. If indeed we look into any family, and the teaching of God is there, we shall find that it is mostly through the means of those that suffer, some one on the bed of sickness or otherwise afflicted, whom God chooses to warn others by their words and their example and their prayers. Even the words of a child in sickness are often such, as seem to speak to others by the Spirit of God: the mouths of suffering babes are found eloquent in His kingdom, and have been known to find access to a heart that seemed closed to all beside, and have opened anew the dried-up fountain of tears.

To be by suffering made meet for doing well; and to do well and to suffer for it; and to suffer, in order that we may do well; this is our calling: and if God finds in us thus any secret resemblance to the Son of Man, He may also lift us up toward heaven, and draw men unto us by suffering. They who would do good to the world in a worldly way, shall be called benefactors; but it shall not be so among you; he that would be great among you in redeeming souls, must be made like unto Him Who gave His life a ransom for many.

To be allowed to do God's own work in the world, to bring forward the great truths of His Church, to convert souls, this is the highest privilege that can be bestowed on man: and he must needs be humbled, who has had bestowed upon him honour so Divine, that no flesh may glory in His Presence. And therefore the high calling to be an Apostle speaks not of converting souls or of a crown of joy, but is contained in these words, "I will shew him, how great things he must suffer for My Name's sake;" and hence that great preacher himself of Christ crucified was himself, even in his very preaching, in "trembling and much weakness and great infirmities:" and another, to whom, if to any, were more signally assigned the keys of remission, had himself most needed the same: and the Psalmist himself, the inspired teacher of God's holiness, in the depth of his afflictions found this comfort, that his sorrows might work for the conversion of others, when, after the deepest expressions of penitential sorrow, he exclaims, "then shall I teach Thy ways unto the wicked, and sinners shall be converted unto Thee."

And even for the penitent, and the sinner above all sinners, there is room for hope, if God is pleased to place him in the school of affliction, that even from this he may be allowed to do greater things than he thinks for; and it may be (so incomprehensible and overflowing is the goodness of God!) that He may render him an instrument to win souls to Him.

Nor do we in this too much exalt repentance. The prodigal son went on his way weeping, and, on returning from a far country to his father's house, had ever on his lips and in his heart and in all his bearing that prayer of humiliation, "I am no more worthy to be called Thy son: make me as one of Thine hired servants." Yet his gracious acceptance was not only beyond his thoughts; but, O the wonderful and mysterious providence of God! even unconsciously beforehand while in this temper of mind, he was being made like unto the Son of God Himself, Who ever delighted to be among men, not as the Eternal Son in Whom the Father was well-pleased, but "as he that serveth:" as one Who came not to be ministered unto, but to minister. What therefore if it be so in His unspeakable goodness, that from the bitterness of repentance may come forth one meet to serve Him in this life, when our sorrows become like the sea even as our sins, and the waterfloods run over us; yet the depths of God's mercies are found therein, calling in answer to the depths of our sins; and we may even from them come forth like Jonah from the great deep, made meet to preach repentance and the unsearchable riches of Christ crucified?

† And not we only, but on whomsoever and howsoever the Cross has come, be it as the evident chastisement of sins, the very consequence of them, or signal punishment for them, yet, if it be borne meekly by virtue of the saving Cross, such, though the poorest or most ignorant, with no other gifts of nature, no speech, nor utterance beyond the simple confession of Christ's mercies through the Cross, becomes, by his very being, a preacher of Christ crucified. Such is the wonderful and mysterious efficacy of the Cross. It has a power and virtue, wherever it descends, infused by Him Who said, "When I am lifted up from the earth, I shall draw all men unto Me." Words of comfort have other power, they speak another language, they speak to

the heart, when uttered by one who has felt the blessed, penetrating, because piercing, touch of the Cross. Words have a power not their own, when given through the inward knowledge of the Cross. They who utter them have a mysterious being and privilege they know not of. Of themselves they know this only, that Christ has, as they deeply feel, for their sins, given them His Cup to drink. But He Who regards not their unworthiness, but has vouchsafed to them His Cross to heal them, giveth to It, in them, Its own efficacy. As they on whom His gifts of healing were shewn, the lame or paralytic or blind or leprous, became, by their very being, living witnesses of His mighty love, so now, whosoever, having been once blind to himself, to the nature of sin, or the holiness of God, now, through the touch of the Cross, sees; whosoever, once bowed down by a spirit of infirmity to earthly things, has now been lifted up to the Cross, and from it beholds his Lord, is, by that very change, a witness that 'unto Christ Crucified and Risen and Ascended, "all power is given in Heaven and in earth." It needs not words. The lowlier, the more real and powerful his witness; for lowliness is the depth of the grace of Christ. As, before, through sin, there hung around him a nameless something, bearing a token of inward decay, so, when turned to God through the Cross, there is a hidden power within him, giving force to words, looks, acts, his very self-abasement and deep sense of unworthiness, not his own nor known to him, but the Presence of that Holy Comforter, Who ever rests upon the Cross and hallows it.

Blessed then, thrice-blessed are ye, to whom your

Virtue of the Cross through love.

Lord has fitted your cross, as He, in His righteous but tender love, saw best for you. Blessed are ye, if ye but learn your blessedness, whatever cross, by nature or by the order of His government, He has placed upon you. Ye will not seek high things, on whom the lowly Cross has been bestowed. But treasure it up for yourselves in your secret hearts; there is no form of it, which is not healing; bury it deep there: it will heal you first, through His gracious Spirit, and when it has healed you, will through you heal others. Only yield yourselves to His Fatherly Hand Who gave it you, to do to you, in you, through you, His loving and gracious Will. So may the very punishment of sin raise you to the very life of the blessed; the chastisement of self-will may conform you, by His grace, to His ever-blessed Will, which is the joy of Angels, the perfection of saints, the bond of all things, the end of the human Life and Death of the Incarnate Son.

Now unto Him Who hath loved us, and washed us from our sins in His own Blood &c.

Almighty God, Who hast given Thine only Son to be unto us both a sacrifice for sin, and also an ensample of godly life; Give us grace that we may always most thankfully receive that His inestimable benefit, and also daily endeavour ourselves to follow the blessed steps of His most holy life; through the same Jesus Christ our Lord. Amen.

SERMON X.

LOOKING UNTO JESUS, THE GROUNDWORK OF PENITENCE.

(Friday Evening. Vigil of All Saints.)

HEB. xii. 2.

"*Looking unto Jesus, the Author and Finisher of our faith.*"

GREAT need have we, indeed, to look to Jesus! As Man, our Way and Pattern and Guide; as God, our Home to Whom we are going; without, the Image Which, day by day, we should seek to have traced upon ourselves; within, the Giver of that Holy Spirit Who traces it; without, in His Life, Death, and Passion, the Object of our Love; within, He poureth in that love wherewith we love Him, through the Holy Spirit which He hath given us. His Passion melteth into love those whose thoughts dwell upon It, and He by His Fire first melteth our stony hearts within, and upholdeth our heavy thoughts that they may rest on Him. He is our Teacher: without, by His gracious and Divine Acts; within, by pouring into us His Light and Love: our Redemption by His Death, our Righteousness by His

Indwelling; Himself, in Himself, the Eternal Righteousness and Wisdom, for which we thirst; our Righteousness here in the way, in that we thirst for Him; hereafter in His Fulness, when they who thirst for Him, shall be filled[a]. He is "the Author and Finisher of our Faith," without us, in that He Who is "the Beginning and the End," is the Object of our Faith, and Alone wrought that Redemption, whereon our faith hangs. He is "the Author and Finisher of our Faith" within us, in that faith is His gift, He gave us hearts to believe; He increaseth, upholdeth, perfecteth our faith; to those who shall persevere to the end, perseverance is His gift. He calleth His own out of the world, guides them by His counsel, upholds them by His Hand, is with them in the valley of death, receives them into glory. "Whom have I, Lord, in heaven but Thee? and there is nothing upon the earth that I desire in comparison of Thee. My flesh and my heart faileth, but God is the strength of my heart and my portion for ever."

And of these ways of beholding our Lord, it must be very dangerous to allow the soul to contemplate Him in either, to the neglect of the other. Our Lord is One Lord. In His humiliation He was God; in His exaltation He is Man, since, as Man only, could the Co-Equal Son be exalted. He was Almighty God, when He "abhorred not the Virgin's womb," lay in the manger, was carried into Egypt, was spat upon, blind-folded, buffeted, was weary, faint, expired on the Cross. As God, He sanctified her who bare Him, received the wise men's gifts, supported

[a] see S. Aug. Ep. 120. § 19.

her in whose arms He was supported [b], gave to each suffering its value for the effacing of the sins of the whole world. And now, as Man, He intercedeth, yea, prayeth, for us, Who, as God heareth us. "No greater gift," says an ancient father [c], "could God bestow on men than that He made His Word, through Whom He created all things, their Head, and united them to Him as members; so that He should be Son of God and Son of Man; One God with the Father and one Man with men; in such wise that neither when we speak to God in prayer, do we separate from Him the Son, nor when the body of the Son prayeth, doth He separate from Himself His own body, but He Himself, our Lord Jesus Christ the Son of God, is the One Saviour of His body, Who both prayeth for us and prayeth in us, and is prayed by us. He prayeth for us as our High Priest, prayeth in us as our Head, is prayed by us as our God." Either were contrary to the Faith, to think that, as Man, He ever did any act except as being also God, or that His acts had not in them a Divine virtue and excellence, because He did them, being God; or that now His Sacred Manhood, although Deified, and passing into the Divine Nature, does not still coexist, never to be severed from His Godhead.

Almost all heresies arise from some misbelief as to that great mystery of godliness, "God manifest in the Flesh." S. John says, "Every spirit that confesseth that Jesus Christ is come in the Flesh is of God, and every spirit that believeth not that Jesus Christ is come in the Flesh is not of God." And so it must also be of great injury to our whole religious

[b] "portans a quo portabatur." S. Bern.   [c] S. Aug. in Ps. 85. init.

habits to think of Him at any time otherwise than as whole Christ. " Own we," says the same father [d], "the two-fold Substance of Christ, the Divine, whereby He is Equal to the Father; the Human, whereby the Father is greater. Yet Both together is not two, but One Christ; else were God a quaternity, not the Trinity. For as the rational soul and flesh is one man, so God and Man is One Christ; and thereby Christ is God, a reasonable Soul, and Flesh. Christ we own in all; Christ in each. Who then is He by Whom the world was made? Christ Jesus; but in the Form of God. Who was crucified under Pontius Pilate? Christ Jesus; but in the form of a Servant. And so of each part whereof the Man consists. Who was not left in hell? Christ Jesus; but only in the Soul. Who lay three days in the tomb, to rise again? Christ Jesus; but in the Flesh alone. In each of these then is Christ named. Yet all these are not two, or three, but One Christ."

It were then very perilous, in dwelling upon the Person or Office of our Blessed Lord, to allow ourselves to dwell, so to say, on one side only of His Divine Truth; to think of Him (as one such case) as our Pattern, without thinking of Him as our Redeemer; or as our Redeemer, and not as our Pattern; or again, as both our Pattern and Redeemer, and not also the Author of all grace whereby alone we can receive Him as either. For so we should divide Him Who is One; and not only do men injure their whole faith, but even that very portion of it, which they set thus partially before them. Thus Scripture says, " Forasmuch then as Christ hath suffered for us in

[d] S. Aug. Tr. 78. in S. Joann. § 3.

the Flesh, arm yourselves likewise with the same mind;" i. e. be this your armour against the Evil one, to be conformed with Christ Crucified, to crucify your sins, to nail to His Cross the desires of the flesh, the pride of life, the love of the world, yea, every longing of the heart which draws away from Him, though the nails pierce you to the quick as they did His Divine and tender Flesh, when, for you, He hung in pains unutterable on the Cross. Suffer with Him, that ye may reign with Him. It were a dream, then, and contrary to Holy Scripture, to think that we could love the Passion of Christ and not engrave it on our lives; that we could be melted by His sorrows, which for us He bare, and ourselves not sorrow or suffer with Him; "delicate members of a thorn-crowned Head;" as though His bitter Sufferings were but to give us ease, to "eat, drink, and be merry," to disport ourselves on this earth, which He watered with His Bloody Sweat, and redeemed with His Precious Blood. The Sufferings of Christ cannot be real to him who never suffers. Again, we know how very coldly they have ever spoken, who have set forth our Lord as the Pattern, Whom we should follow, themselves not meditating upon the Redemption which He wrought, or with what bitter pains He wrought it. It is not, that they deny it; but speaking or thinking of Him as Man, the example of us men, they lose the living faith, that in all He was Almighty God, and think of His Divine Actions after the manner of men, rather than as a Divine law for man.

Again, it is not uncommon to speak of His Sacred Passion, as if It *must* affect the heart of man, whereas we might remain, ice-cold under His very Cross, unless He Himself kindle our hearts with His piercing look of love. He has said, "If I be lifted up from the earth, I shall draw all men unto Me." Truly there is in the Passion a power of love, to draw men and Angels into one, to make men Angels, and all one in Christ; to draw us out of the mire of sin wherein we lay, aloft to Him, to make us hang on Him, cleave unto Him, to lift us up from earth and earthly desires, with that cloud of witnesses by whom we are surrounded, whom we this Eve commemorate, the white-robed^e army of His redeemed, which ever followeth Him, drawn up by the Sun of Righteousness, away from the damp of this earth, gathering around Him, and glorified by His light and reflecting it. Yet this power it has only, because He Who loves our souls, imparts it; He must draw us inwardly, if we are to run to Him, as He has said, "No man cometh unto Me, unless the Father Who hath sent Me draw him." He saith not, "The thought of My Passion, meditation on My exceeding love, thankfulness for the love wherewith I so loved them as for them to become Man, for them so to suffer," but "*I* shall draw all men unto Me." Himself, our Redeeming Lord, is that living Centre of our souls, the Sun of Righteousness to Whom all things are drawn, around Whom all things roll, to Whom all turn, from Whom all look for and have the glow of life and love, through which *they* live whom God brings back into the harmony of His creation. Himself is the True Sun, "from Whose heat nothing is hidden" in His new creation; Him-

^e Rev. iii. 4. vii. 13, 17. xiv. 4.

self the hidden magnet, Who, having no Form or Beauty when He died for us, draws mightily to Himself all who have that which can be drawn, and drawing, holds them to Himself, imparting to them of the virtue which goeth forth from Him, and thereby transforming them into Himself; so that, the closer they are held to Him, the more of His virtue floweth into them, and the more they receive of Him; the more do they, by His indwelling virtue, cleave unto Him, upheld not of themselves but by His Spirit Which dwelleth in them. He, through Whom are all things, Himself, through all, inspirations, Sacraments, hidden drawings, the yearnings and cravings of the soul, prayers, meditations, the Mysteries of His Incarnation, Life and Death and Resurrection, His Sufferings and His Glory, draweth all; Himself as God, the Beginning from Whom all things are, the End to Whom all things tend.

The Passion of our Lord hath in it all sweetness and savour and all manner of delight. In It, as in His Sacred Manhood, are hidden the treasures of His Divinity. It gives power to endure sufferings, and virtue to them, and makes them healthful. It is a remedy against temptation, healing for our wounds, strength to obey, power to love, wisdom to discern, deadness to the world, life to God, freedom from the chains of sin, alacrity to run the way to God, forgetfulness of self, love of God. It is the measure of the depth of our misery whence It raises us, and of the Infinite love of God, to which It draws us, and Whose treasures It lays open to us. It imparts a healthful sorrow for our sins, and makes our sorrow our chief joy; It makes us hate ourselves, and by that hatred and His love, makes us new selves, whom God loves. It turns heaviness into joy, pain into pleasure, shame into glory. It supports the weakness of penitents, the trust of the despairing, shields against relapses, is the holiness of saints, the everlasting joy of all the redeemed. Yet all these and all other wonders It worketh, not in the way of nature, nor of motives to win our affections, nor because our affections *must* needs be drawn by It; for on the contrary It repels the natural man, " to the Jews a stumblingblock and to the Greeks foolishness," and then only avails, when through God's forecoming grace, we yield ourselves to His gracious drawing.

We must then "look unto Jesus;" but our eye must be cleansed by Him to behold Him, strengthened by Him to gaze steadfastly on Him, fixed by Him, that it wander not from Him to the vanities of the world, quickened by Him, every where to discern Him, yea and turned inward upon ourselves, that enlightened by Him, we may know our own utter helplessness even to love Him. We must gaze on Him, with reverence, as our God; with self-abasement and shame, as being, ourselves, through our own sins, guilty of His Death; with wonder at the exceedingness of His love for one so unworthy of all love; with thankfulness for His long-suffering; with contrition for having wasted His love; with longing, again, from His love to receive His love; with purpose of heart to use all the grace He may give, and serve Him with more devoted service, for love of His Love, Who for love of our love vouchsafed to die.

I say not this, brethren, as if it were any new

thing, or what you had not always heard, seeing that these are the very elements of the Faith; but because what we acknowledge in words, we forget in acts; what we own by the understanding, we often receive not in the heart, and if we count ourselves safe and watch not, Satan steals sometimes one part of the truth, sometimes another from us. Who could doubt that he had nothing "which he had not received," that "every good gift and every perfect gift is from above;" that of his own he hath nothing but his sins and short-comings? Who doubts, that as in every breathing the life of the body is retained within us through the secret operation of Almighty God, so for every healthful function of our soul's life we need the continual, forecoming, accompanying, sealing grace of God, in Whom it lives and breathes? Yet he only acts faithfully on this belief, whose whole life is well nigh one prayer; who begins, continues, ends, every course of action, labour, meal, conversation, rest, with some brief mental aspiration to God. Whoever would meditate, speak, preach, on the Passion of our Lord, thinking that It alone could touch men's consciences, would act, as if man could give himself love, or that unloving hearts must melt at once at the hearing of so great love. Blessed be God; the Cross of Christ hath still the same power which It had at the first! It still draws penitents to His feet, twines them around It, that they cannot tear themselves from It, finding sorrow there sweeter than all other joy; It wins even those who once hung hardened on their own cross, converts those who have crucified Him afresh, rends the rocky hearts, awakens those asleep in the dust of forgetfulness, rescues even the prisoners of the grave, raises them, though long since dead, stinking through their corruptions and buried in the graves of their sins, and leads them forth into the holy city, out of the darkness of death into the light of His Presence, the earnest of the Resurrection. "O wonderful power of the Cross!" says a father [f], "O ineffable glory of the Passion, wherein is both the Judgement-seat of the Lord, and the judgement of the world, and the power of the Crucified! Thou hast drawn all things unto Thee, O Lord; and when all day long Thou hadst stretched forth Thy hands to an unbelieving people, gainsaying Thee, the whole world received the power to confess Thy Majesty. Thou, Lord, hast drawn all unto Thee;—for Thy Cross is the fountain of all blessings, the cause of all graces, whereby to them who believe is given power out of weakness, glory out of shame, life out of death." "To none [g], how weak soever, is the victory of the Cross denied; nor is there any, whom the prayer of Christ aideth not."

Yet not the doctrine of the Cross alone, nor its preaching, nor gazing on it, nor bearing it, but He Himself Who for us hung thereon must impart Its virtue to us; Himself, Who bore the Cross to atone for us, applying Its saving efficacy to our souls; Himself, our living Pattern, tracing His own Divine Image on all who "look to" Him. "The Cross of Christ," says the same father [h], "undergone for man's salvation, is both a mystery and a pattern; a mystery, whereby Divine virtue is fulfilled, a pattern

[f] S. Leo, Serm. 8. de Pass. c. 7.
[g] Id. Serm. 15. de Pass. c. 3.   [h] Id. Serm. 2. de Res. c. 1.

whereby man's devotion is aroused; for when he is freed from the yoke of captivity, redemption giveth this power also, that whoso will, may follow it. For if the wisdom of this world in such wise glories in its errors, that whatsoever leader each chooseth, he followeth his opinions and habits and whole mode of life, what shall be to us the communion of the Name of Christ, but inseparable union with Him, Who is, as Himself taught, the Way, the Truth, and the Life; the Way of a holy conversation, the Truth of Divine doctrine, the Life of everlasting bliss?"

"Looking unto Jesus, the Author and Finisher of our faith." We must then first behold Him as its Author, before we look to Him as its Finisher. In both, indeed, He is Himself the Same, Himself our Redemption, Himself the Source of all grace; to the penitent, the Pardoner of his sins; to the persevering, the Giver of endurance to the end; to the perfected, the Crown of the grace He hath given; yet to the perfected also their Redemption and the Remission of their sins, and the Riches of their salvation, to the penitent also, the Author of the grace of penitence. Yet each hath its order. We must cease to do evil, ere we learn to do well; we must die to sin, ere we live to righteousness; mortify the deeds of the body, ere we live the life of the Spirit; bury the old man in the Tomb of Christ, ere the new can be retraced in us; die in His Death, ere we live fully by His Life.

The first-fruit then of the Passion of Christ, is to cleanse the soul in penitence. The vessel must be cleansed of its taints, ere it can receive the good wine. It is in gazing on Jesus that we first learn the foulness of our sins, and gain a deep, loving, healthful sorrow; it is there that, loving much, we are much forgiven. If thou wouldest learn a loving penitence, if thou wouldest have thy sins forgiven, spread out thy sins there. It may be an aweful sight; but there, and there only, mayest thou endure them. To Him, the Judge of men, they are known already; they are known also, in a dreadful way, to the Accuser of the brethren, who taught them. Why should we alone, whom it most concerns, hide them from ourselves, to be revealed to us in the hour of death perhaps, or hopelessly in the Day of Judgement? Then wilt thou love Christ as thy Redeemer, when thou knowest that He is thine own; not, in a vague way, for the infirmities of our nature or as one in the general mass of a sinful race, but when thou knowest thine own sins, and from what He Who died for thee has redeemed thee. Then wilt thou hate thy sins, when thou knowest what they were, one by one, by which thou addedst to that weight of sorrow which He bore; that they formed part of that amazement and great heaviness which He endured; that they sharpened the nails which pierced Him; they were the thorns, which wrung His Brow: to heal them, was His Holy Body torn with stripes; to cover thy shame, did He bear the shame of the Cross. He was forsaken of the Father, that thou, who hast so shamefully forsaken Him, mightest still not be for ever forsaken of Him, the God of thy salvation.

Sit thou, then, when thou canst, apart: there, by the light of His Cross, unfold the book of conscience: much, once written there, is faded from thy sight; He will revive the letters, if thou pray for His light;

in darkness or loneliness much will come back, which is hidden amid the din and glare of the world. But chiefly He will unfold thee to thyself; at one time, one sin will flash across thee, then another; too surely are they thine own; they are the miserable price, at which .thou boughtest thy miserable pleasures: the deadly sweetness has vanished, the bitter memory and the foul spots remain. Couldest thou see them all, thou couldest not endure their foulness or thyself; of thyself, thou canst not cast them from thee, nor their bitter fruits. "We could not," says a holy man [i], "bear a garment so defiled. Who would not vehemently shrink from it, quickly cast it off, cast it from him, as abominable? What when we find ourselves such within, and the defiled soul cannot cast itself from itself? What when we find an inward leprosy, which at great pains and toil he hath gained to himself?" It is an aweful, dreadful, sight often, brethren, page after page, to unfold that miserable book, to see the wretched course of years, calendared by sins; each season of life yielding, perhaps, its own fruits of sin; years, months, days, hours, each swelling the haunting tale; each several sin an act of rebellion against God thy Father, of thanklessness to God thy Redeemer, of despite to God thy Sanctifier! And if each of that ghastly heap be such, what the whole? what the subtler sins, which the conscience was too blinded to perceive? what the canker eating away every seeming good? What seeming good could be the fruit of grace, amid all this which destroys all grace? Where in all this death could have been the life of the soul, which is

[i] Abridged from S. Bern. de convers. ad cler. c. 3.

God within it? Well may we say, "My sins have taken such hold upon me, that I am not able to look up; yea they are more in number than the hairs of my head, and my heart hath failed me."

But, aweful as the sight is, to what end to hide it from ourselves? Better that the loathsome, sickening sore should come to the surface, than that it should putrify within, and become incurable. Fear not! He Who hath borne with thee in thy sin, much more will He upbear thee in thy penitence. It is His voice which hath called thee, "Lazarus, come forth." He hath called thee where thou didst lay, buried under the heavy weight of thy evil habits, hidden in thy conscience from His light, stiffened and bound round with the grave-clothes of thy sins, that thou couldest not move towards Him, and thy face bound round, that thou canst not yet behold Him, He, the depth of light and mercy, calleth to the depth of thy darkness and misery, to come forth from the darkness of thy conscience unto the light of His mercy; He shall loose thee that thou shalt come freely unto Him, and behold His Countenance, and be one of those who sit at the table with Him in His kingdom.

But, first, must we, with Magdalene, kneel at the foot of that aweful Tree, where He, the All-Holy, was made sin for us; He, Who was the Life, died; the Innocent was tortured; the Lord of glory put to an open shame. Would it had been *for* us only! Enough had this been to have caused His Death. But ourselves to have done it! ourselves to be joined with those from whom we shrink, the chief-priests who mocked Him, the coarse multitude who reviled

Him, the thieves (it is almost too dreadful, brethren, to speak) "who cast the same in His teeth." And yet (although it almost makes one dizzy to think of it and chokes one's breath) what says Scripture of any grievous sin? "Seeing that they crucify to themselves the Son of God afresh, and put Him to an open shame." And yet, even thus, His prayer for His murderers may reach unto us, "Father, forgive them; for they know not what they do!" Alas! it is the misery of all sin, that men know not what they do; they know that they are displeasing God; but that they are preferring Satan to their Saviour, a poor bauble or a miserable excitement or a loathsome pleasure to His Precious Blood; that they are giving occasion to devils to triumph in their accursed victories; that they are putting Him Who so loved them as, when sinners, to die for them, to an open shame; this is hidden from them. Too late we find that "too late have we loved Him:" happy, if through any grief or suffering we, by His melting look of pity, be brought to the penitent's confession, "We indeed justly;" to the prayer which translated him from the Cross to Paradise, "Remember me, Lord, in Thy kingdom."

There then let us in His sight spread out before Him the number of our sins, their weight and measure, there (if our heart's best, youngest, warm affections have been wasted upon things of earth, and tears are dried and the heart is seared) let us, at least, with what is yet left us, with shame of face and bitterness of soul, go over our wasted years; our waste of the Price of our souls, His Blood; our waste of His gracious Presence; our ruin of His likeness in our souls, our decay or defilement, and the injury of His Glory. There, in union with His grief and bitter Sufferings, confess we our sins, as He knows them; there offer, if not a broken and contrite heart, yet one that willeth, longeth, that He would break it; say again and again to Himself, "Lord, I would, for love of Thee, grieve that I ever offended Thee; would I had never offended Thee! would I could yet please Thee! would I could have a burning love for Thee!" and He Who drew Magdalene to His Cross, Who, amid the blasphemies of the priests, the false witnesses, the buffettings, the spittings, turned His meek Countenance upon the disciple who had denied Him, He Who softened the heart of the robber who had blasphemed Him, will, whether we hear His Voice or no, say, "Thy sins be forgiven thee." For boundless is the treasure of the Passion of Christ; boundless and overflowing the love of that Almighty Heart, Which for us was pierced; there, in That wounded Side may we bury all our sins, yet It remaineth still "the Fountain open for sin and for uncleanness;" there will He, on true contrition, itself His own gift, again cleanse us; He will rebuild our ruined souls. Of our own we have nought to offer; but if we claim it, all His is ours; for thee He suffered as if there were none beside. Offer with humble heart to the Eternal Father for thine abandoned, useless, wasted life The All-Holy Life and Passion of His Son, and He will cleanse thee from all the sins, for which thou mournest to Him, all thou knowest, and all which, though thou know them not, yet in thy inmost heart thou hatest, and what thou lackest, He, out of the Fountain of His own Mercy, will supply.

Only beware that thou turn not like a dog to his vomit, lest, "if [k] there be no end of sinning, there be at last an end of pardoning." Fearful, though not hopeless, are all serious relapses. In the Passion is thy forgiveness, but in the thought of the Passion must be thy armour. It must be thy refuge not in, but from thy sins; a home for thee, when wearied in the strife, not a mere covert for thy listlessness. "Because," says a father [l], "'the earth is full of the goodness of the Lord,' every where is the victory of Christ close at our side, to fulfil what He said; 'Fear not, I have overcome the world.' Whether then our warfare be against the ambition of the world, or the evil desires of the flesh [m], be we ever armed with the Cross of the Lord." Be this then thy shield in temptation, so to think of His Passion as also quickly to ask, for His Love's sake, His help Who endured It for thee. No sin can long harbour in that breast, which so looks to Christ crucified. Only let it so gaze, as also at all times wholly to depend and hang upon Him, let it so depend upon Him, as also ever to gaze upon Him, and while gazing upon Him in the sacred mysteries of His Love, dart forth continual aspirations after His likeness, and the fruits of His condescension, that through His Birth, He may be born in our hearts, and we, our

---

[k] Tert. de Pœnit. c. 7.   [l] S. Leo, Serm. 2. de Res. c. 4.
[m] S. Leo adds, "or against the darts of heretics." This, although at its own time so very important to bear in mind, was omitted, in order not to distract the mind from the immediate object, which was penitence, by suggesting another extensive train of thought.

earthly selves, die in His Death, rise through His Life, "in heart and mind thither ascend where He is, and with Him continually dwell." For the heart which so gazes after Him, He will draw, more and more, secretly into Himself. Could any be proud, ever gazing on the "lowly of heart?" or impatient, looking ever to the Lamb of God? or avaricious, looking to Him Who, being rich, for our sakes became poor? or hard-hearted, beholding His tears? or indulge in the thought of miserable sin, "in chambering and wantonness," gazing on that Holy Form, stretched and racked on the hard couch of the Cross? or use his hand to violence, or uncleanness, or immodesty, or any other ill, beholding His, so meekly stretched to be pierced for our sins? "This love," says a holy man [n], "is contrary to the desire of the flesh. For what can be sweet to him in the flesh, to whom there is such sweetness in the Passion of Christ?" "I," he says in well-known words [o], "I, brethren, from the beginning of my conversion, in place of a store of merits, which I knew was lacking to me, took care to bind together this bundle of myrrh and to place it between my breasts, gathering it from all the pains and bitter sorrows of my Lord;

[n] S. Bern. Serm. 29, de tripl. dil. Dei.

[o] Serm. 43, in Cant. (on c. i, 13.) The words immediately introducing these, are, "Thou too, if thou art wise, wilt imitate the wisdom of the spouse, and wilt not allow this so dear bundle of myrrh to be plucked away from the chief place in thy breast, no not for an hour, ever retaining in remembrance all those bitter things which He endured for thee, and revolving them in continual meditation, that thou too mayest be able to say, 'A bundle of myrrh is my Beloved to me; He shall dwell between my breasts.' I too, " &c.

first, those endurances of His Infancy, then the toils which He underwent in preaching, His weariness in going to and fro, His watchings in prayer, His temptations in fasting, His tears in compassionating, the snares to catch Him in His words; lastly, His perils among false brethren, the revilings, spittings, buffetings, jeerings, reproaches, the nails, and the like, which ᵖ for three and thirty years, for the salvation of our race, He did and suffered in the midst of the earth. The memory of the abundance of the sweetness of these things will I utter, so long as I live; for ever will I not be unmindful of those loving mercies; for in them I received life.

"These did holy David of old, with tears, seek after, saying, 'Let Thy loving mercies come unto me, that I may live.' These also another of the saints mentioned with deep sighing, 'Great are the mercies of the Lord.' How many kings and prophets have wished to see these things and have not seen them! They have laboured and I have entered into their labour; I reaped the myrrh, which they planted; this health-giving bundle was kept for me; no man

---

ᵖ This enumeration of the Sufferings of our Blessed Lord is repeated by S. Bernard (as his editor notices) in other places, as Serm. fer. 4. maj. Hebd. § 11. Serm. 22, de Div. § 5. It was here closed in the words of the last passage, because the image of the myrrh is carried out in a more imaginative way than we are accustomed to. The whole passage stands thus, "and the like, which that blessed Wood bore, as ye know, so abundantly for our salvation. And here, amid the manifold branches of this fragrant myrrh, far be it from me to pass by that myrrh, which was given Him to drink upon the Cross, or that wherewith He was anointed for His Burial. Whereof in the first, He applied to Himself the bitterness of my sins; in the second, He inaugurated the future incorruption of my body."

shall take it from me; it shall rest between my breasts. To meditate on these I said to be wisdom; in these I formed to myself the perfection of righteousness, in these the fulness of knowledge, in these the riches of salvation, in these the abundance of merits. From these at times there cometh to me a healthful draught of bitterness; from these again the sweet unction of consolation. These upraise me in adversity, keep me low in prosperity, and, amid the joys and sorrows of this present life, guide me safely on either side, as I walk along the royal road, driving back the evils, from which quarter soever they gather over me. These win for me the Judge of the world, shewing to me as meek and lowly Him Who is aweful to the Powers; Him Whom Principalities cannot approach, terrible to the kings of the earth, they shew not only forgiving but imitable." "Wherefore," he says, "these things are ever on my lips as you know; these are ever in my heart, as God knoweth[q]; this is my highest philosophy to know Jesus and Him crucified." May God in His mercy so write by His Spirit on our hearts the Passion of our Redeemer, that It may be seen in our lives, and we follow His steps; else, says [r] that same holy man of himself, "the righteous Blood Which was shed upon the earth shall be required of me, nor shall I be free from that exceeding guilt of the Jews, of being unthankful to so great love, doing despite to the Spirit of grace, counting the Blood of the covenant an unholy thing, treading under foot the Son of God."

[q] S. Bern. adds, "These are very familiar to my pen, as it appeareth."

[r] Serm. fer. 4. maj. Hebd. § 11.

He is, even now, graciously looking on us all, not from the Cross, yet as from the Cross, since even in heaven He deigns in His glorified Humanity to keep those marks, now beaming with glory as with love, which He received for love of us, "the Wounds of His Hands" which He received in the house of His friends. O strange unutterable love, which counted us friends even while we pierced Him, received them from us as enemies, in order by them to make us friends. On us He looketh down in love; may He give us grace to catch His gracious Eye which seeth us, read in it His pitying love, love Him Who loved us, and loving, cleave to Him, and cleaving to Him, follow His steps in the narrow path which for us He trod, that living unto Him, we may die unto Him, and never be severed from Him, "Who, loving His own who were in the world, loved them unto the end." Thou hast said, Lord, "I shall draw all men unto Me." "Draw us forth then, O Lord, out of all the power of the enemy, and evil desires or passions, or listlessness, or manifold cares of this life, which hang around us and clog us and hold us back from Thee; draw us up above the mists which surround us here into Thy pure light; Thou knowest, Lord, that of ourselves we cannot follow Thee; we are weak, but Thou art strong; we are held down by the body of this death, by the cords of our past sins, by the might of evil habits, but Thou hast died that we might live, Thou wert compassed by the snares of death, that we might be freed; draw us then, Lord, as Thou wilt, in penitence unto Thee and to Thy Cross, that bound unto Thee by the cords of Thy love, we may be freed from all besides and follow

Thee; held by Thy hand and upheld by Thy grace, that we may "run the way of Thy commandments, when Thou hast set our heart at liberty," and in this life "drawn after Thee" by Thy grace, may, through Thy Cross and Passion, attain unto Thee, where with The Father &c.

We beseech Thee, O Lord, pour Thy grace into our hearts; that, as we have known the Incarnation of Thy Son Jesus Christ by the message of an Angel, so by His Cross and Passion we may be brought unto the glory of His Resurrection; through the same Jesus Christ our Lord. Amen.

SERMON XI.

LOOKING UNTO JESUS, THE MEANS OF ENDURANCE.

(Monday Evening after the Consecration, Nov. 3.)

HEB. xii. 2.

"Looking unto Jesus, the Author and Finisher of our Faith, Who, for the joy which was set before Him endured the Cross despising the shame, and is set down at the right hand of the throne of God."

THE first stage of penitence has mostly, with deep sorrow, at least some tinge of deep joy. How must it not be joyous, at least, with purpose of heart, to have broken off Satan's yoke, to have been plucked out of the mire of sin and had our feet, as we hope, set upon the Rock, which is Christ; to hope that we are again in our Father's House, in a state of grace; that our Blessed Redeemer unites our sorrows with His Sufferings, our tears of penitence with those tears of Blood which gushed forth from His whole Body, to cleanse that whole Body Which He hath taken, and therein ourselves, the last and lowest and most miserable of His members; that He accepts our very pang that we cannot sorrow as we would out of love for Him and loathing of our sins, as though it were that love itself? How must it not be joyous to us, to hope that the pit, which by our sins we had opened for ourselves, will be closed by Him, that "it shut not its mouth upon us," and heaven which we had closed, is opened to us? How must not our heart bound for joy, at the hope set before us, that we shall one day see Him Who hath so loved and washed us from our sins in His own Blood, nor shall shrink back through thought of our former foulness, when He stretcheth forth His Arms to receive us; that one day our very memory will be cleansed, and we shall be able to look back at all the burning shame of that past, without any hindrance to our bliss; yea that it shall be bound up with our endless bliss and love, and we shall love the more, because we have been so much forgiven? How must we not, though with fainting soul, joy, that, if but the very last in the heavenly courts, we may hope, once, with snow-white souls, to join in that endless harmony of praise, joy in the joy of the highest, though ourselves the lowest, yea joy in the joy of our Lord, and love through the love of God?

Yet must we not think that it will be always so, nor that it is best for us to be thus, nor be downcast if it cease so to be. God deals with us as with children. When weak, He gives to us the milk of His consolations. He gives us some "taste that the Lord is gracious." He gives us an earnest of His endless love, a ray of light which comes from His Divine Presence, which may shine to us in all our darkness and guide us on to the perfect day. But it is rare that He cleanses the whole soul at once. It seems to be almost an universal law of God's holiness, "a man is punished, wherein he hath offended." It may be that, without after-suffering, we could neither loathe our own sins, as we ought, nor feel the depth of the love of God, nor the awefulness of His Holy Majesty which we offended, nor perhaps gain that humility which is a part of true penitence, nor be wholly purified. Yet certain it is, that after a long course of sin, there follow mostly in souls which He leads in the deeper ways of the Cross, seasons of darkness, dreariness, disquiet through evil thoughts, the offspring of the past sin, often strong temptations, misgivings, doubts of God's mercy or of the reality of their penitence, perhaps of all holy truth itself, of the use of self-discipline, fears that they shall never persevere, often an almost seen presence of the Evil one. Against the will of God do men sin, in thoughts of vanity or impurity, or doubt of holy truth, or wilful distractions in prayer, or impatience, or evil thoughts of others, and so, in all other sin; against their own will they are scourged by these same thoughts, when they have parted with their sin and loathe it. And this is indeed of the mercy of God. For thus He tries them, as it were, over again, and by their not consenting to those thoughts, He gives them the victory, wherein they had been defeated, brings them again into the battle, that being faithful soldiers, He may crown them. And so do they obtain an intense hatred of sin, which otherwise they had never known. They could not see its blackness, when they themselves were darkness and walking in darkness; then they see it, when they themselves are in His light and are light in Him.

In darkness we see not all the loathsomeness of the creatures which have nestled in some neglected dwelling; until the light of God's Holy Spirit be poured in, we see not how we have defiled the chambers of our imagery. And so with intense hatred of our sins, we are the more of one mind with God. Hating what He hateth, we learn a deeper love of Him Who loved us, though thus hateful.

"Why," says a father[a], "doth He permit thee thus long to be at strife with thyself, until all thy evil desires are absorbed? That thou mayest understand in thyself thine own punishment. In thyself, from thyself, is thy scourge; be thy quarrel with thyself. So is rebellion against God avenged on the rebel, that he is at war with himself, who would not have peace with God." "Yet begin," he saith, "to the Lord in confession, thou shalt be perfected in peace. Still hast thou war against thyself. War is proclaimed to thee, not only against the suggestions of the devil, 'against the prince of the power of the air, who worketh in the children of disobedience,' against the devil and his angels, 'the spirits of wickedness;' not against them alone is war proclaimed to thee, but against thyself, against thy evil habits, against the old man of thy past evil life, which draws thee to what is habitual to thee, withdraws thee from thy new life. For a new life is enjoined thee, and thou art an old self. Thou art upraised by the joy of this newness; thou art weighed down by the burden of the old; thou beginnest to have war with thyself. But wherein thou art displeased with thyself, thou art united to God; and wherein thou art

[a] S. Aug. in Ps. 75. § 4.

now joined to God, thou wilt be able to overcome thyself; for He is with thee, Who overcometh all things. Hear what the Apostle says, 'With the mind I serve the law of God, but with the flesh the law of sin.' How 'with the mind?' Because thy past evil life displeaseth thee. How 'with the flesh?' Because, evil suggestions and evil thoughts of delight quit thee not. Yet wherein thou art united to God, thou overpowerest what in thee willeth not to follow. For in part hast thou gone onward, in part art thou held back. Draw thyself up toward Him Who lifteth thee upwards. Thou art held down as by the weight of the old self; cry aloud and say, 'Wretched man that I am, who shall deliver me from the body of this death?' Who shall free me from that whereby I am weighed down? 'For the corruptible body weigheth down the soul.' Who then shall free me? 'The grace of God through Jesus Christ our Lord.'"

Thus is the end of these trials, as is the end of all trials in which God guides, in deeper peace, and holiness, and humility, and love. Yet for the present they are grievous. They who so suffer, can often not discern whether the thoughts whereby Satan torments them are not their own. "Can God," they say, "dwell among such foulness? Can this be the temple of the Holy Ghost? Or is there any real love amid all this chillness? any fervour of penitence in all this dryness?" And then perhaps come vehement temptations to think all they hope for, aim at, even believe, a dream, and this life's vain shadow, the reality. And then will come stunning blows, thick perhaps upon each other; God seems not to prosper their work; or what they have laboured to do for

His glory, gives way with one crash. Or God spares not outward trials, in heavy personal visitations, or the deep sins of those they love, or loss of those who, had they themselves been more faithful, might have been less imperfect, until their very soul reels to and fro with their distresses. Sorrows, within or without, will never, through God's mercy, be wanting to the penitent; so that thoughtful men have placed continual prosperity among the tokens of overhanging damnation, as Scripture saith, "if ye are without chastisement, whereof all are partakers, then are ye bastards, and not sons;" and chastisement, though it may be wasted, is still a certain present token of the love of God. So then a thoughtful writer of old tells us, as what he had seen and known in Christian experience, "Sweetness [b] is ever found in the first beginnings of conversion; labour, hardship, disgusts and temptations to struggle with, as it proceeds; peace and repose in its end."

This then is the second fruit of devout meditation on the Passion of the Lord: having learnt by It a loving sorrow for our sins, by It also to learn perseverance amid temptations, from It to draw strength and consolation in suffering. There must, indeed, throughout, be this difference, that He, being sinless, could suffer no trial from within; His was all sinless suffering, the fruit of our sins; ours all tainted with sin, the fruit of our own: His Precious Death was *to* sin, to destroy it; our death in Him was, ourselves to cease from it: His Sufferings were meritorious, ours merited: His, to hallow the nature in which He endured them sinlessly; ours, to purify our own from

[b] S. Isid. Sent. 1. 2. c. 8.

the effects of sin, with which we had defiled it. Yet He vouchsafed to be like to us, even in bearing the likeness of our sinful flesh; and so, in His Death we died, and by His Life we live; so would He come (to speak reverently) as near to us as He can, our Pattern in the endurance of suffering, although the intensity and value of His were Divine, and ours are the sufferings not of men only, but of sinners.

This pattern S. Paul set forth for us in two very solemn ways, the one, as beginners, the other, when we are trained in His school. For Scripture words are so very full, that they mean more or less for us, as we are able to bear it. Either way they are very solemn, for they bring us into the very thoughts of Him Who was God and Man. "Who," he says, "for the joy which was set before Him, endured the Cross, despising the shame." It is a deep mystery to speak of our Lord, as Man, having motives, as we. Yet in that He would heal us wholly, He took our whole nature. He was Perfect Man as well as Perfect God; and therefore although all in Him was ruled by His Divine Nature, and His will was the more free, because it ever followed His Divine Will, yet, Scripture tells us, He had a Human will which He submitted to His Father's. "Not My will, but Thine, be done." And so, as He reformed our whole nature and hallowed it by taking it, so He healed our will also, by having Himself a sinless will, which ever followed, freely yet at once, His Divine Will. And as He was Very Man, so willed He to have all our sinless affections as Man, to hallow all. What condescension, yet what solemn comfort, my brethren, that He vouchsafed with us to weep, to have His soul troubled, to be sore amazed and be very heavy, and, again, in His endurance, as our example, to look forward to the joy set before Him! We might have feared lest it should be too poor a service to toil for a reward: and yet it is a stay to look out of this world's miseries and trials, in the conflict with flesh and blood, and, as we know, with powers also of evil, to the rest in God; to think that each suffering, well endured, makes us, for His sake, more pleasing unto God. And so Scripture tells us how Christ Jesus, Who, in that He was God, could not suffer, but was ever in that ineffable unchangeable Bliss in the Father which He had before the world was, vouchsafed to withhold that bliss from Himself as Man, to look on to it as His future joy, to have it as yet (to speak reverently) in certain knowledge, not as we in hope only, yet, as we too, not yet in possession. There, on the Cross, He saw of the travail of His Soul, and was satisfied; He saw the salvation of our souls, for which He thirsted; saw the reward of the great Price which He was paying, the everlasting joy and glory of all the redeemed; saw us, as many as ever were or are or shall be His, in our every victory over sin by the grace He purchased for us, and our glory, His Gift; saw His own unutterable Glory and Bliss with the Father, and "endured the Cross, despising the shame." And so would He teach us to abide patiently on our little crosses, by His Side, beholding the end of His and the glory which should follow, and knowing that "if we suffer with Him we shall also reign with Him." To His Human Nature that glory was once to come; the heaviness of soul, the pain, the shame, the blasphemies, the forsaking by the Father were to be endured; He foreknew all; to this end was He born; all was ever before Him; we are supported, often, through hopes that we may be spared the sufferings we dread; we know not, beforehand, what they are; when they come, one displaces or deadens another: He hid nothing from Himself, He withheld from Himself nothing but the present consolations of His Divine Nature, and drew from It only the power to suffer more intensely. All that dread hour, from which His human will would have longed to be saved, was in all its Sufferings ever before His Mind. "Now," He saith, "is My Soul troubled, and what shall I say? Father, save Me from this hour; but for this cause came I to this hour."

And not only did He foreknow it, but He chose it. And this is that other meaning[c] of those solemn words, "Who for the joy set before Him endured the Cross," i. e. Who, whereas He might have had joy, chose shame. Free was it to the Eternal Son of God, to remain in His Eternal glory; but He chose for us to become Man; and when He became Man, He need not, had He not so willed, have endured the Cross. He Himself saith, "Therefore My Father loveth Me, because I lay down My life, that I may take it again. No man taketh it from Me, but I lay it down of Myself. I have power to lay it down, and I have power

[c] "Who for joy &c. i. e. He need not have suffered any thing, had He willed, 'For He did no sin &c.' (Is. liii. 9.) as He Himself saith in the Gospel, 'The prince of this world cometh and hath nothing in Me.' It was then free to Him, if He willed, not to come to the Cross. For He saith, 'I have power to lay down My life, &c.'" S. Chrys. ad loc. p. 324 O.T. So also, from him, Theoph. and Œcumenius, and Theodoret quoted by Petav. de Inc. ix. § 7.

to take it again." " He shews," says a father [d], " that not by any penalty of sin did He come to the death of the Flesh; for not without His will did He quit It, but because He willed, when He willed, as He willed." "In His power was it," they say generally [e], "not to be put to reproach; in His power not to suffer what He suffered, had He willed to regard Himself. Yet He willed not this, but regarding us, He regarded not Himself." And so, of all His other Sufferings. "He [f] Who died for us, was first 'troubled' for us. He Who at His own Will died, at His own Will was troubled." "Thou [g] art troubled against thy will; Christ was troubled, because He willed. Jesus hungered; true; but because He willed. Jesus slept; true; but because He willed. Jesus died; true; but because He willed. In His own power was it, in this or that way to be affected or no." What He did, or suffered, He did and suffered through the oneness of His own with the Eternal Father's Will.

And must not that then be good for us, which the Eternal Son chose? Must not that be a proof of God's love to us, which He bestowed upon the Well-Beloved Son? must not that be safest for us, which most likens us to our Lord? must there not be great need for that, which "it *behoved* Christ to suffer?"

So then all things join together, if we are wise, to make us bear the Cross patiently, yea love it. Which of all these were not alone enough, to make us love it? Were it not enough, that it is in the will of the

[d] S. Aug. de Trin. iv. 3.
[e] S. Chrys. on Rom. 15, 3. p. 447. Oxf. Tr.
[f] S. Aug. Tr. 60. in S. Joann. § 2. [g] Ib. Tr. 49. § 18.

All-wise, All-loving God? or that we ourselves need it? or that our Lord Who loved us, for us bore it? or that it is the gift of the love of God? But now to lighten it to us, because it is contrary to flesh and blood, all these are met in one; God wills it for us, because we need it; and He, loving us, gives us what we need; our Lord bore it for us, not only to atone for us, but to impart to our nature the power to bear it, to make us love it, because it likens us to Him Who hath so loved us, and Whom we would love.

All are not taught alike; one is led this way, another that; all ways are right, so that they end in the Cross. Virgin-souls may be most drawn by the love of Christ and the longing for His likeness; "Thy Name is as ointment poured forth" in Thy Passion; "therefore do the virgins love Thee." Penitents perhaps most often hang first, like the robber, upon the Cross against their will; and when, upon the Cross, they, by the secret grace of God, are drawn to say, "we indeed justly," they find themselves near their Lord; then they hang patiently upon it, they thank God for it, they feel its fruits, at last they love it, and would not be without it.

Our first step is patience, "enduring the cross." We cannot expect to love it all at once, not, at least, at the beginnings of our conversion. It will come to us often in some very tender place, piercing us to the dividing asunder of soul and body, so that we are so bewildered with the pang, that we know not what to do; we are stunned or dizzy, and all we can do is, to lie still and motionless and crushed under it. Happy, blessed breaking of the heart, which so bruises in pieces its earthly substance, that it can never come together again, as it was before, but God makes it anew. But that is ever true with us, "What I do thou knowest not now, but thou shalt know hereafter." "No chastening for the present seemeth to be joyous, but grievous; nevertheless it afterwards yieldeth the peaceable fruits of righteousness to them who are exercised thereby." Be not perplexed then, if thou understand it not, nor thyself, if thou know not what God is doing with thee, or art tempted to think that thou profitest not by it, that it is even a token that God has cast thee off, that thou art not bearing it aright, that it cannot profit one who gains so little fruit from it, that it may harden rather than soften thee, that it makes thee worse rather than better. All these and more bewildering thoughts will often come; they are Satan's arts to make us throw aside our cross, or displease God by despairing of His mercy; it is the festering of the nails and thongs of thy sins, which pierce and bind thee to thy cross. Fear not; look unto Jesus by thy side; the nails of thy sins, which pierce thee, have first pierced Him; they have passed through His Blessed Hands, ere they reached thine, and so will heal thee; look out of thyself, and look to Him, the Captain of thy salvation, the Author and Finisher of thy faith.

And to this end, it helpeth much, not to think so much of the outward cause of thy cross, as of the love of God, Who sent it thee. It often makes our cross heavier, and distracts us to think, at one time, that we brought it upon ourselves, at another that it came, as it were, by chance, that had we or others done so and so, or had we been warned, or understood the warning, it had not been thus. "Lord, if Thou hadst been here, my brother had not died." But when the cross has found us, then it is God's will for us. Look not then through whom or what or how it comes, but to Him from Whom it comes. We know Who said, "Not a sparrow falleth to the ground without your Father," "there shall not a hair of your head perish." Rather, the more mysterious it is, the plainer is His Hand, and the greater His love. If He seemeth to do a new thing for thee, and dealeth with thee not after the manner of men, but bringeth thy cross to thee in some strange way, is it not a token the more of His love to thee? Is not His loving Heart set the more upon thee, that His Wisdom inventeth, as it were, some new thing, that He goeth out of the common track of His providence, sooner than leave thee without His chastening love? "Blessed is that servant," says an ancient father[h], "on whose amendment the Lord is bent, with whom He deigneth to be angry!" It is of faith that all which happens, is from God, as either done by Him, if good, or controlled, if evil. Think not then of evil men, if any crosses come through them, except to bless and pray God for them; yea, love them the more, who to thee have been made, by God's mercy, ministers of good, and have brought to thee, though they knew it not, that most precious token of God's love, the Cross of thy Lord. They know not the hidden blessing, whereof they are the bearers to thee; but as, in human joy, our gladness overflows to them who unknowingly bring us good tidings, and we can hardly refrain from sharing with

[h] Tert. de Pat. c. 11.

them our joy, and feel some sort of love and thankfulness to them, although the unconscious bearers of the good which gladdens us; as men would welcome and honour the messenger of an earthly prince who brings them word of some honour or distinction of this earth, and give him gifts; so love thou whosoever brings to thee that choicest gift from the King of kings, the healing Cross. Think not, again, that from them the evil is undeserved. If not deserved of them, it is of God; if we are accused falsely in any matter, we have more evil in ourselves, for which we might be accused truly. And even if the evil is from thyself, and the plain chastisement of thine own sins, lose not patience even with thyself. Be displeased with thyself that thou hast deserved it; thankful to God, Who chastened thee here, that He might spare thee hereafter. "Humble thyself," but be it "under the mighty hand of God," resting as it were under its shadow, trusting in its protection, both against Satan and thyself. "Let the Passion of thy God," it has been said [i], "make satisfaction for thy sins; do thou suffer for love of thy Lord." Think not again that thou couldest bear any other cross better, or wouldest have any other. We may long and pray that "this cup pass from us" before it come, so that we add His blessed words, "nevertheless not as I will, but as Thou wilt." But when it is come, then thou knowest that this, and no other, is best for thee; else His wisdom had not chosen it, nor His love given it to thee to drink. It is a very dangerous deceit of impatience, to think we could be patient under âny other than what God gives us.

[i] Blos. can. vit. spir. c. 10.

Could we be purified or saved in any other way, would He Who saith, He "doth not willingly afflict or grieve the children of men," have chosen this for thee? Be not then impatient with thyself, even that thou feelest impatient, or hateful in thine own eyes, or that thou hast brought the evil on thyself, or that thou canst not amend it; but mourning for thy past sins, commit thy present and future, thy time and thine eternity, into His merciful hands, Who, out of love, made thee and redeemed thee, and now, out of love, would re-make thee to His praise and thy bliss in Him. It has been strongly said, "Although [k] the Lord, as it were, cast thee from Him, and, so cast out, deliver thee in a manner to Satan, so that, abandoned within and without, thou be hemmed in on all sides with extreme calamities, on all sides driven on with dreadful thoughts, on all tormented with unspeakable oppression, yet doubt not, in the least, of the love of thy most loving Creator for thee; allow not a thought, as though thou couldest therefore part from Him, or shrink from thy present trouble, or seek any profitless or forbidden remedy, or give thyself over to any impure consolation; but, bare of all, in faith and love cleaving to Him, give thyself to be bruised and scourged, as and as long as He shall will. Await the issue in silence, according to His ordering and dispensing, saying from time to time in thy heart, 'Let the will of the Lord be done; it can not be evil.' Waver not, I say, in thy holy purpose, although God put not at once an end to thy temptations, but, full of good hope, and with unconquered mind, endure.'" Yet what is this,

[k] Blos. Ib. c. 9.

but what holy Job says, "Though He slay me, yet will I trust in Him." Since His chastening is His love, would we have less of His love? "The wounds of the Righteous are love," says the Psalmist. The deeper, the greater love. Wouldest thou that He should not probe thee to the very quick, that He should leave any swelling unpierced, that so thou shouldest not be healed, that any festering sore of self-love or self-trust, or vanity, or impenitence be left, to destroy thee and eat out thy life? Would we have our dross remain, that we should wish the cleansing fire at an end? Or would we not gladly "pass through fire and water," so that He bring us forth, at last, to that "wealthy place," the rest and refreshment of His love? Rather say we with holy men, "Lord, burn, cut me here, but spare me in eternity;" or as a holy father says [1], "Let then the consuming fire come, let it burn out in us the dross of iniquity, and the slag of sin, and make us pure gold; let Him burn my reins and my heart, that I may think what is good, and desire what is pure."

But that thou mayest endure, thou must not trust in thyself. While we trusted in ourselves we went astray; these sufferings are to teach us at once mistrust in self and trust in God. Part not for a moment with either. Either way, thou partest with His Hand. It matters not in which; whether thou think that thy weakness is strength, or that His strength will not be perfected in thy weakness. "Look unto Jesus, the Author and Finisher of thy faith," that "as He has begun, so He will finish His good work in thee." As He has brought thee into

[1] S. Ambr. in Ps. 118. 1. 3. §. 1.

the fire, so He will bring thee through it and out of it.

"Look unto Jesus," enduring the Cross, so shalt thou never be weary of thine. "Truly," says a father [m], "He scourgeth every son whom He receiveth. Every son? Yes, the Only-Begotten Son was without sin, yet not without the scourge. Whence the Only-Begotten Himself, bearing thine infirmity, and prefiguring in Himself thy person and that of His whole body, when He drew nigh to His Passion, in His Manhood which He bore, was sorrowful that He might gladden thee, was saddened that He might comfort thee." Let us shrink from any form of the Cross, if He bare it not first for us. "And we indeed justly." He bore the very same, if sinless, and for our sins, their punishment. Be it what it may, of body or spirit, He bore all, to sanctify all to us. "Thou endurest suffering for a time," says a father [n], "thou shalt not endure it for ever. Brief is thy trouble; eternal shall be thy bliss. For a little while thou grievest; endless shall be thy joy. But beginnest thou to give way, amid suffering? Thou hast too the pattern of the Sufferings of Christ set before thee. See what He suffered for thee, in Whom was nothing, wherefore He should suffer. Suffer what thou mayest, thou shalt not attain to those mockeries, to those scourgings, to that robe of derision, to that Crown of thorns, to that Cross." He took our very meanest, poorest, every-day ills, that we might be ashamed of none; He took deeper infinitely than our very deepest, as infinitely greater as God is than man, that we might fear none. He

[m] S. Aug. in Ps. 31.   [n] S. Aug. in Ps. 36. S. 2. § 4.

compassionates our least, Who bore each for us, upbears us in each. And He bare all of His own Will, to teach us to will it. "All earthly goods," says the same father [o], "He despised, to shew they were to be despised; all earthly ills He endured which He bid to be endured, that neither in the one might happiness be sought, nor in the other, unhappiness be found. He hungered, Who feedeth all; thirsted, through Whom all drink is created, He Who spiritually is the Bread of the hungry and the Fountain of the thirsty; He was wearied by an earthly journey, Who made Himself our Way to heaven; was dumb, as it were, and deaf before His revilers, through Whom the dumb spake and the deaf heard; was bound, Who loosed from the bonds of infirmities; was scourged, Who expelled from the bodies of men the scourges of all sorrows; was crucified, Who ended what excruciated us; died, Who raised the dead?" Does poverty harass us? think we of the Manger. Or homelessness? of His Sacred houseless Head. Or being forsaken of friends? how the disciples forsook Him and fled. Or unjust revilings? how to the Holy One it was said, "Thou blasphemest;" (not to name all those awful coarse blasphemies, which God's Holy Word records.) Or malice of enemies? see His whole Life, from the cradle at Bethlehem to the Cross. Or shame? the stripping of His raiment and those awful spittings. Or any one bodily pain? behold His whole Body, from His thorn-crowned Head to the nail-pierced Feet, one Bruise! Or false witness? think of the mock-judgement of Caiaphas. And if it pursue thee to thy death, did it not even

[o] S. Aug. de cat. rud. c. 22. § 40. Select treatises pp. 229, 230 O.T.

follow His Resurrection? Or that thou art disbelieved? "Neither did His brethren believe on Him." Or that thy good is evil-spoken of? Of Whom was that said, "He deceiveth the people?" "For a good work we stone Thee not?" Or sorrow in others' grief? go to the grave of Lazarus, or see His Mother by His Cross, when the sword pierced her own soul also. Or seeming abandonment of God? Think of that mysterious cry, " My God, My God, why hast Thou forsaken Me?"

O blessed art thou, who, by whatever pain or sorrow, art in any way brought nigh unto thy Lord! Only pray for patience, to endure by His Side. If thou look away from Him, the cross would be but, as to the impenitent thief, the foretaste of Hell; look to Him, and, for His sake, it is, as to the penitent, the gate of Paradise. The very least will fret thee, if thou look at them or to thyself; the very greatest, if thou look to Him, will but lift thee nearer unto Him. Thee too shall the Cross lift up from the earth, and, by His grace, place thee nearer to Himself. O blessed holy loneliness of the aching heart, if thou mourn only to Him! Blessed widowhood of the soul, which finds no earthly comforter, that the Heavenly may in His time descend upon her! Blessed solitude of the Cross! in which, raised up for a while from among the throng of men, thou art nailed motionless, canst not reach forth thy hands to their pleasures, art severed from them, and alone with JESUS! Blessed void, which nothing can fill except thy God! Blessed hours of unrest, in which thou canst on all sides find no repose for thy weariness, so it teach thee to repose in Him! Blessed bareness and nakedness of the soul, in which, reft of all, it may receive some likeness of its Lord, bared for it upon the Cross, in which all falls from it which hid it from itself, or which it would hold fast, besides its God! Blessed depression and death of the heart, in which all living things die unto thee, and thou diest unto thyself and to the world, and art buried in thy Saviour's Tomb, tastest of the sweetness of His Death and of rest in Him, thence to rise with Him to newness of life, loving Him Alone, seeking Him Alone, living in Him Whom thou seekest, and seeking Him that thou mayest live. "O good Cross," shall all the redeemed say [p], "receive me from men and give me to my Master, that He through thee may receive me, Who through thee redeemed me!"

Be not dismayed, then, that thy sins brought thee to it, nor though it be mingled with inward shame, or be the direct fruit of thy sins; humble thyself the more, but let nothing within thee or without, nothing, if so be, in the human instrument of them, no suggestion of Satan, no sense of thine own unworthiness, no unlikeness to Him, no foulness of thoughts or of temptations, draw thee off from 'looking unto Jesus.' Whatever we have been, trouble itself, if God give us but the longing to be patient out of love to Him, is a token of His Presence. He draws nigh to the soul, Who has said, "I will be with him in trouble," "when thou walkest through

[p] Words which were very probably S. Andrew's, at the sight of the cross whereon he was to suffer. The Acts, although not genuine, seem to preserve things which are genuine. "O good cross, which hast received glory from the Limbs of the Lord, long longed for, anxiously loved, unceasingly sought, and at last prepared for my longing soul, receive me, &c."

the waters, I will be with thee ᵠ." He will (He seems to say) be near thee then in some special way, as though before He had not been with thee. He will then, in a manner, begin to be with thee; for He is with thee, by a secret presence, through the cross He gives thee. "When thou walkest through the waters," He joineth Himself, as it were, unto thee, and upbears thee, thou knowest not how. He, Who was with the three children in the fiery furnace, shall not let "the flame kindle upon thee." Yea, although "He draw nigh to us" in "another Form" and in the guise of "a stranger ʳ," it shall but be, that He may "teach us concerning Himself," and "tarry with us" in the end, when "it is towards evening and the day is far spent." If He seem to "make Himself strange unto us, and speak hard things unto us," it shall be but to bring us to ourselves, and when we confess "we are verily guilty," to "bring us near unto" Him, and "make Himself known unto" us, and sustain us, and "save our lives with a great deliverance ˢ."

Fear not then. Suffering is the bridal ring, by which He espouseth the returning soul unto Himself. The very endurance is a mark of His Presence in thy soul. Alone thou couldest not endure them; thou must faint under them; thou wouldest consent to evil in them or through them, but for His secret, even if unfelt, aid. In itself, chastisement would but harden the heart, unless God softened it. Such is the dreadful picture in Holy Scripture ᵗ. "Men were scorched with great heat, and blasphemed the Name of God, which hath power over these plagues;

ᵠ Is. xliii. 2. ʳ Luke xxiv.
ˢ Gen. xlii. 7. 15. ᵗ Rev. xvi. 9. 10. 11.

and they repented not, to give Him glory..... They gnawed their tongues for pain, and blasphemed the God of heaven because of their pains and their sores, and repented not of their deeds." It is of the Lord's mercy, that it is not so with any of us. Receive, then, thy crosses, in whatever form they come, as most precious pledges of His undeserved love; thank His Fatherly hand Who gives them; pray for grace to endure under them; think of every pang, as a separate gift of His love; unite each, as far as thou canst, with the Cross of thy Lord, and He will give to each a part of Its virtue; the deserved buffetings of Satan shall, by His grace, prepare thee for the society of Angels; the loathsome memory of sin shall be a means of cleansing thee, through His Precious Blood, from all sin; the aching unrest of a broken heart, which but for His love were but the gnawing of the never-dying worm, shall prepare thee to enter into His everlasting rest; the badge of shame shall be thy entrance into His glory. Only "tarry thou the Lord's leisure; be strong, and He shall comfort thy heart, and put thou thy trust in the Lord."

Now unto Him that loved us, and washed us from our sins in His own Blood, &c.

Almighty and everlasting God, Who, of Thy tender love towards mankind, hast sent Thy Son, our Saviour Jesus Christ, to take upon Him our flesh, and to suffer death upon the Cross, that all mankind should follow the example of His great humility; Mercifully grant, that we may both follow the example of His patience, and also be made partakers of His Resurrection; through the same Jesus Christ our Lord. Amen.

SERMON XII.

UNION WITH CHRIST INCREASED THROUGH WORKS WROUGHT THROUGH HIM.

(Feast of All Saints [a].)

S. JOHN xv, 9, 10.

"*As the Father hath loved Me, so have I loved you: continue ye in My love. If ye keep My commandments, ye shall abide in My love; even as I have kept My Father's commandments, and abide in His love.*"

THIS should be a day of subdued, holy, joy, peculiar to itself. On other festivals, we praise God for some portion of His work of mercy in our Redemption, or for some of that holy band of Apostles and Evangelists, through whom the light of the glorious Gospel has reached to us; to-day we praise Him for having perfected what He began, for having completed *in* man what He wrought for him. To-day is the festival of all the redeemed, whom He perfected. All, whatever we may be, if we have any good in us, may find our likeness there; young or middle-aged or old; men or women; masters or servants; rich or poor; in authority or subject to it; honoured

[a] Also before the University in the Cathedral Church of Christ in Oxford on the Feast of All Saints, 1840. See Advertisement.

or despised; learned or unlearned; joyous or sad; in virgin or married or widowed purity; or purified anew through penitence; yet, more among those who were poor, and despised, and mourned, and were, in this life, "of all most miserable." Still, in every people, amid every outward or inward circumstance of life, mind, temper, endowments, feelings, gifts, has He sanctified His own, and so translated them to Himself; assuring us that, what He wrought in them, He will work in us too; that, if we be not becoming saints like them, not His grace is lacking, nor are our trials too heavy, but we are feeble because our will is unfaithful. All have an interest in that goodly band, because all have in that endless variety of "the just made perfect," those who once bore their very likeness, "the image of the earthly," even as we may with them "bear the Image of the Heavenly." As upon them, being what we are now, that Image was once re-traced through the same Sacraments and hidden operation of the Holy Spirit, so may we too, day by day, be transformed secretly into that Divine likeness which now they bear. Whatever our peculiar trials be, many of them have passed through the very same, victorious. All, whose examples kindled our early faith, Patriarchs, Apostles, Prophets, Martyrs, Confessors, Teachers, Ascetics, Penitents, are there; all are at rest from their various labours; all have come out of their varied tribulations, and have washed their robes in the Blood of the Lamb; all are at rest in Abraham's bosom, "in peaceful abodes," "in the keeping of the Lord[b]:" they are restored to our lost, yea a more

[b] S. Aug. see Note C. on Tert. p. 117, 18. Oxf. Tr.

blissful Paradise; they are "with Christ," behold Him by sight not by faith; "see Him ineffably;" joy in His Countenance; see light in His Light; have begun their endless praise of God. Yea, it is to be hoped that all of us have a still closer interest there; all, in some gone before, have their portion in Paradise; all have some who long for and await their coming, in patience, hope, and peace, and prayer; all have some link of human affection with the unseen world; all some treasure there, that their hearts may the rather be there also.

Well might we say, "It is good for us to be here!" In their peace we forget for a while this world's feverishness; in their rest, our own faithless disquietudes for ourselves or those whom God has lent us, or for the Church of God; in their purity, the defilements, which from every corner of our land go up to bear witness against us, and our own, and we long for purity such as theirs and the day when we too shall be wholly cleansed; we long with their praises to mingle ours, under their feet, and for the time (if it may be) to praise God less imperfectly, as feeling ourselves in communion with those who praise Him perfectly, and being joined, as we confess, " with Angels and Archangels and all the company of heaven," catch for the while some faint but cheering gleam of their undying fervour. It is good to find ourselves "in the city of the living God, the heavenly Jerusalem, amid an innumerable company of angels, the general assembly and Church of the firstborn which are written in heaven, and the spirits of just men made perfect;" to feel that we are one Church with them, though we in weakness, they in strength; we hard-beset by foes, they conquerors; we seeing in a glass darkly, they face to face; we weighed down by "the body of this death," they freed; we imperfect, they perfected; we in the land of the shadow of death, they in the land of the living; the issue of our conflict uncertain, they, in peace, awaiting their crown. But in what is all this to end? Our Church, with our Lord, sends us back from the holy Mount into the world of duties and of trials, bids us gird ourselves (as we pray) to "follow His blessed saints in all virtuous and godly living," and in the Gospel, selects for us, not a picture of the heavenly Jerusalem, but the blessing pronounced by our Lord upon faithful duty; teaching us how they became saints, and how we are to follow their steps.

On this, then, their holy day, I would forego the privilege of speaking of communion with them, in their and our Lord, and would endeavour, in conformity with this guiding of our Church, to say somewhat on the way in which they became saints, and in which we must become such, if we would be as they; how good works, wrought in Christ, produce an increase in (we may not shrink from the word) "righteousness and holiness before Him," and union and acceptance in Him. To this end, as it is difficult to gather into one the comprehensive teaching of the Beatitudes, I have chosen words, in which our Lord Himself declares the value of good works as a condition of abiding in Him; as in the parable of the Vine, whereof they are the close, He tells us also their office in increasing that union with Him, whereof they are themselves the fruit. A patient consideration of that parable would, more readily perhaps than any other Scripture, dispel the errors and misconceptions, which prevail on the whole subject, it being one of the clearest forms, in which we can mould our thoughts of the origin and course of our Christian life.

First then, against the Pelagians, it declares that of ourselves we are nothing: "Without Me ye can do nothing." There is no question then of "works before the grace of Christ and the inspiration of His Spirit[c]." By nature we were wild plants, bearing a bitter fruit; the parable exhibts us as *in* the Vine, taken out of our state of nature, made partakers of the richness of Him Who is the True Vine, and so enabled to bear fruit through the nourishment which He supplies, even His Holy Spirit, which He diffuses abundantly through all the true branches. Throughout the parable, our Lord speaks not, how we were brought into the Vine, but how, having been brought in, we are to *remain* in it. "*Abide* in Me," He saith. They must have been *in* Him before. "Every branch *in* Me," "if a man *abide* not in Me." "*continue* ye in My love;" "ye shall *abide* in My love;" "I *have* loved you." Eight times, in scarcely more verses, does our Lord speak of being *in, continuing* in, *abiding* in Him and in His love. The whole subject then of our primary justification, whereby, in S. Augustine's words, "for sinners we were made righteous," is antecedent to, and presupposed in, this teaching. Not only could we not, of ourselves, have become righteous,—much less, in that transcendent way, of being members of Him Who is God and

[c] Art. xiii.

Man,—but having been made righteous, neither, of ourselves, can we do works of righteousness, without the continual inflow of His grace, preceding, accompanying, upholding, perfecting each several act we do. "Without Me, ye can do nothing." And thus, further, the parable corrects not the heresy of the Pelagians only, but a cold form of doctrine, now nearly past away, which seemed almost to regard the grace, whereby we can bear fruit, as an external state or condition, in which we are placed, once for all; and that thus taken out of our state of nature we possess grace as the gift indeed of God, yet rather as a gift implanted in us, than as continually supplied to us, and derived into us by the Giver. As though we had it altogether *in* ourselves, and being endowed with it, had it as our own endowment, much as our natural faculties are, although a superadded gift. Rather it is a stream like the life-giving sap, continually anew infused into us, keeping us ever in a blessed dependence upon the Vine, cementing us into It, attesting our union with It, so that our life is not our own, not an imparted life, yea not a life bestowed by God and from God, but a yet more glorious and awful privilege,—His Life in us. "I live," saith S. Paul[d], "yet not I, but Christ liveth in Me." "I am the Way, the Truth, and the Life." "Because I live, ye shall live also." It is our privilege, our glory, that we have not our own, but that which is "Another's." It were far less to have a life of our own, than to live, through God living in us, and quickening us that we might live.

But though our life from the first is God's and

[d] Gal. ii. 20.

supplied continually by God, man has yet the aweful power to exclude it, forfeit it; and so the doctrine that man "cannot fall finally from grace given," is likewise shut out by this teaching of our Lord. For it is of those who have been *in* the True Vine, grafted in, not assuredly as dead branches, but now dying, because by dead works they shut out its life, that it is said, "Every branch *in* Me that beareth not fruit, He taketh away." The branches which shall be cast into the fire and burned, were in Him once, lived in Him once.

Lastly, as by not bearing fruit, these lost their life, so it is by bearing fruit that life is increased; not, again, of itself, since *in* Christ nothing is of itself, but all of Him and to Him and through Him: still, bearing fruit is the appointed means, whereby life should be enlarged. For such God the Father tendeth; "every branch that beareth fruit He purgeth it, that it may bring forth more fruit." He cuts away what is yet dead in it by the sharp knife of suffering; He cutteth short what is luxuriant and would be leaves only, fair shew, and promise, and feelings, that the life, restrained and condensed, "may bring forth more fruit." In such, God the Son abideth; "if ye keep My commandments, ye shall abide in My love; he that abideth in Me, and I in him, the same bringeth forth much fruit." In such, the Holy Spirit more fully dwelleth, filling them more largely as they are enlarged to receive It, since it is through Him that the Son dwelleth in man. "If ye love Me," our Lord says a little before, "keep My commandments; and I will pray the Father, and He shall give you Another Comforter, that He may abide with you for ever; the Spirit of truth, Whom the world cannot receive, but ye know Him, for He dwelleth with you and shall be in you." So then, love, given by God, keepeth the commandments; and, upon keeping the commandments, the Father giveth Another Comforter, Whom the disobedient world *cannot* receive, but which obedience, which He gave the power to render, fitteth the more to receive.

And in each stage of man's transformation "from glory to glory," the former stage becomes as nothing. For all which man attaineth to in this life is but the beginning of what is to be ripened in eternity; God's saints seem to themselves to be ever beginning; and so Holy Scripture speaks of each degree, as if what is spoken of, then for the first time existed. Thus it is so often said, "And His disciples believed on Him," as though the belief, which they before had, compared with each enlarged degree of belief, were unbelief. And so here, "Herein is My Father glorified, that ye bear much fruit, so shall ye be My disciples." Only as His disciples, could they bear fruit, much less "much fruit;" yet bearing much fruit maketh them in such sense His disciples, that what they had been before, became as nothing.

And on "bearing much fruit," there seemeth to be yet a further stage opened, in which they shall so be taught what to ask, that whatsoever they shall ask, shall be given them. As it is said in the Psalms[e], "no good thing will He withhold from them that live a godly life," so here, "he that abideth in Me and I in him, the same bringeth forth much fruit; if ye abide in Me and I in you, ye shall ask what

[e] Ps. lxxxiv. 12.

ye will, and it shall be done unto you." And again[f], "Ye have not chosen Me, but I have chosen you, and ordained you, that ye should go and bring forth much fruit, and that your fruit should remain; that whatsoever ye shall ask of the Father in My Name, He may give it you." We, for the most part, it is to be feared, cannot speak of these great promises, but as a dim guess of what we know not; they who in older times obeyed more faithfully, knew what they were; yet, as obedience is the condition of all acceptable prayer, so to these higher measures of obedience there seems a higher promise annexed; a bolder, nearer access to the Father, which should ask what it willed, and have what it asked, because, filled with His Spirit, it could not ask amiss, but His Spirit in them "made supplication according to the will of God." "Thou hast asked a hard thing," said the Prophet who was the type of our ascending Lord, to him who asked "a double portion of his Spirit," "yet if thou see me when I am taken from thee, it shall be so unto thee[g]." And so these, ever gazing upwards and seeing their ascended Lord, though taken from them and Unseen, have what they ask; they see what others see not; long for what others understand not; obtain what the souls of others are too narrow to receive.

Imperfect even their obedience, while yet in the flesh, must still have been; imperfect, because that which is perfect is not yet come; imperfect, because the infection of nature yet remaineth; imperfect, because perfection is not in this life, not until, through death, death and the sting of death, and corruption,

[f] ver. 16.   [g] 2 Kgs. ii. 10.

are swallowed up in incorruption and life and victory. But although imperfect, still it was real; although it could not stand before the Holiness of God, yet it bears a semblance of that Holiness; although acceptable only through the Obedience of Him Who had no sin, it had a likeness to that Obedience, through which it was accepted. For so our Lord continues, "If ye keep My Commandments, ye shall abide in My love, *even as* I have kept My Father's Commandments, and abide in His love." The source of the love of the Father to the Man Christ Jesus, and of His unsinning obedience, (to speak reverently of so aweful a mystery,) one may yet say, was the Hypostatical Union, with "the Well-beloved Son, in Whom the Father is well-pleased;" yet did not this hinder the other truth, that through that unsinning obedience the Man, thus united with the Godhead, abode in the Father's love. No more then does the fact, that it is through God's good pleasure, predestinating, calling, justifying, sanctifying, that they who were "by nature children of wrath," become the objects of His love, hinder that it is by keeping His commandments, that they abide in the love, wherewith they were first loved. "It will not suffice," says S. Cyril[h], "to our entire peace of mind, or to the sanctification, which is to exhibit[i], as it were, Christ Who sanctifieth us, that we be received, in the character of branches; but upon this must we also sincerely follow Him by a perfect and unfailing love. For hereby chiefly may the might of the super-human gluing and joining-together in the Spirit be well

[h] In Joh. l. x. in v. 4.
[i] τὸν ὡς ἐπὶ ἐκθέσει τοῦ ἁγιάζοντος ἡμᾶς Χριστοῦ.

maintained and preserved." Our Lord again shews, that the source of our acceptableness is His love, "As My Father hath loved Me, so I have loved you;" His love, fore-coming, made them objects of love; yet being so made, it was for them to abide in it, not to cast themselves out of it; "continue ye in My love;" and that, by keeping His commandments, "If ye keep My commandments, ye shall abide in My love;" and that, a real keeping, in kind though not in degree like the Obedience of our Lord Himself, as Man; "*even as* I have kept My Father's commandments, and abide in His love;" so shall that transcendent love, wherewith the Father loveth the Son, redound to those who by keeping His commandments abide in Him and in His love.

Such is a faint outline of the teaching of this great parable, and of the truths, which on its surface it declares; more they will see, who deserve to see more; yet, thus far, it sets forth the history of the Saints we this day commemorate; that all which was good in them they had from being engrafted into the True Vine, Christ Jesus; that they remained in the Vine, while others, equally engrafted once, fell; that by bearing fruit, or good works, the one abode in It, as, through not bearing them, the others were cast out and withered; that bearing fruit they were the more cared for by God, and purged that they might bring forth *more* fruit; so did they bring forth *much* fruit; and were for that cause yet more filled with the Spirit, so that they might ask for yet higher measures of grace, and love, and attainment, and "the secret intercourse of the Lord, which is with them that fear Him," and what they asked, was given them. So was the Father glorified in them; so did they abide in their Saviour's love, even as He in the love of the Father; so continuing in His love to the end, were they translated hence to His endless love, even to Him, Who is Love.

To say that "by keeping the commandments" we abide in the Saviour's love, and that by obedience our faith is enlarged and perfected, is one and the same thing. For we can "abide" only, by making progress; it is a law of spiritual, as well as natural life, that not to grow is to decay; natural life has its bounds; it reaches its full strength, and then stays not; forthwith it begins to decay; spiritual life has no bounds; but if a bound be put to it, and it increase not, it too follows the same law, and decays. The heathen proverb, "not to advance is to fall back," must be much more true in things Divine, in which we are upheld not by our own strength; in which strength, unused, is gradually withdrawn; and they from whom it is withdrawn, must fall back to perdition. Would we "abide" in Christ, we must, by keeping His commandments, advance. "Ever," says S. Augustine[k], "be what thou art, displeasing unto thee, if thou wouldest attain to what thou art not yet. For whereat thou art pleased, there thou stayest. But if thou sayest, "*it sufficeth,*" thou art lost. Ever add, ever walk, ever onwards; stay not in the way, return not, go not out of the way." We can, then, only abide in the love wherewith our Lord loved us, by keeping His commandments; and by that obedience we, by His own gracious appointment, grow in that love, which, through the Infinity of its

[k] Serm. 169. fin. (p. 871. Oxf. Tr.)

Nature, ever diffuseth itself, wherever it can be received, and has no bounds, except our incapacity to receive it. And through the increase of love, obedience is increased, since "love is the fulfilling of the law." To love is to obey; since love hath no will to please itself, but what it loves. Love obeys, because it is glad to be employed in His service Whom it obeys; obeying, it understands more readily His Will Whom it obeys, as being by obedience brought more in unison with His Will; understanding more, it performs more; performing more, it loves more; and thus it spreads in an ever-widening circle, love enlarging obedience, and obedience giving strength and substance to love, until, being filled by the Holy Ghost, it "bringeth into captivity every thought to the obedience of Christ," expandeth itself to the compass of the whole law; embraceth, with a perfection relative to its earthly state, the whole range of duty to God and man; and realizing it according to its capacity, is looked upon by God as though it fulfilled it. "The righteousness of the law is fulfilled in them." And this not by any natural law, whereby habit is strengthened by action, (although this moral law is a type of the spiritual rule,) but because to obedience there is given enlarged knowledge, and a holier, enduring Presence of the Ever-blessed Trinity, the Father and the Son through the Spirit Enlarged knowledge; since our Lord says, in connection with this same teaching, "He that hath My commandments, and keepeth them, he it is that loveth Me, and he that loveth Me shall be loved of My Father, and I will love him, and will manifest Myself to him;" so that to obedience our Lord manifests

Himself in a new way, a way of which the world knows nothing, understands nothing, can receive nothing, because it is given to faith not to sight, is a spiritual not an earthly reality: a holier, fuller Presence; since our Lord so explains His own words, "If a man love Me, he will keep My words, and My Father will love him, and We will come unto him, and make Our abode with him." i.e. (on so great a mystery I had rather give the comment of the holy Augustine than my own,) "Lo! in the holy, the Holy Spirit also with the Father and the Son maketh His abode; within, namely, as God in His own temple. God, the Trinity, Father and Son and Holy Spirit come to us, while we come to Them; They come by aiding, we come by obeying; They come by illumining, we come by contemplating; They come by filling, we come by receiving; so that to us there is of Them no outward, but an inward, Vision, and in us there is of Them no transitory, but an ever-lasting abiding."

One dares not speak as if words of our Lord needed confirmation even from other Scripture. Since, however, Scripture-teaching as to the value of good works has, of late, become unfamiliar and distasteful, it may be useful to dwell briefly on some other passages, not as to their value generally, (which would be too large a field,) but in this one point, how "good works which are the fruits of faith, and follow after justification [1]," increase our acceptableness to God in Christ. "I will never forget Thy precepts," says the Psalmist, "for with them hast Thou quickened me," or "given me life [m];" not assuredly by the

---

[1] Art. xii.   [m] Ps. cxix. 93.

outward commands, or by the outward law; for "the commandment which was to life, I found," S. Paul says, " unto death;" not then by any outward law, but because He put the law into their hearts, that they might do it, and was Himself their law and guided and led them; yet was it by the law thus placed within them that He gave them fresh, renewed, increased life; "with them hast Thou quickened me."

In like way, S. James, speaking of the last act by which Abraham's faith was tried, that last crowning act, wherein he saw the Day of our Lord, which he had longed to see, whereof the Angel of the Lord said, " Now know .I that thou fearest God," speaking of this act, S. James uses the very words, " by works was faith made perfect." "Was not Abraham our father justified by works, when he had offered Isaac his son upon the altar? Seest thou how faith wrought with his works, and by works was faith made perfect?" The works proceeded from faith, and thereby became acceptable; "faith wrought with his works;" but that inchoate faith, so to say, was perfected by the works wrought through it; "by works was faith made perfect," not manifested only, (although this is true, before men and angels) not evidenced only to be a living faith, but " perfected." Faith, being brought into action, developed out of the bud into the fruit, transplanted from the heart into the life, acted upon, itself, the Apostle says, gained thereby, was "perfected." And so man's trial throughout is not a mere exhibition, but a strengthening and maturing of the faith itself by each separate act of faith; as also faith is weakened by each act of want of faith, not merely the want of it evinced. And so S. James goes on to say, "And the Scripture was *fulfilled*, which saith, Abraham believed God, and it was imputed to him for righteousness," i. e. what had been said of him at first without works, was then *fulfilled*, realized, had its completion by his works; his righteousness still flowed from his faith, but now, by works and especially by this mighty deed of faith, was in a higher and fuller degree realized or "fulfilled." "And he was called the friend of God." This too is the title of faith perfected by obedience. Abraham was so called, S. James says, because, believing, he offered up his son. "Ye are My friends," saith our Lord to His Apostles immediately after the parable of the Vine, "if ye do whatsoever I command you[n];" and again, "And I say to you, My friends[o]," in connection with suffering for His sake. And so God at first shewed Himself to Moses awefully in the flame of fire in the bush, so that "Moses trembled and durst not behold[p]," and God bade him put off his shoes from his feet; but, after he had been long tried and faithful amidst the threatenings of Egypt and the gainsaying of his own people, Scripture saith, "God spake unto Moses, face to face, as a man speaketh to his friend[q]:" to him, *as being faithful in all his house*[r], God saith, "I will speak mouth to mouth," not as to others distantly in visions and in dreams and in dark speeches.

What S. James inculcates thus more fully is taught also by S. Paul: "As ye yielded your members ser-

[n] S. John xv. 13.   [o] S. Luke xii. 4.   [p] Acts vii. 32.
[q] Ex. xxxiii. 11.   [r] Numb. xii. 7, 8. Deut. xxxiv. 10.

vants to uncleanness and to iniquity unto iniquity, even so now yield your members servants to righteousness unto holines[s];" i. e. as each act of uncleanness and iniquity led you, step by step, to further iniquity, and growth in iniquity was the result and end of each act of it, so now shall growth in holiness be the fruit and tendency of each separate act of obedience. And after a few verses, "Now, having been made free from sin and become servants to God, ye have your fruit *unto holiness;*" i. e. ye yield and have an abiding fruit of good works, as our Lord promises, "and your fruit shall remain," and that fruit tending to, and issuing in, holiness. And not sanctification only, but man's righteousness or acceptableness before God, S. Paul teaches is thus increased; and that, in reference to the very works which the Ancient Church, in consonance with Holy Scripture, so dwelt upon, as obtaining mercy, covering past sin, works of charity to the poor. S. Paul first declares the same truth out of the Old Testament; "As it is written, He hath dispersed abroad, he hath given to the poor; his righteousness remaineth for ever[t]." The 112th Psalm, which S. Paul here quotes, is in itself very remarkable for its relation to the 111th, in that what the 111th declares of God, the 112th declares of the good man; that he is merciful as his Father is merciful; and both declare, the one of God, the other of man, "his righteousness endureth for ever;" as though Scripture would say, that they who, fearing and trusting the Lord, imitate His goodness, shall have His Righteousness imparted to them; their righteousness, like His, as being His

[s] Rom. vi. 19.   [t] Ps. cxii. 9.

imparted to them, should abide for ever; and that, " because as He is, so are they in this world;" "they have dispersed abroad, they have given to the poor, their righteousness endureth for ever." S. Paul proceeds; " Now He that ministereth seed to the sower, both minister bread for your food, and multiply your seed sown, and increase the fruits of your righteousness [u];" that is, (for a prayer in Holy Scripture for the faithful is a prediction of what God would give if they persevere,) God should requite their deeds of love with a threefold reward, of things temporal and eternal. First, He would feed them who fed His poor; "minister bread for your food;" then, He would enlarge their means that they might ever continue on their works of love; "multiply your seed sown;" but, more than all, He would repay them the spiritual seed which they had sown, in a harvest of righteousness; "increase the fruits of your righteousness." He first gave them the seed; He, as in earthly things, would give the increase. And He too would crown the increase which He had given. Still man's sowing was the condition of that increase, and to them who thus cultivated the soil of heaven, He promises a heavenly recompense, the increase of their righteousness or acceptableness in His sight here, and abundant and rich reward, when they should "come again with joy and bring their sheaves with them." And so, by the Prophet Hosea, He teacheth the same truth in the same image. " Sow to yourselves in righteousness, reap in mercy, for it is time to seek the Lord, till He come and rain righteousness upon you [x];" i. e. work righteousness and place it

[u] 2 Cor. ix. 9. [x] Hosea x. 12.

with God as a deposit, and He shall repay you, not by any measure of deserts, but in proportion to [y] His own mercy; not as you work, but according to the abundance of His gift; "sow in righteousness," and He "will come and rain righteousness upon you;" bestow "grace for grace;" "give to him that hath;" enlarge the righteousness of him that worketh righteousness, and that by coming to him, "until He come and rain righteousness upon you;" as our Lord says, "If a man love Me, he will keep My words, and My Father will love him, and We will come unto him, and make Our abode with him [z]."

S. Paul says again [a], "God, condemned sin in the flesh, that the righteousness of the law might be fulfilled in us, who walk not after the flesh, but after the Spirit," i.e. that, walking continually and holding on in the course wherein they were placed, guided by the Spirit Which dwelt in them, at last the righteousness which the law requires might be fulfilled in them. And for the Ephesians he prays the Father of our Lord Jesus Christ [b], "that He would grant unto them, to be strengthened with might by His Spirit in the inner man; that Christ may dwell in their hearts by faith; that they being rooted and grounded in love, might be filled with all the fulness of God." From God he begins, in God ends; begins by the mighty strengthening through His Indwelling, ends in the satisfying fulness of His beatific Presence. Yet the course and order of the Christian life is, that the Holy Spirit strengthens them mightily, penetrating [c] the inner man, and Christ dwelleth in

---

[y] יפְּ [z] S. John xiv. 23. [a] Rom. viii. 4.
[b] Ephesians iii. 14—20. [c] εἰς τὸν ἔσω ἄνθρωπον.

the heart by faith: yet so strengthened, they remain strong, unshaken, immoveable, " rooted " in that Rock, "grounded" on that Foundation, unyielding to any assaults of passion or the world or the Evil one; and then through His love within them, they "know His love which passeth knowledge," and are "filled with the Fulness of God," even the abundance of His grace, and consolation, and love, yea all wherewith He, Who Alone filleth all things, Who Alone can fill the soul, filleth the faithful heart which abides rooted in His Love. All is of God; yet it is through remaining stedfast in the love which He gave, that they attain to the depths of His love, and are filled with His Fulness.

And of himself S. Paul says, "for this cause we faint not; but though our outward man perish, yet the inward man is renewed day by day," i. e. in proportion as the body was worn down by sufferings for Christ, were soul and spirit, day by day, renewed and enlarged; the life which he lived became less his own, more the life of Christ within him; as he had said just before, "always bearing about in the body the dying of the Lord Jesus, that the life also of Jesus might be made manifest in our mortal flesh." Ever dying with and for his Lord, he lived more and more; his was, day by day, more and more a real life; the life of Jesus day by day expanded more and more, took more possession of him, "was made manifest," displacing death by life.

S. John inculcates the same as S. James and S. Paul. "Whoso keepeth His word, in him verily is the love of God perfected[d];" perfected, namely, by His in-

[d] 1 S. John ii. 5.

creased In-dwelling Who is Love. The words are a brief summary of our Lord's promise, "If a man love Me, he will keep My words, and My Father will love him, and We will come unto him, and make Our abode with him." And so again, "If we love one another ᵉ, God dwelleth in us, and His love is perfected in us; hereby know we that we dwell in Him and He in us, because He hath given us of His Spirit." "He that keepeth His commandments, dwelleth in Him and He in him. And hereby we know that He abideth in us, by the Spirit That He hath given us." "Herein is our love made perfect, that we may have boldness in the Day of Judgement, because as He is, so are we in this world ᶠ." What S. Paul saith of faith, S. John saith of love, where*by* it "worketh" and differeth from the belief of devils, as S. James of deeds, where*in* it worketh. Love is the first gift of the Spirit; so that whoso hath love, "not" a "love in word nor in tongue, but in deed and in truth," knoweth that God hath given him His Spirit, whereby He "sheddeth abroad His love in our hearts ᵍ." Whoso loveth, in him God dwelleth, and by indwelling enlargeth and perfecteth his love, so that loving after the likeness of God, he may have confidence in approaching Him. "Begin to love," says S. Augustine ʰ, "thou shalt be per-

---

ᵉ 1 S. John iv. 12, 13.   ᶠ Ib. iv. 7.

ᵍ "This very thing, that 'He hath given thee of His Spirit,' whence knowest thou? Ask thy inward self. If it is full of love, thou hast the Spirit of God. Whence know we, that thou canst know from this that the Spirit of God dwelleth in thee? Ask the Apostle Paul. 'Because the love of God is shed abroad in our hearts through the Holy Spirit Which is given us.'" S. Aug. Tr. 8. in Ep. S. Johan. c. 4. § 12. pp. 1201, 1202 O.T.   ʰ Ibid.

fected. Hast thou begun to love? God hath begun to dwell in thee; love Him Who hath begun to dwell in thee, that by in-dwelling more perfectly, He may make thee perfect." Or in his well-known words, " Love commenced is commenced righteousness; love advanced is advanced righteousness; great love is great righteousness; love perfected is perfected righteousness, but love out of a pure heart and a good conscience and faith unfeigned [i]."

To conclude, as we began, with our Lord's own words, almost the closing words of the book of Revelations [k], our Lord's last words to His Church, declare the same, " The unjust, let him commit injustice still, and the filthy defile himself still: and the just, let him do righteousness still, and the holy, let him be hallowed still." In which our Lord teaches, how bad and good are continually, the bad by despite to His grace in their acts, the good by their use of it in theirs, working out each their completed state. The evil, being at the last abandoned to themselves, " shall increase to more ungodliness;" " the path of the righteous shall shine more and more unto the perfect day;" and not only so, but on occasion of the very growth of evil in the wicked the holy shall be aroused and warned to increase in holiness. The overhanging ruin of the cities of the plain shall urge the more "the just man" to escape from among them to the mountain, lest he be consumed. Standing at the close of the Revelations, the words seem to point to the close of all things, that, before our Lord's final coming, the kingdoms of light and darkness will take more distinct possession of the

[i] de Nat. et Grat. c. ult.   [k] Rev. xxii. 11.

world; the light of heaven and the darkness of hell will each send forth tokens more manifest of their approach; darkness and light will be more visible, less mingled; the "blackness of darkness," as it gathers itself for its last conflict, will, by collecting over against the kingdom of light, be the darker and heavier; the brightness of the sun will shine the more clearly, when the mists, which now often gather over it, have separated, and concentrated themselves over against it. But, as a general truth, the words declare the will of our Lord, that the just, by increase in righteousness, should become yet more justified; the holy, by growth in holiness, yet more hallowed; in our language, that both justification and sanctification, in some sense, increase in the justified and sanctified.

Such also, Scripture history attests, was the way which they trod, whom we this day commemorate. Lesser trials prepared for greater, lesser obedience obtained grace for the more difficult. Such was the course of the father of the faithful from his first leaving his country until he offered up his only son; such was the patience of Job, yielding up first possessions, then his children, then his body to a martyrdom of disease, then his soul to be held out as a hypocrite, the enemy of God Whom he served; such of Jeremiah and John the Baptist, who were sanctified from their mother's womb, to their martyr-death, through suffering, privation, the nethermost dungeon, the desert, until, having borne witness through their martyrs' lives, they were at last permitted to seal them by martyrs' deaths; such of all the noble army of martyrs; one conflict sent them on prepared for another; each dint on their shield was a pledge of the final victory; but the glories of martyrdom were too great a gift to be bestowed on those undisciplined by a corresponding life; those unprepared, (such as we are now,) sunk under the extremity of suffering, and denied their Lord. Such was the course of all that white-robed army; step by step they won their way, until "going on from strength to strength," they at last "appeared in the Presence of" their "God, in" the "Zion" which is above.

Thus may we contemplate them, and it will be well. Contemplate we them in their trials, victories, endurance, self-devotion, unwearied prayers, fastings, abnegation of self, love to man, fixedness on God, the honours which God vouchsafed them here, earnests of their present bliss, preludes of the greater bliss and glory hereafter. "For their works do follow them." Contemplate we them in their contrast with ourselves, how they shewed forth their faith by their deeds, and by works was their faith made perfect, until we be ashamed of our great professions of the purity of our faith, with our laggard steps, our self-indulgence, penurious almsgivings, unsacrificing ease, vacillating obedience, the things of nought upon which we have at some time wasted our energies, the ashes which most of us have, at some time, eaten for bread! How shameth it us, that they were men of like passions with ourselves, who were so purified that they could bear, in the flesh, to see God and lived; to whom He deigned to speak familiarly as a man to his friend, and hid not from them what He would do; whose intercession or whose zeal He accepted for a whole rebel people; whose "covenant

He kept for a thousand generations[1], and cast not off their children for their sakes;" whose voice He listened to and stopped the course of the sun, or the seasons; who had power with Him, and prevailed; with whom He walked in the fire, or stopped the mouths of lions, subjecting all nature to them, because they subjected themselves first unto their God. By whose tongues again He spake, filled their minds with His Spirit, and fitted them to reveal His counsels; bears witness that they were "full of the Holy Ghost;" deigned to be called especially "their God;" made them and their actions, singly, types and images of His Son; revealed to them wisdom in visions of the night; converted nations by their labours; and their earthly course over, honoured the very vessels which they had left, and shewed the healing tokens of His Presence in their very ashes [m]. How must they have been sanctified, whose very earthly tabernacles He so honoured, and testified that "right dear in His sight is the death of His saints!"

And we, how little has God wrought by us, how little has He deigned to speak by us, (since our words are feeble and bring so little fruit; His, mighty and return not void!) How faint His presence, since He "maketh men to be of one mind in an house," and our house is so torn and distracted, and we can so little "understand one another's speech!" Our Ark is hemmed in, and we see not the issue; [the [n]

[1] Ps. cv. 8.   [m] 2 Kgs xiii. 21.

[n] This heavy description is here retained, as it was preached in 1840. At Leeds, what follows was omitted, both lest it should be applied to our immediate sorrows, and because the picture is gloomier than seems true to the writer as to the present day. The evils prevalent among us have not diminished: some, perhaps,

very light which gleams among us, shews us but the darkness of our heavens; our fresh life which He has, we trust, infused into our Church, but shews the extent of the presence of the former death. Our enemies are fierce, and we cannot win them; our sheep are scattered, and we cannot re-unite them; our people are wayward, and we cannot restrain them; our labourers few, and we cannot obtain others from the Lord of our Vineyard. "We have not wrought any deliverance in the earth, neither are the inhabitants of the world fallen º."] It may be a sore loss, greater than we can imagine, that, although confessing in our Creeds, "the Communion of saints ᵖ," we, for the most part have so little felt the privilege of being "fellow-citizens with the saints, and of the household of God," of belonging

and the very "root of all evil," the "love of money," have indeed, in the world, even increased. But the tokens of God's Presence with our Church, both without, by His Providence, and, more especially, by His deepening grace within the souls of men, make even our very evils cease to be appalling. No one can think of our great towns, without an oppressive sense of the magnitude of the evil; yet when God gives the heart to desire to repair past negligence, even the amount of past evil is a token of the mercy and long suffering of Almighty God, Who, even thus, has had compassion upon us. º Is. xxvi. 18.

ᵖ "The belief of the Communion of Saints is necessary to inflame our hearts with an ardent affection towards those which live, and a reverent respect towards those which are departed and are now with God.—And if all the saints of God living in communion of the Church deserve the best of our affections here on earth, certainly when they are dissolved and with Christ, when they have been blessed with a sight of God and rewarded with a crown of glory, they may challenge some respect from us, who are here to wait upon the will of God, expecting when such a happy change shall come." Bp. Pearson on the Creed, Art. ix. fin.

to a body, of which such glorious hosts have been already perfected, of being struggling members of the one Body. Not realizing that they now live to God, live a higher life than we, being "freed from the body of this death," their histories appear like by-gone tales of what has been, not the living victories of those still "living to God," present in His sight Who wrought these things in and by man. We hear of them, read them, and forget that they are written as our ensamples; that "the Lord's arm is not shortened that it cannot save;" but that "our iniquities have separated between us and our God." Exalting ourselves, as though we were the living, they the dead, we have received the just recompense in ourselves, and are abased.

Be we followers of them, as they of their Lord. Imitate we them in little things, if we cannot in the greater; if not in their glorious close, yet in their outset. Mighty as they became, yet were they too weak and unformed once. By yielding themselves in little things to God's moulding Hand, His Hand formed and fitted them for great. Daniel's first trial was in meat and drink; David's in protecting his father's flock; Joseph's in filial obedience and constancy amid the evil deeds of his brethren, which he reported to his father, and then in continence, as fearing "to do that great wickedness and sin against" his unseen "God." Yet such were the first steps, whereby David became the man after God's own heart; Daniel one of the three men, chief with God; Joseph, the saviour of his brethren and the emblem of his Redeemer. To that moulding Hand yield you yourselves; you, at least, are not bound round, it is to be hoped, by enduring custom; ye are plastic still to His Hand, to Whom we would all be like clay to the potter. Blessed, thrice-blessed, are ye, if it be thus with you. Yet, even at the worst, nothing is too hard and dry, for that Almighty Hand to shape to a "vessel for" everlasting "glory," so that it harden not itself amid the fire, whether of inward or outward grief, by which He would soften it. Whatever we be, only yield we ourselves to the stroke of that Divine rod, which brought water out of the flinty rock so that it gushed out like the great deep, and He will, out of our stony hearts, even if tears are dried, bring forth the healthful streams of penitential sorrow which shall flow on to life everlasting. Blessed then too are you, if now, at the last, you yield yourselves, to whatsoever severe, but loving, discipline His righteous and Fatherly Providence shall see good for you; temporal losses, bereavement, pains of body, dreariness of mind, fierce temptation, harassing thoughts, whereby He shall bruise, crush, destroy, what you have become amiss, make you hate what you have been, and long to be renewed according to that blessed Image in which He re-created you.

Wherever we are in the road, one step lies immediately before us, the next; to break off something which we know in ourselves to be displeasing to God, to acquire by His grace, some grace acceptable to Him. If we cannot yet reach the footsteps of the blessed saints who have gone before us, their Divine zeal, their entire deadness to the world, their super-human charity, at least seek we Him Whom they sought, if not in high things, yet in ordinary duties, seeking to please Him and not man, to gain honour from Him, and not from man. Seek we Him, in the three great classes of duties which our Lord points out, self-discipline in fasting, devotedness to God in prayer, love to man, in self-denying charity, and He will fit us for whatever He has in store for us. The lowliest office, the commonest every-day task, the most undignified suffering, if done or borne for Him, in His faith and fear, will, through His merits Who gave the power so to do and bear it, "work out an eternal weight of glory." Yet, if, as it seems, evil days are coming upon the Church, and (it may be) the approach of the kingdom of darkness is ushering in the Coming of our Lord, duties and sufferings of a higher class may be reserved for those who in simple obedience, humility, self-denial, patience and prayer, are preparing themselves lowlily to receive whatever office our gracious Master may deign to call them to. This then be your ambition, in whatever task of life, to please God; this your pleasure, to be acceptable in His sight; this your "meat and drink," lowlily to do His will; this the object (as it is the end) of your life, to gain Him Who shall Himself be "the exceeding great Reward of the faithful;" to fit yourselves to receive Him Who, although we are altogether "unworthy that He should enter under our" decayed and defiled "roof," yet "dwelleth in the contrite and lowly of spirit [m]," and "looketh to him who trembleth at His word [n]." So, lowly though the outward lot of any here be, may their prayers prevail with God to spare a guilty nation, and purify and restore His returning Church; so may those to whom He has here lent talent, or station, or wealth,

[m] Isaiah lvii. 15.   [n] Ib. lxvi. 2.

or firmness, be even here foremost in carrying on His work, and have high posts of duty assigned them, of which as yet they rightly dare not even dream, if they be foremost too in disciplining themselves to obey; so may all, if, with stedfast though fearful heart, they set themselves to keep His commandments, abide in His ineffable Love.

The time is short; a few more years, and, borne on our Saviour's Cross, the waves of this troublesome world will be passed, our haven won, and we at rest, where we would be, in Abraham's bosom, with all whom He hath loved to the end: a few struggles at most, few in proportion to the joy set before us, and the last struggle will resign us over to the end of our struggles, even endless peace, of which the peace vouchsafed to each faithful struggle is the earnest and the preparation: a few years past, and what will it concern us, under what outward circumstances we have passed our life, so that our lot is then with God's saints? What will matter then, privation, sorrow, disappointment, dejection of heart, failing of the eyes, suffering of body? Yea rather, as our loving Lord this day spake unto us, how blessed it will have been to have "mourned," if by His Mercy we may then "be comforted;" how blessed to have been " poor in spirit," if then, through His merits, ours be "the kingdom of Heaven;" how blessed any self-denial, or toil, or pain, or chastisement, whereby purity of heart shall have been retained or restored, if, when we shall close our eyes upon the vanities and distractions of this passing world, and open them upon eternity, we shall "see God." Which may He of His infinite mercy grant, not for our worthiness, but to our unworthiness, for the Worthiness of His Ever-Blessed Son, in Whom He "hath made" such as we are, and can make us also "to be meet to be partakers of the inheritance of the saints in light;" to Whom with the Father &c.

O Almighty God, Who hast knit together Thine Elect in one communion and fellowship, in the mystical Body of Thy Son Christ our Lord; Grant us grace so to follow Thy blessed saints in all virtuous and godly living, that we may come to those unspeakable joys, which Thou hast prepared for them that unfeignedly love Thee; through Jesus Christ our Lord. Amen.

SERMON XIII.

HOPES OF THE PENITENT.

(Saturday Evening, Feast of All Saints.)

S. LUKE xv. 7.

"I say unto you, that likewise joy shall be in heaven over one sinner that repenteth, more than over ninety and nine just persons, which need no repentance."

THIS morning, I spoke of the course marked out for the Christian in the order of God's love for him, how having been "made a member of Christ," he should through "faith working by love" abide in Him; how by love his faith should be heightened, and by the increase of faith his love be deepened, and his deepened love issue in fuller obedience, and by acts of obedience should faith and love again be strengthened, until faith and obedience and love should together be perfected to that fulness, which God in His eternal purpose designed for him, and faith should end in sight, and love be purified in the blissful Presence of Him Whom it should for ever love. But were this the only course, how were it with most of us, my brethren? With how many of us has this order of God been broken! This speaks of going from "strength to strength," "giving all diligence to add to faith virtue, and to virtue knowledge, and to knowledge temperance, and to temperance patience, and to patience godliness, and to godliness brotherly kindness, and to brotherly kindness charity," and in all these " abounding more and more : " and we have mostly at some time been going back, not advancing ; wasting, too many of us, His gifts of nature as well as of grace, our best natural feelings, our early affections, on worse than vanity ; and now in all this waste and with some poor fragments only left, what, might we say, have we to do with the victories of saints, the crown of continued, faithful, service ? If this be all, where are we ? and what our hope ?

Blessed be God, my brethren, this is not all. I said, "all of us, even penitents, have our likeness there." Close by the Virgin-Mother at the Cross, was the woman who had been a sinner. He Who was born of a Virgin, names no other in the sacred line which leads up to Him, but a heathen woman, an incestuous, and an adulteress. He whose Son He specially deigned to call Himself, the Son of David, was the royal penitent; and yet the man after God's own heart. The chief of the Apostles was the only one who denied his Master. And that other glorious Apostle, "not a whit behind the very chiefest Apostles, though he be nothing," "the chosen vessel to bear" his Lord's "Name," what title does he take, but "the chief of sinners?" Love is of God, and the depth of love shall be the measure of our bliss, since it will be also of our nearness to God Who is Love. No depth then of our fall may hinder from any height of glory, as of love. We must be much loved, who have been so much forgiven; and much forgiven, we may hope to love the more Him Who has so much loved us.

Not then the need of deep penitence, but the absence of it, forfeits heaven or any degree of bliss. Dreary indeed and lonely, in itself, were the outset of penitence; dreary as to the past, full of perplexity the present, full of fears the future. For what is the past? One blank. Yea would it were one blank, would that there were nothing written there! Would, the penitent must feel, that waste were all, that he could now begin, with but the loss of past years, of missed opportunities, of past grace forfeited; himself, it may be, advanced in the course of years, in his course to heaven but at the entrance; the work of a life to be compressed perhaps into a fragment of its term. A dreary review were this alone. For what is waste of grace, but waste of the Presence of God, narrowing the soul so that it cannot receive, as it might, His love; paralyzing it, that it cannot stretch forth to attain to Him? What is it but to be a stranger to the ways of God with the soul, and that secret intercourse which He has promised to them that fear Him? What is it, but to be a stranger in its Father's house, not to know its Saviour's voice, which it has not obeyed; to be in darkness, since God by His grace is the light of the soul; cold, since He is its warmth; sick, since He is its health; yea well nigh dead, since He is its Life; knowing not God, to Whom it would go, nor the way by which it should go, nor itself which is to be moved; happy in this only, if it have light enough to see its own darkness!

Yet such might be the fruits of sloth only. But man, as he cannot serve two masters, so he must serve one. If he obey not God Who is above him, he must obey his own inferior nature. Set between heaven and earth, and drawn to both, if he refuse the drawing heavenwards, he must sink earthwards. Partaker with the Angels, in his spiritual nature, "man, being in honour, and understanding not, becometh like the beasts which perish." What is the awakened sinner's past? A dreary, confused, heap of sins, recollection thronging upon recollection, sin calling up the memory of sin, some standing out perhaps more marked, and casting a deeper shade of blackness upon the rest; some wounds of the soul giving a deeper pang; and yet perhaps more dreary still, that countless mass of sin, which has passed unheeded from his memory; so that those darker spots seem to him but tokens, as it were, of that foul leprosy which has infected and defiled his whole frame, and forces from him the leper's cry, "Unclean, unclean!" I know not which to the sinner is the most overwhelming, those outstanding sins, the memory of which ever haunts him, or that entangled impenetrable mass of sins, negligences, and ignorances, which he cannot recall, which seems the thicker, because he cannot distinguish them, the daily, hourly, unceasing sins of a life passed in forgetfulness of God.

What then were an awakened sinner's present? Could it be described, it were less miserable. Its very misery is, that having lost its Centre, God, the soul tosses to and fro, (Holy Scripture says,) "like a troubled sea;" restless, amazed, stupified, ever shifting from one misery to another; itself loathsome to itself, how much more, it must think, to God! covered, within and without, with the innumerable ulcers of its past sins, and these exhaling an intolerable stench, sickening to himself, offensive even to the inhabitants of heaven. Nothing has it in that wide waste of past life, whereon to rest; its best deeds flash upon it as self-deceit; pleasing itself in itself or in man's praise for its natural graces, and so marring even these, and making itself or those around it, its idol instead of God. How has it laboured for the wind! what ashes hath it eaten for bread! how hath it changed its glory for that which doth not profit! Behind, is a desolate wilderness; before, it is as death. Within, a decayed spirit, a dried heart, its spiritual senses dulled, its strength weakened, its limbs bound as by grave-clothes, its evil customs an iron chain; the soul become the servant, the appetites lords, the will enslaved; the light of faith darkened; it sees what is right, only to think it hopeless, if not to begin, at least to persevere. The Holy Spirit it has grieved, and defiled His temple. Will He indeed return to that so unhallowed? Its Saviour it has sold for thirty pieces of silver; yea, for what more miserable price, for what defilements hath it bartered His precious Blood! Hath then His Blood indeed been shed even for those who waste It and trample It under foot, and count it an unholy thing? To the Father it has preferred His creatures, defaced His Image, wasted His gifts, fled far from His house, dishonoured His Name, disobeyed Himself, obeyed His enemy. To whom, will it often ask, do I now belong? To Him Who made me and whose work I have marred, to Him Who redeemed me at so costly a Price, and Whose Price I have wasted, to Him Who sanctified me, and Whose motions I have rejected; or to him whom in all this I have served? Am I yet indeed the dwelling-place of the Trinity? Do They yet inhabit a mansion so broken, so decayed, so defiled? or are these thoughts of pride, or vanity, or grosser sin, tokens of another inhabitant, whom by my sins I have invited to enter in and dwell there? "By one consent to sin did Adam" (a holy man has said [a]) "lose the brightness of innocence, the robe of immortality, the incorruption of the flesh, purity of soul, sweetness of contemplation, liberty of spirit, the kingdom of heaven, the fellowship of Angels, the friendship of God;" and his own are on him in multitudes. For fewer sins, must he well think, have many been cast into hell! how shall he escape? Or would he think now, thus late, of the joys of heaven, are they indeed still in store for him? Is the society of angels, the ineffable sweetness, the infinite love, the brightness of glory, the torrent of pleasure, the Face of God, are these for one who has but the bitterness of soul for the remembrance of past evil to offer? Will God bestow Himself on one who misused His creatures and despised Himself? will He gather up such fragments as these, refine these dregs?

"An evil thing it is and bitter to have forsaken the Lord thy God;" and through weariness and aching of heart must the sinner often be brought to feel what he has lost. Truly he has lost all, who has lost Thee, O Lord God!

[a] S. Laur. Justin. Serm. in Fest. S. Joann. Ev. Opp. p. 530.

Yet heavy as the clouds must often be, which man's sins have spread between him and his God, suspending, as it seems, all influx of grace from God, stopping his prayer that it should not pass through, Holy Scripture pierces it for us. While all seems dark below, above that veil of cloud is He, the Unchangeable, in light and serenity and love, forsaking none who forsake not Him finally; meeting us, when fleeing from Him, in displeasure, that we may turn to Him in love; drawing us, although unseen, that we, though bound by the chains of our sins, may have power to come to Him. On the penitent's first tear, there is joy in heaven. O wondrous power of penitence, which can increase the joy of heaven! The blessed Angels, who ever behold the Face of our Father, ever joy ineffably in the Divine Presence, ever fulfil His Will, and are filled with His glory, and ceaseless praise, Holy, Holy, Holy! they, possessed already of their everlasting bliss, partakers of the Eternity, the Truth, the Will of God, and in Him possessing the fulness of light and of immortal wisdom, who, even while ministering to us, never part from the blissful contemplation of God, the food of whose life is God Himself, can their bliss be increased? can it be increased by the sight of one, still so loathsome to himself, and so burdensome? "There is joy in the presence of the Angels of God over one sinner that repenteth." In him, who seeth not as yet himself, doubtful of himself and his own stedfastness, doubtful almost whether God can love him, the Angels, in Divine light, see their future fellow-citizen in bliss; joy that one more is recovered from our lost world, that the lost is found. Loving with the love of God, they joy to see one more to fill up their ranks broken by the evil angels' fall, to swell the praise of heaven, to join with them in the endless song, to love with them and reflect the glory of our one Head, Who kept them from falling, restores us, when fallen.

But deeper, more marvellous, mystery yet! what marvel that Angels enlarge their joy, when He, the Lord of Angels and their God, is said to rejoice! Ye know, my brethren, Who is that Good Shepherd, Who when out of the perfect number of His creatures, His hundred sheep, that one sheep, man, fell, and the number of those who should love and worship Him, was broken, left His Father's glory and those ninety-nine sheep, the Angelic hosts, safe indeed and fenced still and encompassed by His Almighty Hand, in what seemed, as it were, a desert, because man, its heir, had forfeited it. Ye know Who sought His own lost sheep, lay down His life for him, and returned bringing with Him the firstling of His flock, a penitent; translating him first of all from his cross to Paradise, and then taking with Him the souls of those who had awaited His Coming. And how brought He him? "Rejoicing." We dare not speak of these mysteries in other words than Holy Scripture giveth us; we dare hardly clothe them with our own thoughts; we know that with Him, the unchangeable Light, is no shadow of turning; that to Him, to Whom all His works are known from the beginning of the world, joy cannot be like our human joy, who are gladdened by some source of joy we knew not of before. But He, Who vouchsafed to take our nature upon Him, speaketh in our language of

Himself; and, as the Father Who doeth nothing but what from all eternity He foreknew that He should do, is said to "repent," when He doeth other that He had before done, yet according to His own secret and unchangeable counsel; so the Son joyeth over the repentant sinner, or our lost race, when His unchangeable love can pour itself out upon His creature which He had changed, and what before was alien from Him can receive His love. The Father, Holy Scripture saith, "shall rejoice in His works[b]," when, in their new and final birth, they shall once again be all "very good," and His "glory shall be for ever," streaming forth from Him and to Him returning, unhindered by our evil; and that ineffable complacency and love, wherewith He beholdeth the image of His own Divine perfections, may rest upon His restored creation. So also the Son, Who is One with the Father, is said to have joy in the perfecting of His new creation, the work of His Redemption. As the deepest mysterious meaning of those sacred words, "I thirst," is understood to be, His longing for the completion of the counsel of His love towards us, and that He "thirsted" for our salvation; as, by the well of Samaria, He hungered and thirsted, not for material water, Who had that "living water" to give, whereof "whoso should drink should never thirst," nor for our earthly food, which when His disciples brought Him, He refused, saying "I have meat to eat ye know not of;" but He thirsted for the faith of the Samaritan city, and His food was His Father's Will and man's salvation, so it is said, "He shall see of the travail of His soul and shall be satis-

[b] Ps. civ. 31.

fied," in that " by His knowledge" should "He justify many." And again, " from the ivory palaces," i. e. from the royal, large, pure, beauteous, hearts of the saints, "hymns shall gladden Thee." He, it is said, "the King," "Lord God," Husband of the Church, should "desire" that "beauty" wherewith He had Himself endowed her, and made her "all-glorious within." He rejoiced not alone, but "exulted for joy," that the Father had "revealed to babes" the mysteries "hidden from the wise and prudent." Yea, over His fallen but restored Church, it is said, " He will save, He will rejoice over them with joy, He will rest[c] in His love; He will rejoice over them with jubilation[d]." O unutterable condescension of

[c] lit. (as in the Margin) " He will be silent in (or through) His love." This seems more in accordance with the context, before and after, than that of the Chald. and S. Jer. " shall be silent" (as to their sins.)

[d] רן, רנה, generally denote the inarticulate sound of joy, which cannot express itself. S. Augustine often comments thus on the words "Jubilo," "jubilatio," by which הריע, תרועה are expressed, as being " a marvelling for joy which cannot be expressed in words." (in Ps. 46. § 7.) Thus on Ps. 32. (33.) Enarr. 2. § 8. " This it is to sing well to God, ' to sing with jubilation.' What is this? To sing within the mind; not to be able to explain in words, what is sung in the heart. For they who sing, whether in the harvest or the vintage, or in any other fervid work, having begun to vent their joy in words of song, as though filled with such overflowing joy that they cannot express it in words, pass away from syllabled words into the sounds of jubilee. Jubilee is a sound signifying that the heart yearneth with what it cannot utter. And whom doth that jubilee beseem but the Ineffable God? For He is Ineffable Whom tongue cannot utter. And if thou hast no utterance for Him, yet mayest not be silent, what remains but thou make jubilee, that the heart joy without words, and the boundless breadth of joys should not be confined within the limits of sylla-

our God, Who thus deigns to shadow out His love to us sinners under the words of the deepest love which He hath given us! All holy love shadoweth forth some portion of His; Father, Mother, Husband, would He be to the soul in His protecting fostering, In-Oneing love; and as our intensest love and joy cannot be uttered in words, but joy vents itself in unformed sounds, and love rests in silence over the object of its love, so He saith, "He will rejoice with the cry of jubilee, He will be still over us in love." O wondrous stillness, image of that everlasting rest wherein in all eternity He rested in the love of His Coequal Coeternal Son, that without spoken words, or image of sense, or motion of the mind, He is felt in silence by the soul. And this for sinners!

Yea, so much does He make our joy His own, that as He maketh known to the Heavenly hosts,—"His friends," because they ever do His Will, "His neighbours," as being nearest to His unapproachable glory, and ever enjoying His blissful Vision [e],—He saith (holy men have observed [f]) not "rejoice *over* this My sheep which was lost and is found;" not, rejoice *with* it, created with yourselves to see My Face, and now restored to be with you in bliss;" but "rejoice

---

bles?" (see also S. Greg. Mor. viii. 52. § 88. p. 489. Oxf. Tr. and xxiv. 6. § 10. xxviii. 15. § 35. who follows S. Aug.) In this wonderful expression of Divine love in Zephaniah, both are combined, the depth of love as expressed first by silence, then in unformed words; the word also rendered "joy," in the second place denotes, as is known, the exultation of joy. There is also the threefold division so remarkable in the O. T. as a hidden symbol of the Trinity. It is thrice repeated in different words that God joyeth.

[e] S. Greg. ad loc.   [f] as S. Greg.

with *Me*, for *I* have found *My* sheep that was lost." So would He speak His tender love towards us, as though our salvation were *His* gain, Who needeth nothing, to Whom nothing can be added, since of Him and by Him and through Him are all things.

And this His joy is not only over our whole redeemed race; it is, Holy Scripture says, in all its fulness over each single penitent sinner. Holy Scripture speaks of all as one, since all, though many, are one body in Christ; and yet, again, all which is true of the whole, is true of each single living member, so that each member may in the Psalms or Canticles or the Song of Songs, as being in the body, take the words of the body. For His love, being infinite, is bounded not in itself, but by our power to receive it; whom He loveth, He loveth infinitely, for His is an infinite Love. As we are taught to say to God in the words of the Psalmist, " O God, Thou art *my* God," though He is the God of all, visible and invisible; so of God our Redeemer S. Paul saith, " I live by the faith of the Son of God, Who loved *me* and gave Himself for *me*[g]." "The measure of His love to each," saith a holy father[h], "is as great as to the whole world," so that we might boldly say, "So boundless was His love, that He would not have grudged His Sufferings though but for one;" the joy which He hath in the redemption of the world, He hath in the conversion of a single soul; and "we owe Him as deep a debt of love, as though He had come for us alone;" yea, deeper, far, since the salvation of others is our gain, not His; for the bliss of all shall increase the bliss of each, while each in each

[g] Gal. ii. 20.   [h] S. Chrys. ad loc.

beholds the glory of God reflected, and in the glory of each shall we have our own special joy.

Needs any more comfort yet? There is a yet more mysterious aweful comfort to the penitent; for it is on occasion of his very sins. "There is joy in the presence of the Angels of God over one sinner that repenteth, more than over ninety-nine just persons which need no repentance." It is so awful a doctrine, that I dare not name it without a prayer to Almighty God, that none of you abuse it (as men do all the doctrines of grace) to your hurt. Full of soothing were these words in that meaning, that while self-righteousness [i] mars the value of works, else of real good, neither past sins nor present infirmities hinder the joy in heaven over one once so evil. More condescending yet were the words, if we may think that God vouchsafes to speak after the manner of men, and so speaks of His joy over those all but lost, as greater than that in those who never fell, (as the Angels,) or those who fell less deeply. As we for the time joy more in the frail health of one dear, recovering from deep sickness, than in the strong health of others also as dear; as the victory is gladlier after peril, the haven to those all but wrecked; so would He clothe the exceeding tenderness of His love for us sinners in words of our sympathy [k]. More wondrous miracle of mercy yet, in that their plainest fullest meaning, that there are restored sinners, over whom God indeed joyeth more than over others in whom He still joyeth; that God

[i] S. Aug. de quæst. Ev. ii. 32. See Catena Aurea, Oxf. Tr.

[k] See a passage of great beauty in S. Aug. Conf. viii. 3. p. 138, 9. Oxf. Transl.

Who createth all good, directeth to His good ends all evil, does overrule to good even the past falls of the penitent. "We must weigh this," says S. Gregory the Great[1], "why He alloweth that there is more joy in heaven over converted sinners than over the righteous who stand. Why but what we know and see in daily experience, that mostly they who know themselves to be oppressed by no burden of sin, stand indeed in the way of righteousness, do not things unlawful, yet pant not anxiously for their heavenly home, and allow themselves the more in things lawful, as they remember they have not committed things unlawful? And mostly they remain sluggish as to the performance of any more excellent good, because they feel themselves very safe that they never committed the more grievous evils. Whereas sometimes they who remember that they have done some things unlawful, stung by their very grief, burn for the love of God, practise themselves in great virtues, seek all which is difficult in the holy strife, forsake all things of the world, flee honours, rejoice in reproaches, are on fire with holy longings, pant for their heavenly home, and considering that they have gone astray from God, compensate their former losses by their later gains. There is then more joy in heaven over a converted sinner than over many a righteous who standeth. For so too in battle, the captain loveth more that soldier, who returning after flight, presses bravely on the enemy, than him who never turned his back, yet never did aught bravely. So the husbandman loveth more that field, which, after thorns, bringeth forth large fruit, than that

[1] ad loc.

which never had thorns and never produceth an abundant harvest." And so, when our Lord, rebuking the temper of such, as having borne the burden and heat of the day, would grudge the equal reward of those who had stood idle until the eleventh hour, subjoins, "so the last shall be first and the first last [m]," He means among other things, surely [n] this, that some converted late in life, should, through the depth of their penitence and the vehemence of their love, be higher in heaven than others who had not gone so far astray, nor yet had afterwards loved so fervently.

Not then in this life need any utter Esau's exceeding bitter cry, "Hast Thou not reserved a blessing for me?" "Hast Thou but one blessing, O my Father?" Thou needest not, thou weary soul, sit down in heaviness and gloom, as though all were hopelessly lost, because thou hast squandered in a far country, far from God in thine affections, His first bright inheritance. Our Father is not so poor as to have one blessing only, nor are His "many mansions" open to redeemed of one sort only. Were it so, who could hope? Hast thou lost that first bright crown of virgin-souls, who have loved God Alone, have ever loved Him, loved Him with their first, pure, spotless, ardent, undivided love, yet who can tell the brightness of her crown, who once despised of man, despising herself yet more, with unashamed shame which maketh not ashamed, burst through to the Feet of Jesus, and washed them with a sinner's burning tears? Crippled, seared, dried, distracted, weak, unstable, nay, polluted, as thou

[m] S. Matt. xx. 16.   [n] S. Chrys. ad loc. see Cat.

mayest feel thyself, all, the least, is too hard for thee, but what too hard for God's Omnipotence, what too sick for the Heavenly Physician, what too sinful for Him to heal, Who " was made sin for us, that we might be the Righteousness of God in Him?" In thine own strength thou wentest astray; not in thine own strength must thou return: well is it, if at last we feel our weakness, that so His strength may be made perfect in us. Fear not then, lest the way be long; He thy Lord is thy Way. Fear not lest thou faint by the way; He to Whom thou comest for heavenly Food, will not send thee away fasting, who art come to Him from far; He, the Gospel says, "receiveth sinners and eateth with them," He is Himself their Food. Fear not, because thou hast, it may be, but the fragments of a wasted life to offer Him, for Whom too little were its earliest and best. He bid "gather up the fragments which remain," that nothing be lost; He needeth not time, His own creature, to perfect those whom He maketh His, so that thou give thyself up now at the last, as the clay to the potter, to be unmade of what thou hast made thyself, remade by Him to that for which He made us. Hide thyself not, nor thy sins, like Adam, from Him. Hide thyself no longer wilfully under the defilements, the mire, the manifold vanities of this world, and He, the Eternal Wisdom, will, through them all, behold on the lost piece of silver His own kingly Image and Likeness; He will draw it forth and cleanse it, will retrace His own Eternal Form upon it, His own Holiness, His Purity, His Righteousness, and will lay it up, rejoicing, amid His jewels in the everlasting treasury. Flee not still further, and He, the Good Shepherd, will not chide ° the sheep which He has found. He will not leave us, wearied and wasted by manifold wanderings, our steps unsteady through our many falls, *ourselves* to follow Him. He saith not only, " I will lead thee by still waters," " My sheep hear My voice, and I know them, and they follow Me," but " He layeth it on His shoulders, rejoicing." He bowed Himself from heaven to earth ; He stooped to our lowliness ; He folded us in love in His Bosom ; in His lowliness on His shoulders which bare the Cross, He bare us ; there would He have us lay down our sins ; there would He have us rest our wearied limbs and our aching hearts ; with His own pierced Hands would He hold us ; there would He admit us nigh, not from afar, wishfully to behold His own Blissful Countenance of love ; there would that thorn-crowned Head incline towards us, melt our stony heart with His look of tenderness, and cleanse us anew with that Precious Blood, gushing from the Wounds which the thorns of our sins had opened. Not on our own frail feet, not by the weak longings of our spirits, are we upborne from earth to heaven ; but, "beneath thee," He saith, " are the everlasting Arms." Not to Angels only hath He given thee in charge, to bear thee up, but He Himself hath folded thee around Himself, hath bound thee like an ornament around His Neck, hath clothed Himself with thy mortality, that with thee, as part of Himself, " His Body and His Bones," He might ascend again to the Bosom of His Father, and Himself rejoicing, amid the rejoicing choirs of Angels, bring thee into the joy of thy Lord.

° See S. Greg. Nyss. Hom. de Mul. Pecc. in Cat. Aur.

But are we then alone, my brethren, the sheep of Christ? Are we alone the lost and found? If found ourselves, and we indeed hope, that when lost and astray He sought us, can we help yearning, with His own love, over His other sheep yet scattered in this evil world, that they too may be gathered, and be one fold under One Shepherd? Can we, in the wide wilderness of this land, where so many souls are, with the prodigal which we once were, "perishing for hunger," while, not for any deserts of ours but according to His mercy He has drawn us back to His own House, has spread a Table before us, given to us Angels' Food, and the good Shepherd feeds us with His own Blood,—can we not long for those who might be gathered and are not? He Who hath so loved us, loveth them; He Who died for us, died for them; He Who, in part through the ministry of others, has sought us, would, through us, seek them. If as, one by one, He regained us who had erred and strayed, like lost sheep, in negligence or still deeper sin, uplifted us when fallen, bound us when broken, and laid us on His shoulders rejoicing, there was joy in heaven, how much more, when many, at once, are gathered! And shall we hope that Angels have joyed and do joy over us, and not long that, through us, they should joy over others also, like us lost, but not, like us, (as we hope,) as yet restored? Shall we, who are admitted to the citizenship with the Angels, not ourselves joy with Angels' joy? Could we not almost think that we could hear the echoes of the Angels' joy, when these houses of God arise, as folds for repentant sinners, to gather in His returning sheep? Or if we share not this their joy, think we that we shall be owned by Him with Whom they rejoice, because He hath found the sheep which was lost?

My brethren, lukewarmness about the salvation of our brethren is no good token for ourselves. Knew we from what pit we had ourselves, as we hope, been saved; knew we, by what undeserved Mercy we had been sought, and, as we hope, found; knew we Him, by Whose Love we had been gathered, and if we are saved, on His Shoulders rest; could we be careless, while those around are not found, because we seek them not? Our very blessings condemn us, if we impart them not. To be careless about others' salvation is to risk our own. For they only are saved who love. And can we indeed love God, if we long not that all around us should love Him Who has so loved us, in Whose love we have found our rest?

Love is the mark of His sheep. The Good Shepherd Who laid down His life for His sheep, has said to us by His Apostle, "And we should lay down our lives for the brethren." He Who stooped so low to our misery and sin, that He might raise us so high, to be "with the princes of His people," before His Father's Throne, yea, to "sit down with Him in His Throne," saith to us, "Bear ye one another's burthens, and so fulfil the law of Christ." Bear we then indeed the tokens of Him, Who was wounded and bruised in His search for us, Who "was Himself led as a lamb to the slaughter, and was as a sheep dumb before His shearers," if we part with none of our luxuries or comforts or ease to bind up that which was bruised or bring back that which is astray? If we care not for those who are, with us, the flock of Christ, shall we be placed at the last Day among that flock we cared not for? are we indeed His sheep, or are we not rather, of "the goats?"

Oh think ye then what it was, once to have been lost; what had it been, to have been left as lost; what it is, to have been found by Him; what at the last Great Day, to be found *in* Him; what to share the Angels', yea your Master's joy, (nay, is it not a foretaste of everlasting joy, to joy with Him over them, who with you shall joy in Him for ever?) and as He hath loved you, love Him in them! In whatever lawful way God opens to you, by all acts of love and tenderness, by tender warnings where you may, by loving care for the lambs of Christ, by gentle ministering to the bodies and souls of the sick and afflicted when the soul is most open to holy influences, by making peace, by helping, if it may be, to restore the fallen, by self-denying toil or alms, by the charity of daily prayers for the conversion of your fellowsinners, shew forth your love; and He, the Fountain of your Love, shall Himself be its everlasting Reward; He Who giveth you to joy with Him here, shall in His everlasting kingdom joy over you and in you; His "joy shall remain in you, that your joy may be full."

Now unto Him Who hath loved us, and washed us from our sins with His own Blood &c.

Almighty God, Who shewest to them that be in error the light of Thy truth, to the intent that they may return into the way of righteousness; Grant unto all them that are admitted into the fellowship of Christ's Religion, that they may eschew those things that are contrary to their profession, and follow all such things that are agreeable to the same; through our Lord Jesus Christ. Amen.

SERMON XIV.

BLISS OF HEAVEN, "WE SHALL BE LIKE HIM."

(Sunday Morning, Nov. 2.)

1 S. JOHN iii. 2.

"Beloved, now are we the sons of God, and it doth not yet appear what we shall be: but we know that, when He shall appear, we shall be like Him; for we shall see Him as He is.

IT is a common, misgiving, thought, when men would turn to God, or even when they are in some way religious, "how can I be happy in heaven? what will be its happiness?" And according to men's tempers, they will further say, "Here I am ever doing; the duties of life give me what to do; I study, it may be, or labour or do the works of my calling, and I can picture to myself being happy, if I have something wherein to *do* God's will; but I am soon weary when I would think of God; if I use prayers given me by holy men, or the divine Psalms, I cannot fix my thoughts long upon God; even, when He gives me most grace, and I feel borne out of myself, in love, or praise, or thankfulness, and for the time could forget myself and all created things, in the sweetness of the love of God, I soon fall back in weariness; it is good to cleave fast to God, but I am weak and cannot hold on; I could think that Eternity could be happy, were it all like such moments as these, but how can I love and praise for all Eternity, and be unwearied still? Change is my very refreshment here, can I then find joy in the one single love of God?"

Such thoughts imply a state more or less imperfect. They are doubtless sometimes sent by God, to make us feel how imperfect our state is; that we are too much taken up with the things of this life; that Heaven being little in our thoughts, and so a strange place to us, we cannot understand the joys of those who dwell there; that our hearts are too much scattered among outward things, and so cannot think what it could be to be wholly knit and gathered up in God; that we, dwelling little on the thought of God and His Goodness, seldom conversing with Him, have but a faint love, and so cannot understand what it would be to love on for ever. In part, they are true, that, we cannot in this life imagine what the bliss of heaven will be. For, "now we see through a glass darkly:" how can we think what it will be, "face to Face to see God?" Now "we know in part;" what a mystery then to us, that we "shall know God, even as we are known," enter into the very secrets of His love, share in His Knowledge, His Wisdom, His Power, His Will, His Glory, His Beauty, His Bliss, His Love which is His Bliss, know God with the same knowledge wherewith He knows us, save that we are bounded, He unbounded, or Infinite! Still, after our measure, we shall have entrance to all the thoughts of God, see things without Him as He sees them; see within Himself, in a manner, as He sees Himself; we shall be ourselves within Him, enfolded by His Essence and Essential Glory and Love; and as He knows us, by His Presence in our souls, so we shall know Him by being taken up within Him, there to contemplate Him, to read His Excellence and His Goodness eye to Eye, more than, in the face we here best love, we can read the deepest love, with which any in God here loves us. Truly, "eye hath not seen, nor ear heard, neither have entered into the heart of man, the things which God hath prepared for them that love Him." For the "good things which God hath prepared" are God Himself; and, "no man, while in the flesh, can see God and live." Sooner could the worm, which encased in a hard crust of wood or pebbles, lies lifeless, imagine what it would be, when it rises, as it were, from its grave and flies free and aloft to the day; sooner could the child in its mother's womb, imagine the power and strength and understanding of the full-grown man; sooner, one born in a dungeon imagine, out of its darkness, the glories of the richest gladliest day; than we, out of this our prison-house could, even from those rays of light wherewith God at times bedews the faithful soul, tell what it will be to be within the full Light of His Countenance. S. Paul, when rapt up into Paradise, "heard unspeakable words, which it was not lawful for a man to utter;" S. John saw the Vision of our Lord in glory, and heard the heavenly harps, and the new song of the redeemed, and saw the glory of the Heavenly City, and Him that sat upon the Throne, and the blessed company round about the Throne, as "they worshipped Him That liveth for ever and ever;" yet neither S. Paul nor the beloved disciple knew what the full bliss of heaven would be; for S. Paul still says, "it hath not entered the heart of man," and S. John, "Beloved, now are we the sons of God; and it doth not yet appear what we shall be."

It may then be some contentment to us, yea surely it is an earnest of the greatness of our bliss, that no one in the flesh can understand it. Picture we all the joy of the whole world, not those fleeting miserable joys which the poor "world which lieth in wickedness" seeks after, but all the purest, brightest, most transporting joys, which ever filled the soul of any saint of God; think we of the calm bliss of S. John, when he knew in himself that "he that dwelleth in love, dwelleth in God, and God in him," or of S. Paul, when he said, "to me to live is Christ;" and "not I, but Christ liveth in me;" or of martyrs, when for the abundance of joy, they joyed in spirit, while their flesh was consumed; or of S. Stephen, when he saw heaven opened, and his Redeemer standing to defend him, and ready to receive him, and place him by His Side, on His Throne; or any who have so loved that they could say with the spouse in the Canticles, "I am faint with love;" "I am my Beloved's and my Beloved is mine," and could hardly support the fulness of the consolations of God; these had some foretaste, but they could not, as yet, even conceive the bliss of Heaven; for it "hath not entered into the heart of man." O deep Ocean of joy and bliss and love, wherein we shall ever freely range, ever longing yet ever satisfied; ever filled yet never sated; ever loving yet never weary; ever receiving fresh streams of love and glory and bliss from the exhaustless Fountain of all Good, which is God.

It were then the part of faith to believe, that, if we love God, we must be happy, because we have His word for it. If He willeth to make us happy, how should we not be so? If He says, "Enter thou into the joy of thy Lord," into His own very joy, must we not joy, when He has thus enfolded us with joy? Shall His Almightiness fail, that He cannot make us happy? or His love Who became Man to die for us, that He will not? or His own Fulness of Bliss, wherein He hath been Himself "Blessed for ever," that It should not suffice us, when He filleth us with all the love which we can contain?

There are, indeed, those in whom this fear, whether they could be happy, comes from their own present real unfitness to be so, and whom some ensnaring sin keeps back from the grace of God; or in many of us, it may be that we have been too much taken up with outward and earthly things, earthly business or pleasure, or even lawful delights, to taste of His inward sweetness, or hear His secret voice of love. And, in most cases, it may be, that some real hindrance may be to be removed, some secret subtle sin, some undue love of self or of His creatures, that they may know the surpassing love of the Creator. But, besides all this, it may be that our mistake is, a secret over-trust in self, as if our bliss in heaven were to come from our own powers of loving, dwelling on, embracing, God, instead of being filled with Himself, when He "shall be All things in all," and we shall love Him with His own love, wherewith He shall first have filled us, in an endless flow and reflow of love, ever poured out anew on us, ever from us returning back to Him from Whom it comes.

Yet, further, to help us to think of this bliss, that so, through the sweetness of eternal bliss, we may despise and trample on the tempting, debasing, sweetnesses of things of sense, God tells us how, without this our earthly pleasure, we may hope there to have unwearied bliss.

"When He shall appear, we shall be like Him." Then shall every hindrance to spiritual bliss cease. "We shall be like Him." Then shall all which is unlike Him drop off from us. And this it is which hinders our bliss. What is it, but "the corruptible body, which presseth down the soul," "the body of death" in which we are imprisoned, "the law of sin in our members which warreth against the law of our mind," the temptations of the flesh, the world, and satan; the memory of past sin, the present infirmities, the distraction of inward and outward cares? These give no rest to ths soul; they fight against it from without, if no longer admitted within; they weary it by their ceaseless strife; cast it down, when it would rise up towards God; bring a cloud before it, when it would gaze unto Him; drown by their din the sweet whisper of His secret voice. How can we then now paint to ourselves that everlasting rest, when He shall for ever "have healed the stroke of our wounds," have blotted out our sins, bruised Satan under our feet, rescued us from the lion ready to devour? How can we imagine now what it will be, when corruption shall have put on incorruption, what is sown in corruption, in weakness, in dishonour, shall be raised in incorruption, in power, and in glory; when the world and the lusts thereof shall have passed away; and we, if we have loved God, remain alone with Him in the company of the blessed; the very body which clogs us now, made like unto the glorious Body of our Redeemer, itself spiritual, capable of spiritual joys, a partner in our bliss and adding to its fulness? What should there then be to abate or hinder the fulness of our joy, when "death shall be swallowed up in victory, through our Lord Jesus Christ," and nothing around, above, below, within, shall withdraw us from the love of God? For all around shall reflect His love; all we see shall, with ourselves, be full of His glory; in all, and in ourselves, we shall behold God; yea in Himself, in Whom we shall live, we shall behold, know, love, Himself. "Blessed," says a father[a], "are 'they who dwell in Thy House; they shall evermore praise Thee.' This shall be our whole employ, a neverfailing Halleluiah. Think not, brethren, that ye will be weary then, inasmuch as ye here last not out, if ye would long say, Halleluiah: some need recalleth you from that joy. And whereas what is unseen hath not the same delight, if, amid the very oppression and frailty of the flesh, we, with such alacrity, praise What we believe, how shall we praise What we see! When death shall have been swallowed up in victory, when this mortal shall have put on immortality, and this corruptible shall have put on incorruption, no one will say, 'I have stood long;' none, 'I have been long fasting, watching long.' For greatly will they be then up-stayed, and the very

[a] S. Aug. in Ps. lxxxiii. (lxxxiv.) §. 8.

immortality of our body shall hang upon the contemplation of God. And if this His word which we give forth to you, can keep the weakness of our flesh so long standing, what shall that joy do for us there! How shall it change us! For 'we shall be like Him, for we shall see Him as He is.' Being then 'like Him,' how shall we fail? Whither turn aside? Fear we not, brethren. The praise of God, the love of God, will not cloy us. If thou canst fail to love, thou canst fail to praise. But if love shall be everlasting, because that Beauty can never cloy, fear not lest thou be unable to praise for ever, Whom thou shalt be able to love for ever. So then, 'Blessed are they who dwell in Thine house; they shall evermore praise Thee.' Sigh we for this life." "When [b] I shall with my whole self cleave to Thee, I shall no where have sorrow or trial; and my life shall wholly live, being wholly full of Thee. But now since whom Thou fillest, Thou upliftest, since I am not full of Thee, I am a burden to myself."

Much, too much, were this for us, to be freed from infirmity and sin; but too little for the love of God. Much were it, and perhaps all, of which many think, that we shall, if we attain thither, be freed from this life's ills, " shall hunger no more, neither thirst any more;" that God " shall wipe off all tears from our eyes, and there shall be no more death, neither sorrow, nor crying, neither shall there be any more pain." Yea, much is this too, because God has promised it; it is His Gift, the token of the full doing away of sin, when its wages too shall cease. Sweet is it to think of an everlasting rest,

[b] S. Aug. Conf. x. 28. p. 204. Oxf. Tr.

in which there shall be no strife with sin, no rebellion within us, no temptation without, no fear of falling, no enemy to watch against, but all shall be one blessed, everlasting peace, in God and with God. Yet too little is this for the boundless love of God, too slight reward for the Sufferings which our Lord endured upon the Cross for us! This we could imagine in some holier seasons, when our whole souls are hushed in the Presence of God, and our whole will is absorbed in His, and the soul is all knit up in one to love, and is dead to all without and to itself, or in some thrill of joy which He bestows on penitence, or some ray of light which He sheds on the soul, bathing it with His sweetness or melting it with His love, or drawing it up unto Himself. But this is not our bliss; since this "the heart of man can conceive;" all this is but the means whereby we may receive His Bliss; it is not our Bliss itself; for that is, GOD.

Elsewhere it is said, we shall "be equal unto the Angels." And what were not this? for us, who lay on our "dunghill," sunk in the mire and foulness of our sins, to be "set with the princes of His people," the ministers of His Presence, who have ever done His will! for us, who had made ourselves "like the beasts which perish," to be like the most perfect of His creation, the highest created wisdom and beauty, who ever kept their high estate and their nearness to God, and did His Will and never defiled His Image, perfect in their degree, free from all passion, partakers of the immortality of God, ever beholding the Face of the Father. But now the greatness of our bliss and theirs is told us in more solemn overwhelming words, "we shall be like Him." Like Whom? Like God. The very gift, which Satan taught Adam, by disobedience to seek to gain for himself, not to receive of God: that same surpassing Gift, through the obedience and death of Him, Who is God and Man, will God bestow on man, to be like Himself. "Ye shall be as God," said the tempter, and man through lust fell. "I have said ye are gods, saith God, and ye shall all be children of the Most High;" "that we, having escaped the corruption which is in the world through lust, might be partakers of the Divine Nature;" not by Essence, since that belongs only to the Holy Trinity in Itself; not Personally, since that belongs only to the Incarnate Word; but still by grace, although not by nature; by His indwelling in us, now in each according to his measure, more perfectly in glory. "The Word was made Flesh," says a father[d], "in order to offer up this body for all, and that we, partaking of His Spirit, might be made gods; a gift, which we could not otherwise have gained, than by His clothing Himself with our created body. For hence we derive our name of 'men of God,' and 'men in Christ.'" "For [e] therefore did He assume a human body, that having renewed it, as its Framer, He might make it god in Himself, and thus might introduce all us into the kingdom of heaven after His likeness.—For therefore the union was of this kind that He might unite what is man by nature to Him Who is in the Nature of the Godhead, and man's salvation and deifying might be sure."

[d] S. Athanas. Nicen. Def. c. 3. fin. p. 23. Oxf. Tr.
[e] Orat. 2. c. Ariann. § 70. p. 380, 1.

"We shall be like Him." A likeness we had by nature and by grace, ere it was lost by Adam's fall. About us God vouchsafed to consult, and in our creation was the sacred mystery of the Trinity in Unity first revealed, as in our Baptism it is renewed. "And God said, Let Us make man in Our image, after Our likeness." Like God we were by nature, in our royal birth, the lords of all the animal world, the end for whom it was made, as God Himself is the End of all things; ourselves to obey God Alone, and then all beside to obey us. Of Him we were a shadowy likeness, as the created and finite can be of the Uncreated Infinite God, in that we, by His gift, had a soul one and incorporeal as He is; immortal, by grace, as He by nature; possessed of understanding, will, and memory, and these free, as made free and upheld by Him; uniting, in a manner, heaven and earth in ourselves, in that we had in part the nature of angels, in part that of the things below us; yea, for us, heaven and earth and time itself are, since when the number of the elect is finished, heaven and earth shall be changed, and time itself shall be no more, and "God shall be All in all." And this image of God flowed over upon the body too. In that it was formed upright, to gaze upwards to heaven and towards God, its very form shewed that, although of earth, it was not made for this earth, not, like the beasts that perish, to seek the things of earth, but for its home in heaven and in God. Our very look bears witness for Whom we were made. Why look to heaven, if thou grovellest on earth? Yea, if any of us dare scarce look up to heaven, it is because like the publican, we feel that, but for God's mercy, we have lost it.

We were then an image of God by nature, and this image, in part, we never lost, can never lose. "The image," says a holy man [f], "can be burnt in hell, not burnt away; it can be all on fire, but not destroyed. Whithersoever the soul shall go, there will it also be. Not so the likeness. It either abideth in good, or if the soul sinneth it is miserably changed, being likened to the beasts that perish." Our truest, fullest, likeness, was in that gift above nature, the soul of the soul [g], Divine grace. By this was man, ere he fell, clad and gifted with original righteousness, from which by nature we are now far gone: by this, was he capable of receiving, not all knowledge only, so as to grasp in himself, and order, and mould, all thoughts of all created things, but he could receive all wisdom, virtue, blessedness, the sight of God, the Spirit of God within him: by this was he a likeness of God in His everlasting rest: for no passions were at war within him, his appetite was subdued to his reason, his reason to God: and so his will was one with the Will of God, and his soul, holding converse with God, as He walked in the blissful garden, reflected his Maker's Will, as clear water gives back the face of heaven, or a mirror flashes back the brightness of the earthly sun which shines upon it.

This likeness through Adam we lost; through Christ we more blessedly regained. For now are we holy, not only by the gift of God, but by Him Who vouchsafes to be called His Gift, because He is given to us, His "Holy Spirit Which dwelleth in us."

[f] S. Bern. Serm. 1. de Annunt. § 7. [g] S. Aug.

Now have we a likeness of God, not because we were so made only, but because we were more blessedly "re-made, being renewed after the Image of Him Who created us." And this Divine Image is engraven upon our souls, not in any outward way, nor even by the grace of God alone, but also by the Spirit of God within us, "else," as saith a father[h], "we had been called the image of the grace, rather than the image of God Himself." And our Lord said to the Apostles, "Receive the Holy Ghost," whereby, through the inbreathing of the Saviour, they became partakers not of grace alone, but of the One Holy Spirit. By the Holy Spirit, Scripture saith, we have been sealed; but, says a father again[i], "The seal hath the Form of Christ Who sealeth; and of this Form do the sealed partake, being formed after It; as the Apostle saith, 'My little children, of whom I travail again until Christ be formed in you.' But they who are so sealed, well are they said to be 'partakers of the Divine Nature,' as Peter said. And through the Spirit are we all said to be partakers of God. 'Know ye not, he saith, that ye are the temple of God, and that the Spirit of God dwelleth in you?'" Not through any creature could we be made partakers of God; not Angel or Archangel could dwell in the soul, but God Alone Who made it for Himself. "So," says a father[k], "have we the rich gift, that He Who is by Nature and truly God, is our Indweller and Inhabitant, in that from Him we receive the Spirit Which is both from Him and in Him, and His Own, being, by Name and in Truth,

[h] S. Cyr. Dial. vii. de S. Trin. p. 638.   [i] S. Ath. Ep. i. ad Serap. § 23, 24.   [k] S. Cyr. Dial. vii. de Trin. p. 641.

equally Lord with Himself, and to us replacing the Son, as being by Nature One with Him." "He sent to us the Comforter from Heaven, through Whom and with Whom He is with us and dwelleth in us, pouring into us no foreign but His own Spirit, of His own Substance, and of That of the Father." And so our Blessed Lord says again, "If[1] any man love Me, he will keep My words, and My Father will love him, and We will come unto him, and make Our abode with him." And lest any one think that the Father and the Son only, without the Holy Spirit, make Their abode with those who love Him, let him consider what was said just before[m] of the Holy Spirit; "Whom the world cannot receive, because it seeth Him not, neither knoweth Him: but ye know Him; for He dwelleth with you, and shall be in you." "So," adds a father[n], "cometh the Spirit, as cometh the Father; for where the Father is, there also is the Son, and where the Son is, there is the Holy Spirit. But He cometh not by motion from place to place, but from the grace which quickeneth to the grace which sanctifieth, to transfer us from earth to heaven, from decay to glory, from slavery to the kingdom. The Spirit so cometh, as cometh the Father,—in Whom, when He cometh, is the full Presence of the Father and the Son." O the depth of the riches of the condescension and love of God, Who hath not only pardoned us and delivered us from death, but has given us righteousness and sanctification; has not given them us only, but, as Scripture says, Himself made His Son such to us, by taking our nature into God, and in our nature dying for us; and not only so, but imparting

[1] S. John xiv. 23. [m] ver. 17.
[n] S. Ambr. de Sp. S. L. i. c. 11 § 122, 3.

His grace; and not grace only, but making us sons; and not sons only, but members of His Only-begotten Son; not heirs only, but co-heirs with Christ; to have in our measure what He has, the everlasting Love of the Everlasting Father; and of this He hath given us the earnest, His Holy Spirit, Who with Him is One God, to dwell in us, in His Own Holy Person, and unite us with Him.

My brethren, if such be the first-fruits, what shall the harvest be? if such the earnest, what shall the full gift be, whereof it is the earnest? if such our clay, when gilded [o] over by the glory of sonship, what when it shall be wholly conformed to His glorious Body? if such through the veil, when we feel only after Him, what when, face to Face, His glory shall shine upon us? if such in "the region of the shadow of death," what shall it be "in the land of the living," whereof God Himself shall be the Light and Glory and Beauty, and "in His Light we shall see Light?"

"We shall be like Him." I have said hitherto, brethren, rather *that* we shall be really like Him, not *how* that likeness to Him shall come to us, nor *what* it is to be like Him. *How* we shall become like Him, the Apostle goes on to say, "for we shall see Him as He is," (and on this I hope to speak this afternoon,) "What it is to be like Him," Who but Himself can tell?

Yet, to gain some thought of our future bliss, think we, for a little moment, of some of the Perfections of our God. In some way, indeed, they cannot be, except in God Himself; for God Alone can be

[o] S. Cyr. Dial. vii. de Trin. p. 646.

Infinite and Incomprehensible; and the Creator; and as far as His Wisdom and Power and Goodness are Infinite, they cannot belong to the creature. What received these, would be God Himself. Scripture says not, "we shall be He," but "we shall be like Him." But we should not be like Him, if we had not, after our measure, and as far as creatures can contain them, the qualities (so to speak) of Almighty God. Such is the love of God, so does His Goodness love to bestow Itself, that He would withhold nothing of Himself, which His creatures can receive [p]. God is All-Holy, Himself the Source of all holiness. We then, if we be brought thither, shall be, in every part of us, holy. Nothing unclean entereth there. Within and without we shall be filled and clothed

[p] In this passage, some older writer was followed. S. Anselm, in more than one place, speaks of the power which the Blessed shall have, because, having no will but that of God, all they will shall be. See below in Serm. 16. end; and Epist. l. ii. 22; "Whosoever shall be found worthy to reign there, whatsoever he shall will, shall be in heaven and in earth, and whatsoever he shall not will, shall not be, either in heaven or in earth. For so great shall be the love between God and those who shall be there, and between these one to another, that all shall love one another as themselves; but all shall love God more than themselves. And therefore no one shall will there, save what God wills; and what one shall will, that will all will, and what one or all shall will, that will God will. Wherefore whatsoever any shall will, this shall be, as to himself and all besides, and all creation, yea and as to God Himself. And so each shall be perfect kings; for what each shall will, that shall be; and all together with God shall be one king, and as it were one man, because all shall will one thing, and what they will shall be." And Rusbroch; "In that life there shall be the whole compass of wisdom, inasmuch as we shall know perfectly whatsoever we shall will. There shall also be every sort of power, for we shall be kings and sons of God; and shall do what we will, &c."

with the Holiness of God. It were not heaven, if, in its whole compass there were one speck, not changed into the Holiness of God. In Presence of His Holiness, it were more unbearable than the pains of Hell. God is All-Wise. We then, seeing Him, shall read in Him the treasures of His Wisdom, the mystery of our being and of His love. God is All-Powerful. Our Blessed Lord hath said, "To him that overcometh will I give to sit upon My Throne, even as I also overcame and am set down with My Father on His Throne;" and to all the elect, "Thou hast been faithful in few things, I will make thee ruler over many things." God is all-glorious; and glory "is the very name of our future being." To "bring many sons to glory" was the very end of the Sufferings of our Lord. "When He shall appear, then shall ye also appear with Him in glory." Glory shall fill the elect above the brightness of the sun, shall make them transparent with light, all-bright, all-pure; and that, with the imparted light of God. And what should I more say? God is Love. And when faith is turned into sight, and hope into its substance, then shall "charity abide" and be perfected; then shall we love with the love of God, shall love God as God loveth Himself, ever through His love cleaving unto His love, ever borne to God, uplifted, filled, overflowing, receiving, giving back so as again to receive, the unutterable love of God, and by His love changed into His own Unchangeableness.

My brethren, who might not dwell for ever on these words? And yet I have told you, as yet, nothing of their reality; nor can I tell you; for what have I been speaking of? The Wisdom, Holiness, Power, Glory, Beauty, Love of God. And to know these, we must see Himself. The ear cannot catch them; the tongue cannot speak of them: to the inmost heart which loveth, God revealeth but some faint gleam of them. They are laid up in store for them who love Him.

And shall we, then, my brethren, for whom these things are in store, to whom, if we are saved, there is reserved, according to our measure, such fulness of the love of God and likeness to Him, shall we any longer be wasting that likeness, wasting bliss everlasting, amid the fleeting, fading, sickening, vanities of this world? "So much the more unlike," says S. Augustine [q], "is the soul of man to Him, the Incorporeal, the Eternal, the Unchangeable, the more he loveth the things of time and change." If we would be "like Him" in glory, we must in our degree be "like Him" here by grace. If we would have His Image for ever, we must bear even now the Image of the Heavenly, after which, by His mercy, we have been renewed; if we would behold Him in bliss, our heart must be made pure here, that by faith it may here see, Whom by the eye of the body it sees not.

That likeness here is renewed, in proportion as is our love; since God is love. It is begun, when we are wearied and sickened at ourselves, that we are so unlike Him, so far removed from Him. It is enlarged, when with penitent love we return from the far country whither we had strayed, to confess our unworthiness in our Father's Presence. It is carried

[q] De Civ. Dei ix. 17.

on by His grace, through every act of self-denial, or virtue, or love, or penitent suffering, for love of Him; through every groan, that we are unlike Him; every longing to be like Him; every fervent momentary prayer we breathe for His love: for fervent prayer is not our own, but the unutterable groanings of His Spirit Which dwelleth in us. It is renewed by that Heavenly Feast, the Food of Angels, wherein (in the words of our Church) " our sinful bodies are made clean by His Body, and our souls washed through His most Precious Blood," yea " we dwell in Christ and Christ in us, we are made one with Christ and Christ with us." It shall be perfected, in those who, by His grace, persevere to the end, in that blessed everlasting Sight, when our vile body shall be made like unto the glorious Body of our Redeemer, our soul shall see the Ever-Blessed Trinity, and in that sight receive of the ineffable Beauty and Glory and Majesty and Love which it sees.

Oh defile we then no more that Royal image, in which He formed us; which, when sunk in the mire of sin, He came to cleanse anew by His own Precious Blood; which He sought out so diligently, by toil and suffering; which He longs to shew on high, rejoicing, to His friends and neighbours in the heavenly courts. Come we to Him, " not with the feet but with the heart," and " be enlightened, that our faces be not ashamed," looking, in trust and penitence and hope and love, to His Divine Countenance; desiring that His Divine Features be, one by one, retraced on our souls. Long we to be cleansed, and He will cleanse us; long we for His Indwelling, and He will come to us; treasure we His Sacred Presence, when we have received It, and He will cleanse us more and more; hide we no part of our sinful heart from Him, and He will by His light brighten the dark corners over which we grieve; and all, sorrow or joy, dryness or refreshment, the light of His Presence or His seeming absence, shall but the more kindle our longing and cleanse our souls for that unvarying, unceasing, unspeakable Presence in bliss. "We shall be like Him, for we shall see Him as He is."

Now unto Him that loved us and washed us from our sins in His own Blood, and hath made us kings and priests unto God and His Father, to Him &c.

O God, Who hast prepared for them that love Thee such good things as pass man's understanding; Pour into our hearts such love towards Thee, that we, loving Thee above all things, may obtain Thy promises, which exceed all that we can desire; through Jesus Christ our Lord. Amen.

SERMON XV.

BLISS OF HEAVEN, "WE SHALL SEE HIM AS HE IS."

(Sunday Afternoon, Nov. 2.)

1 S. JOHN iii. 2.

"Beloved, now are we the sons of God, and it doth not yet appear what we shall be; but we know that, when He shall appear, we shall be like Him; for we shall see Him as He is."

"WE shall see Him as HE IS." My brethren, I said, I hoped, by the grace of God, to say something to you of these amazing words. And yet the more I would try to speak, the more I seem driven back into my inward self, to worship in silence what I cannot speak of. How should we speak of what we have not seen? and yet, in the flesh, "no man can see God and live." What could the blessed John say, he who had lain in the Bosom of Him Who, although veiled in our flesh, yet was God? Even he could only say those two words, "we shall see Him," and that, "as He is." And what should we say, who are "of unclean lips, living in a people of unclean lips!" Even when some ray from that heavenly Brightness, Which is God, has streamed upon the hearts of saints, it has been but as a flash which came and was gone; it kindled, for the time, the whole mind, and filled it with light, and seemed to bear the spirit into another world, and left an unutterable sweetness and longing; but it stayed not, and what it was, the soul could not utter. What if the boundless Beauty and Goodness of God could be gathered into one created mind, and that while yet in the flesh, weighed down and clogged by its corruption? "In Thy Light shall we see Light[a]." Through God Alone can we behold God. Yea, in the Ever-blessed Trinity shall we see Itself. "With Thee, O God the Father Almighty, the Fountain of life, was the Coequal Son, Who" in the Beginning "was[b] with Thee and ever was, because He was with Thee, through Whom and in Whom all things were made, and He is the Life of all, and He maketh Thee known to us, that the hearts of men might be enlightened to know Thy Majesty." Of Thee[c] the Light, Who art the Father, shall we see the Light, the Son, in the Light, The Holy Spirit. Invisible He is in Himself to all created being, The Son as the Father: the brightness of His Presence is the hiding-place of His Power: not Angel or Archangel could bear the brightness of that unapproachable Light wherein He dwelleth, unless He strengthened their sight. To Him

---

[a] Psalm xxxvi. 9.   [b] S. Ambr. in Ps. xxxv. § 22.

[c] S. Greg. Naz. Or. xxxi. § 3. "This is it also of which David was fore-instructed, when he said, 'in Thy Light shall we see Light;' and now we too have both beheld and preach, receiving from the Light the Father, the Light the Son, in the Light, the Spirit, a concise and simple confession of the Trinity:" and Or. xxxiv. § 13. "Be thou enlightened with David who saith to the Light, 'in Thy Light shall we see Light;' i. e. the Son in the Spirit, than Which what can be more radiant?"

darkness is light, and to us His sight would be darkness; for His very Brightness would blind us. He dwelleth in light, yea He Himself is that Surpassing, Unbounded, Uncreated, Ineffable Light wherein He dwelleth, (for He Who is not in space, nor bounded, can dwell in nothing but Himself,) and "yet clouds and darkness are round about Him;" for, as another Psalm saith, "He covereth Himself with light, as with a garment." The Light, which He is, is to us the covering which hides Him. "Invisible is He for the excellence of His Brightness, and unapproachable through the exceeding abundance of the outpouring of His super-substantial Light[d]." No created being, however high, could, of its own power, and by its nature, behold God. None but God can, of Himself, see God; the Ever-blessed Three in One, Which God is, Alone hath beheld from Eternity His own Glory, Majesty, Beauty; Himself resting within Himself, and in Himself finding the One Object of His Perfect Bliss. Whatever else hath seen Him, or seeth Him, seeth Him through the Divine Light; else would not that be true which Holy Scripture saith, that "it cannot be approached."

And this may be some help to us to imagine the exceeding Glory and Beauty of Almighty God, that all created beings must be lifted above themselves and their own nature, and receive of the Glory of God, in order to behold Him. Far less were it, could It be beheld by any natural power. Now not only is the Nature of God Incomprehensible, that is, such that it cannot be taken into the mind and grasped by any the very highest created mind, ("for who,"

[d] Ep. 5. ad Doroth. ap. S. Dionys. Opp. t. ii. p. 81.

saith Scripture, "can find out the Almighty to perfection?") but even the outskirts of His Glory cannot be seen, unless He Himself give to the mind a power of seeing, above its own nature. So above all created things is He Who created them, such a chasm is there between Him and even those nearest to Himself, that they cannot, as it were, pass over to behold Him, except by Him; they cannot see Him, except by Himself in them. Such is the height and depth of God: the Beginning not to be approached by us, the Compass not to be taken in, by those whom He enables to behold Himself; the deep things of God none can search out, save He, Who is of the Father and the Son, even the Holy Spirit. As no man knoweth the depths of man, and his secret thoughts, and his heart which is very deep, save the spirit of man within himself, so, Scripture says, "none knoweth" the "hidden" depths of God, the Abyss of His Majesty, save He Who is within the Eternal Godhead, "the Spirit," Who being God, hath One Godhead, Essence, Knowledge, and Almightiness with the Father and the Son.

And so, again, may we the more see, how in this life we can form no thought of the real bliss of the life to come, and yet think how that bliss will fill our whole souls, take up our whole souls, overflow us with Divine joy, and uphold us that we fail not from its excess, and weary not of its fulness. In one word, we (if we be found worthy) shall see Whom we now see not, and we who shall see, shall be other selves, and have other powers wherewith to see, even His, Whom we shall see, God. Now, both God is hidden, and we are weak and unworthy of that Great

Sight. Then God shall disclose Himself, and give us sight, that we may see. And this Sight shall be His own. It cannot then fail, because it will be Divine. "In Thy Light shall we see Light." It shall be we, who see that Light which is God, yet in His light, the light of Glory wherewith the souls and bodies of the Blessed shall be filled. Even here, where what we love or gaze on, is created, yet as long as we can gaze, our minds are filled the more, the more we gaze. Even in deep human love, the longer the soul dwelleth on that which reflects heaven in the object of its love, the intenser and more entrancing is its love. If we gaze stedfastly on the earthly sun, as long as we can bear it, the sight becomes intenser; not its beauty, but our sight fails. How much more, when that Blissful Beauty shall be Infinite, and instead of dazzling us shall give us strength to gaze, shall draw us into Itself; and yet Its Loveliness is Infinite, so that we shall find no end! In God and through God, shall we see God; in God and through God, shall we love God. Which shall fail, that so we should cease to love, the love of God with which He shall fill us, or the Love and Loveliness Which He is, Which is Infinite? We fear lest we should change, but there is no change there; because all which is imperfect shall be done away, and "God shall be All things in all." We shall still be, for it is said, He "shall be in all;" all then shall still be: we shall be ourselves and yet shall be other selves; because "God shall be All things in us." The iron[e] is still iron, when it has

[e] The beautiful passage of S. Bernard, followed here, is in the tract. de dilig. Deo c. 10. " on the fourth degree of love, in which

ceased to be cold, and having been steeped in fire, has a heat and brightness not its own, and while it there remains, its light and heat pass not away : the air is still air, whether filled with mists which are breathed forth from this earth, or, as now, with light from above, so that it is, as it were, all one brightness ; a drop of water ceases not to be, when in a vessel full of wine it has only the richness and colour of the wine. Even so we shall not cease to be; but God being All things in us, we shall be other selves, and, S. John says, "like Him;" our powers of mind shall be ours; our substance, ours; but all, full of God. Even here all we have of our own, is sin; our substance is of God; our will, memory, reason, are of God, though we, through passion, bend our will awry, and cloud our reason, and defile our memory with hurtful things: our power to love is of God,

man so wholly loves God, as to love himself only on account of God." This S. B. supposes to belong to the state after the Resurrection. "So to be affected is to be deified. As a little drop of water, poured into much wine, seems wholly to cease from itself, while it assumes both the taste and colour of the wine; as iron, white with heat, is very like unto fire, being deprived of its own previous form; and as the air perfused with the light of the sun is transformed into the same brightness of light; so must then, in the saints, all human affection, in a certain ineffable manner, melt away from itself and be wholly transfused into the Divine Will. Else how shall God be All things in all, if in man aught of man remaineth? The substance indeed will remain; but in another form, another glory, another power. When shall this be? Who shall see it? who possess it? 'When shall I come and appear before the Presence of God?' O Lord my God, my heart hath said unto Thee, 'Seek ye My Face ; Thy Face, Lord, will I seek?'" (quoted partly by Pet. de Inc. x. 1.) The first comparison of the "iron" occurs in S. Cyril Jerus. xvii. 11. p. 227. Oxf. Tr.

even if we therewith love vanities. But there, shall "God be all things in all;" not as now the Holy Spirit "distributeth to every man severally as He wills," and what each is, he is by His gifts; not only as Christ is to us "Wisdom, Righteousness, Sanctification, Redemption," since here we have all things in part only; but "God shall be all things" perfectly in each according to his measure. There shall be no remains of a contrary will; nothing of man's own; else God would not be All. There, says a holy man¹, "He Who filleth the soul with good things, shall HIMSELF to the reason be the fulness of light, Himself to the Will the abundance of peace, Himself to the memory the lastingness of eternity. O Verity, Charity, Eternity! O Blessed and blessed-making Trinity! To Thee my miserable threefold self miserably sighs, because it is haplessly banished from Thee."—"O wonderful serenity, which the Truth, that is God, shall shed on us; fulness of sweetness, wherewith God, Who is Love, shall bedew us; eternity of safety which Power most High, that is God, shall give us. So shall God be All in all, when our reason receiveth light which cannot fail; our will, peace which cannot be troubled, our memory cleaveth eternally to the never-failing Fountain of all good." How can we ever cease to love, when we love unceasing Love with His own Love? Nought shall there be there without, to draw us from God; for all who shall be there, shall alike be full of God. In all shall we see nothing but God; all shall be as mirrors, flashing forth and back the rays of the Glory and Beauty and Love of God; God shall be All in

¹ S. Bern. S. 11. in Cant. § 5, 6.

all, so that in each we can but love God. Nought shall there be there within, to draw us down from God, nothing to care or provide for, no bodily needs, no weakness; for we ourselves shall be full of God.

"We shall see God." Yet this does not yet tell of all our bliss. In some little measure God hath been seen; and yet must that be true, "No man hath seen God at any time." "God appeared unto Abraham[g]," not seen by him by the power of nature, but because God willed to be so seen: and Jacob wrestled with God, and said[h], "I have seen God face to Face, and my life is preserved:" and the "Lord spake with Moses Face to face, as a man speaketh unto his friend[i]:" and this was a gift above all prophets, that him alone the Lord knew face to face[j]: and, Isaiah says, "I saw the Lord of Hosts sitting on a Throne:" and our Lord hath said, "Whoso has seen Me, hath seen the Father," and S. Stephen saw Him in His Glory standing at the Right Hand of God, and S. John saw One "like unto the Son of Man, and His Countenance was as the sun shineth in his strength," and when he saw Him, so aweful was the Sight, he saith, "I fell at His Feet, like one dead:" and the wicked shall see Him at the Day of Judgement; yet is it the blessing of "the pure in heart" alone, that they "shall see God."

There is then one sense, in which holy men have seen God; another sense in which no man in the flesh hath seen Him, or shall see Him, but which shall be our joy, when we shall be "like unto the

[g] See S. Ambr. in S. Luc. l. i. c. 24. (on i. 11.) and S. Aug., commenting on the passage. Ep. 147. ad Paulin. de videndo Deo.
[h] Gen. xxxii. 30.   [i] Ex. xxxiii. 11.   [j] Deut. xxxiv. 10.

Angels," who, in the unbroken repose of that bliss-giving Sight, " do alway behold the Face of the Father." Holy men have seen Him, as He was pleased to shew Himself unto them; but not, "as HE IS." For then had they seen Him all in one way, not in different Forms [k], for He changeth not, but in One simple Essence. And when God was speaking unto Moses Face to face, he still prayed [l], "I beseech Thee, shew me Thy Glory," and He shewed him not Himself, but some fainter parts of His Glory, not Himself Who "hath no parts." And so all who saw Him saw yet through a glass, darkly, what He vouchsafed to discover of Himself, not His Very Divine Nature. And they who saw our Lord in the Flesh, and to Whom the Father revealed that He was God, did in Him see the Father, with Whom the Son is One: yet not with the bodily eyes, but with the mind, did they see or acknowledge either the Son or the Father. In His Divine works, they to whom the Father gave eyes to see, beheld the Divinity of the Son; and in the Son Who was God they saw the Father, Who in Nature and Operation is inseparable from the Son. Outwardly they saw (which alone the wicked shall see) the form of a servant: with the eye of faith, they discerned that He was God: yet the Form of God, of which He had "emptied Himself," they as yet saw not. It was kept in store for them and us (if we will) in bliss.

This, then, is the bliss of the Blessed, that we shall see Him as HE IS. This has in itself all bliss; all through this shall flow into us. We shall, as it were,

[k] S. Chrys. Hom. xv. in Cat. on S. Joh. i. 18.
[l] S. Aug. l. c. c. 8. § 20.

while keeping our being, be changed into Himself, for so Scripture says, "we shall be *like* Him," and how can we be like Him, if, in all which He can impart, we are in any way unlike Him? His own Being and Substance none can have, save Those Who are of Him, but Uncreated, The Son and The Holy Ghost. But all, which He can give and we can receive, He will give; and this, through the Sight of Him: "we shall be like Him," "*for*," Scripture says, "we shall see Him as HE IS."

Yet although "we shall see Him as HE IS," still this is even a part of our blessedness, that no created being can see Him wholly. For He is Infinite. Thus we repeat in the Creed, that "the Father, Son, and Holy Ghost are One Incomprehensible," i. e. that They cannot be wholly taken in by any mind. There is a fulness of knowledge, which lies in the Bosom, (as Holy Scripture calls it,) or the Depth of God, "Which enfoldeth and embosometh[1] all things, Itself boundless," which none can know, but Who is One in Nature with God. "The Invisible Incomprehensible Trinity" can be known perfectly, as HE IS, to Itself Alone. But less blessed were it to behold God, were His Perfections not infinite. Now, says a father[m], "the mind whether of Angels or of men, as it pants after that Light which knows no bounds, shrinks together, as too narrow, in that it is a creature; it stretches onward above itself by its

---

[1] Clem. Al. on S. Joh. i. 18. "In that he calls that which is Invisible and Ineffable, 'the Bosom of God,' certain have hence called it 'the Deep' [Bosom], in that it enfoldeth and embosometh all things, Itself unattainable and unbounded." Quoted by Petav. de Deo. 7. 4. 2.

[m] S. Greg. Mor. x. 8. (p. 589. Oxf. Tr.)

advancement, yet not even when enlarged can it compass His Brightness, Who encloseth all things, at once surpassing, upholding, filling them." He filleth, yet overfloweth[n]; containeth all things, is in all, and yet contained by none; "filling [o], He surroundeth, and surrounding, He filleth; upbearing, He transcendeth, transcending, He upbeareth."

And so may the soul the more for ever delight itself in the Sight of God, because it shall see Him truly, yet cannot grasp Him wholly. Where shall be an end of loving, where love is endless, infinite? or of gazing on Beauty Infinite, where that very Beauty by our longing and its Sight shall draw us more into Itself; where is no weariness, no satiety, but a blessed union of thirst and satisfying fulness; where desire shall have no pang or void, and fulness shall but uphold desire; for both shall be Perfect, Unfailing, Love, unfailing through God's Gift, as the Very Essence of God, Who is Love. If God, Who is the Source of Love, can fail, then might the bliss of those fail, Who see Him, love Him, in Himself.

"Thine eyes shall see the King in His Beauty," yet not then, as far off, but brought nigh, yea within God. Even now "in Him we live and move and have our being;" both by nature, since He is everywhere and there is no place out of God; and more blessedly by His Providence which compasses us around, and by His grace which dwells within our souls; "and[p] we live in Him, as in Life Eternal." But

[n] S. Aug. Conf. i. 3.   [o] S. Greg. ib. xvi. 31.
[p] S. Ambr. de Bono Mort. c. ult. § 55. "We move in God, as the Way; we are in Him, as the Truth; we live in Him, as in the Life Eternal."

how much more there, where is the fulness of His Presence, and we shall see Him, Who now also is around us, although we see Him not! "For," says an early father[q], "as they who behold the light, are within the light, and partake of its brightness, so they who behold God are within God, partaking of His Brightness. For the Brightness gives them life; they then shall partake of life, beholding God. The beginning of life comes from the partaking of God; and to partake of God is to know God, and enjoy His Goodness. Men then shall see God, that they may live, by that sight made immortal and reaching unto God."

O what shall be the bliss of those who shall enter into that boundless Ocean of everlasting joy, that Goodness which is the Source of all good, that Beauty of which all things fair are but the shadow, and hide It from us rather than reveal It, that Light of lights, which lighteneth the eyes not of men only but of Angels; to behold in His own Wisdom, the causes of all things that have ever been, the orderings of His Providence, by which He "sweetly disposed all things" for good; to behold by His own love, the love wherewith He hath loved us; to know in Himself His "love which passeth knowledge," and that "peace which passeth all understanding;" in His Holiness to be hallowed as He is holy, and in His Perfection to be perfected. What joy shall it be beyond all joy, besides which there is no joy, to see that great Sight, for which Moses longed, which comforted Job in his sufferings, for which our whole nature has fainted and groaned until now; "with

[q] S. Iren. 4. 20. 6.

our eyes, and not another's," to see the Living God! to see Him in Himself, to "know Him" perfectly, "even as we are known" of Him; that nothing of His Glory or Majesty or Love should be hidden from us; for "we shall see Him as He IS," in His own unchanging Essence, and be freed from death and change and corruption by beholding Him Who is Life unchanging and incorruption! What, my brethren, must be the greatness of that bliss, wherein the Ever-Blessed All-Holy Trinity rests in all eternity, even Its own everlasting joy, to which nothing can add, nothing can lessen it, for all things exist by It and out of It! And yet He, our Saviour, the Coeternal Son, shall bid those who love Him, to "enter into" that His joy, "the joy of our Lord." Him, before Whom the Seraphim veil their faces, shall we behold, eye to Eye; we shall know Him Who in the depth of His Being is known only to the Coeternal Son and the Spirit of Both; we shall "see the Everlasting Father and His Consubstantial Son, equal to Him in Goodness and Eternity and Glory and Majesty; Begotten without beginning or time or end; and the Holy Spirit, proceeding from Both, the indissoluble Bond of Love, the Blessed Embrace of mutual charity [r]."

"We shall see Him as He IS." He saith not, "was" nor "shall be," but "as He IS" unchangeably, in Whom there is no "Was" nor "shall be," but "IS" in His own unchanging Essence; not as things here which "are" not, because they "never

[r] S. Laur. Justin. de obedient. fin. Opp. p. 550. He adds before the last words, "pacis suavissimum Osculum," quoted by Pet. de Trin. vii. 12. 8.

continue in one stay;" but "IS," because He abideth, changing all things, Himself unchanged, and the endless Rest of all which now changeth. So shall His blissful Vision abide, and we abide in it, because He changeth not. HE IS, and we shall be in Him. How shall our joy pass away, when He Who shall be our Joy, abideth ever? "When," says a holy man [r], "shall that longing eagerness be cloyed, or that sweetness withdraw itself, or Truth defraud, or Eternity fail? But if that longing and power to see last for ever, how shall bliss not be full? Nothing shall be wanting to those who ever see; nothing shall be too much for those who ever long."

Yet although we shall see Him, as He IS, Unchangeable, and thereby ourselves become free from change, still must there ever be in Him new and exhaustless treasures of Wisdom, Power, Love, unfolding to us; since, although we shall, not in mirror, or by aid of any other thing, nor dimmed by any thing between, see Him Who is Infinite Wisdom, Power, and Love, no created being can see Him infinitely. Nothing shall He hide from those who love, nothing withdraw; they shall see Him in His Simple Being; see, Whom we now believe, "the All-Holy Trinity, Father, Word, and Holy Ghost, One God, in Persons distinct, in Substance Co-eternal, in Power Equal, in Operation Inseparable, in Will Harmonious; and through that Vision," continues the holy man [s], "shall the reason be ever filled with the light of Truth, the will overflow with most

---

[r] S. Bern. in Cant. Serm. 31. init. where he dwells on the "est," not "fuit" or "erit," following S. Augustine.

[s] S. Laur. Justin. l. c.

burning love, the memory, ever cleaving inseparably by one simple act to Him Who IS, shall be satisfied with a blessed fruition." Still may we truly see Him, and yet must we be unable wholly to contain Him in our souls. Else, we should be Himself. As a holy father [t] has used the likeness of earthly things, "if through a very slight opening we see the sky, we say truly that we see it," yet we see it not wholly; or " if from a high mountain we behold the sea," we see it truly, yet we see " neither its breadth, nor length, nor depth, nor hidden recesses, nor the effects which it produceth;" so and much more must there be in Him, the Cause of all causes, the Infinite Source of all which is or can be, in Whom lies hid all which can be, even though it never be, a depth of Wisdom, and Power, and Love, whose being we shall know, but whose marvels shall be ever new. We shall, if we attain, love and admire and praise and cleave to Him the more, because we shall see Him Infinitely to have all worthy of praise and love and admiration, yea Himself to be Infinite Perfection and Beauty and Love, yet be ourselves encompassed by, not compass, His Infinity.

Oh what shall it be to range freely within that boundless bliss, to be admitted into its very depths, or (to speak [u] with holy men) " to be translated into the Glory of God;" to move, to think, to see, within God; in Himself and by Himself to see Himself; " clearly to see, love, and by eternal fruition possess

[t] S. Epiphanius Hær. 70. § 8. quoted by Petav. de Deo vii. 3.

[u] Most of this solemn language is from Rusbroch de fide et judic. Opp. p. 191. quoted also by Blos. sacell. animæ fidelis c. 23. and margarit. spirit. § 8.

God," and by God in turn to "be possessed [x];" "by love to comprehend, and by love to be comprehended;" "to know Him in everlasting brightness, love Him with everburning desire and delight," "to have [y] Him present within us, as our Life, to feel in the substance of our souls the Godhead, indwelling, overstreaming, a torrent of pleasure for evermore," and, "united with Him, to rest with Him, in" His unutterable "bliss." And, within God, united with the Eternal Word, what shall it be, (which we can more think, though above all thought,) to see the Glorified Manhood of our Divine Redeemer; to see His Face, shining above the brightness of the sun, yet in rays of love; to see that look which brought us to ourselves and Him; to hear the Voice of love, which called us, and we followed Him; to see, all bright and pure and radiant with light and Divine lustre, the glorified Scars which for us and for our salvation He received, and which ever since have in the Presence of the Eternal Father been pleading witnesses of His Love and Suffering for our guiltiness, withholding His anger from us; and, in that sight, "to have our heart and all our senses filled with His glory, and for joy and love dissolved," but

[x] "This then shall be our bliss, the possession of God. What then? shall we possess Him, and shall He not possess us? How then saith Isaiah, 'Lord, possess us?'" He possesseth then and is possessed; and all for us. For that we may from Him be blessed, He is possessed by us; but not, that He may be blessed, doth He possess us. He both possesseth us, and is possessed by us, to this only end, our bliss." S. Aug. in Ps. 32. (33.) Enarr. 3. § 18.

[y] Blos. Ench. Parv. ii. 6. Opp. p. 551. perhaps from S. Laur. Justin.

that the Love which melteth shall sustain us. And because no created heart can contain such love, we shall joy in the bliss of others, as our own[z]. Nothing is there but love; and so, such as one's self, of all the meanest, if by His gift, he may attain thither, shall in the higher joy and love of all the rest of the saints in bliss, joy as if it were his own. In all we shall behold, in all love God. The praise of all shall gladden us; each voice, which has learned the new song, shall swell with its own special beauty, the everlasting harmony; the glory of each several star in that more blessed firmament, shall shed its own special lustre. While all joy in those "unfailing[a] streams of Mercy, Goodness, Majesty, and Love, and sweet Peace," which shall issue forth from the Redeemer, "all shall encompass Him with longings of burning love, and shall render all thanksgiving and praise," thanking Him that they are His and of Him, and casting their crowns before Him, joying most of all that "they are justified by His grace, redeemed by His Blood, saved by His love, glorified by His merits."

And shall we not then, my brethren, while yet in the flesh, turn aside, if not to see, as Moses, the shadow of it, yet with him to long after this "great Sight?" Shall we not long to be hid in the shadow of the Rock, the Word made Flesh for us, and there, apart for a while from the noise and tumult of the world, the strife of the camp below, "the voice of

[z] See more fully S. Anselm quoted at length Serm. 16. end. "No one shall be imperfect there, for what any shall not have in himself, that through love he shall possess in others." Blos. l. c.

[a] S. Laur. Just. l. c.

them that shout for mastery, or the noise of them that sing" but not "the songs of Zion," long and pray to have our eyes cleansed, that we may see but the outskirts of His glory, see His Presence reflected around us, see It in our brethren, receive some gleam of It in our souls? Shall we, "having this hope," not "purify ourselves," not cleanse our hearts, and pray that He would cleanse them? Shall the eye again wander among forbidden things, "the lust of the flesh, the lust of the eye, the pride of life," which is to behold God? Shall the heart fill itself with the pomps and vanities of the world, which it renounced when the Name of the Trinity was named over us, with which, if it be pure, we shall see God; which is formed for God, to receive the love of the Infinite God? Beautiful is the glistening of gold, the sparkling of gems, or wine when it giveth its colour in the cup, or countenances which deceive the heart of man to its perdition; dazzling is the possession of wealth, or power over others, or eminence in this world's station; soothing our luxury and ease; but what is the fleeting beauty of all created things to the Infinite Beauty of God? what is all gladness to the Joy of our Lord? what, all riches to the treasures in heaven which fail not, His everlasting Love? what, all which sight could grasp in heaven and earth, compared to Him Whom as yet we see not, but Whom, if we be found worthy to stand before Him, we shall, when heaven and earth shall have passed away, "see as He IS?" Oh waste we then ourselves and our hearts no more in the busy chase of this world's cares and riches and pleasures which abide not, nor, if we could keep them, could fill our hearts. Mourn we in our inward hearts that we ever followed them; pray we that God will forgive us the past; that He would cleanse our memories of the stains we too sadly know; empty we our hearts of all beside Him and what we love in Him and for Him. Long we that He may enlarge our hearts, and enlarging, indwell them, and indwelling, purify them, that we may one day see Him, Who vouchsafeth Himself to be the exceeding great reward and joy of the blessed. Many of us have this day answered, " we lift up our hearts unto the Lord." " Oh be that true which we have said [b]!" Grovel we no more on earth; seek we not the things of earth; bury we not in earth, by seeking "our treasure" here, the hearts, which we have owned should be in heaven; but with hearts and eyes, and faith and hope and love, follow Him, whither He is "gone to prepare a place for us," that "when He, our Life, shall appear, we may appear with Him in glory," and "may be like Him, for we shall see Him as He IS."

Now unto Him that loved us &c.

O God, Who by the leading of a star didst manifest Thy only-begotten Son to the Gentiles; Mercifully grant, that we, which know Thee now by faith, may after this life have the fruition of Thy glorious Godhead; through Jesus Christ our Lord. Amen.

[b] S. Aug.

SERMON XVI.

BLISS OF HEAVEN—GLORY OF THE BODY.

(Sunday Evening, Nov. 2.)

PHIL. iii. 20, 21.

"*Our conversation is in heaven, from whence also we look for the Saviour, the Lord Jesus Christ, Who shall change our vile body, that it may be fashioned like unto His glorious Body, according to the working whereby He is able even to subdue all things unto Himself.*"

CAN then any thing be added to their bliss, who have the sight of God? Nothing surely, as the source of their bliss; since He is the Blessed, overflowing Source of all good. Yet in some way can bliss be added to them, who now, eye to Eye, behold God. For it has ever been believed in the Church, that they who laid down their lives for Christ, "the noble army of martyrs," at once enjoyed the full Presence of God. Holy Scripture tells us [a], how "they who were come out of great tribulation, and washed their robes and made them white in the Blood of the Lamb," "being slain for the Word of God and the testimony which

[a] Rev. vii. 13—15. vi. 9—11.

they held," are "before the Throne of God, and serve Him day and night in His Temple." And yet these same souls, under the shadow of the Altar of God, to Whom they had offered their lives a sacrifice acceptable to Him, in union with His in Whom and through Whom they suffered, "cried with a loud voice, How long, O Lord holy and true, dost Thou not judge and avenge our blood on them which dwell upon the earth." What else is it," says a father[b], "for souls to utter the prayer for vengeance, but to long for the Day of final Judgement, and the restoration of their lifeless bodies. For their great cry is their great longing." "And a white robe," it goes on, "was given to every one of them, and it was said to them that they should rest for a little season, until their fellow-servants also, and their brethren that should be killed as they were, should be fulfilled." Each had "a white robe," even holy and complete purity, and rest and the blessedness of the soul[c], given them; for so our Lord had promised to them that should overcome, "the same shall be clothed with white raiment," "and they shall walk

[b] S. Greg. Mor. ii. 7. § 11. p. 75. Oxf. Tr.

[c] "Before the Resurrection they are said each to have received one robe, for that as yet they have the joy of blessedness of mind alone; two they will then receive, when, with the perfect joy of their souls, they shall be clad with incorruptibility of bodies." S. Greg. Pref. ad Mor. fin. (p. 30. Oxf. Tr.) He is followed by S. Bernard, Serm. 3. in fest. omn. Sanct. § 1. "They have each received a robe; but with the two robes shall they not be clad, until we also are so clad, as the Apostle says of the Patriarchs and Prophets, 'God providing some better thing for us, that they without us should not be made perfect.' For that first robe whereof we spake is the bliss and rest of souls, but the second is the immortality and glory of bodies."

with Me in white;" the robe of immortality and innocence and brightness, shining with the light of their Lord in His radiance, clad by Him and with Him, Who, when in His Transfiguration He allowed some portion of His Essential Glory to stream forth, "His raiment was made white as snow." Yet have they not yet all which they shall have; for they are bid to "rest for a little season," and to wait until " the number of their fellow-servants should be fulfilled." Their waiting troubles not their rest; for they wait in the Presence of God, under the shadow of the Heavenly Altar, in the Light of His Countenance; their will is wholly one with the Will of God; their souls, perfected in His Presence, "cleave [d] in the bosom of their inmost secrecy to Him," and seeing light in His Light see all things which they see as He sees them. Of Him Whom they behold are they taught what to ask; and He Who has bid us pray, "Thy kingdom come," (whence we too pray, that " God would shortly accomplish the number of the elect and hasten His kingdom,") wills that they should both ardently long for the end and the restoration of their bodies, and yet be satisfied with their present bliss and their knowledge that the rest shall be when He wills. The soul which really loves God, is happier far that things are as His Wisdom willeth and His Love chooseth for it, than if it had all which itself longeth for. And they, in the Presence of God, cannot, by any the faintest motion of their own will, which is now for ever made one with His, will for any thing except what they read in His bliss-giving Countenance that they should will.

[d] S. Greg. Mor. ii. 7. whose thoughts the following are.

There they see His Will, and seeing are blest. So then, both because He willeth them, with the deep fervour of their longing, to pray for the end, when His glory shall be fully revealed and Himself be All in all, they cry with a loud voice, saying, "How long, O Lord, holy and true?" and because they know that as yet He willeth it not, they too as yet will it not, and are at rest. They would love Him less, did they not desire with this burning longing, what shall be His full glory in His creation and in them. It were a less perfect will, if they longed that it should be, ere He wills it. And He, to perfect His creatures, both willeth that it should be the sooner, on account of their prayers which He teacheth them, and that they should ardently long, and love the more for their ardent longing. So are they doubly perfected by the delay, in that they long the more, and yet that longing finds its rest in the hidden depths of His love and All-holy Will. He bids them "rest awhile, until the number of their brethren be fulfilled." And so they are blessed both in the hope of the increase of their blessed company, and in that the Glory of God is enlarged, and His Will fulfilled, both in the prayers which He teacheth, and the burning longings which He giveth, and the refreshment and rest which He infuseth, and the final consummation which He delayeth. And they shall receive large increase by the delay, in the number of those who, with them, shall joy in God, and whose joy they shall ever share, joying in beholding and loving God, in them as in themselves.

Yet for the time are they imperfect. Without us shall they not be perfect, nor yet without their own bodies. "It becometh not," says a holy writer[e], "that entire bliss should be given, until man to whom it is given shall be made entire; nor that the Church as yet imperfect [in the number of her members] should receive perfection." Such mysterious dignity hath God bestowed on this poor body;—the Flesh which, sinless, God the Son vouchsafed to take, that without it the bliss of the blessed should not be perfect. How should it not be, that an exceeding mystery should belong to this poor, corruptible, suffering[f], body, when He, Who is God, vouchsafed for ever to take it, in its real substance, although holy and undefiled, into God; to make our flesh the bond of union, between the Creator and the creature, taking it into Himself, and Himself now dwelling in our corruptible bodies? My brethren, let us think with reverence of the Body of our Lord, because of His exceeding love both in taking it and in glorifying it; so may we too have some thought of the glory of those who keep it undefiled, or, through penitence, have it restored to them, cleansed through His Precious Blood and conformed unto His.

"The Word became flesh;" not Itself changed into flesh or ceasing to be God, being the Unchangeable, nor changing the flesh into the Word, nor as confounded with the flesh, nor yet again merely joined to it, nor taking the flesh only, (for "flesh" here, as the "soul" elsewhere, in Holy Scripture

[e] S. Bernard, l. c.

[f] "Whence is this to thee, thou miserable flesh, thou foul, thou decayed, whence this to thee? Holy souls, which God adorned with His own Image long for thee; souls which He redeemed wait for thee; and without thee their joy cannot be fulfilled, their glory perfected, their bliss consummated." S. Bern. l. c.

denotes our whole nature; only, to shew the love and condescension of God, he speaks of that which is the basest part of us, and which we had most degraded). These are the heresies of carnal men, stumbling at the humility, wherewith God would heal man's pride. He took our whole nature wholly; "took the manhood into God," uniting in His Divine Person our human nature with His own Divine. And what had our nature become [g]? "Man being in honour and abiding not therein, was like unto the beasts that perish." Sin had made our flesh worse than a brute's nature. By nature we were the last of the rational creation; by sin, we had sunk below the irrational. And He the Creator came down and became as His creature. The Invisible God becomes seen of man and as Man. Not ceasing to be in the Form of God, He hides It under the form of a servant. Incapable of suffering, He takes our weakness that He may suffer. He willeth to have all our sinless infirmities, pain, hunger, weariness, thirst, weakness, mortality, death. So wholly was His Godhead veiled, that the deceiver who had deceived the whole world, was himself deceived, and thought Him man, and slaying the Innocent, lost his hold of us the guilty [h]. O marvellous device of Divine Wisdom

---

[g] "He took a servant's form, putting on that flesh which was enslaved to sin." S. Ath. c. Ar. i. § 43. 241. Oxf. Tr. and ib. note h. "It was necessary for our salvation," says S. Cyril, "that the Word of God should become Man, that human flesh, subject to corruption and sick with the lust of pleasures, He might make His own; and whereas He is Life and Life-giving, He might destroy the corruption &c... For by this means, might sin in our flesh become dead." Ep. ad Succ. i. p. 138. see further l. c. n. h.

[h] See S. Greg. Mor. L. 33. c. 7. and others in Pet. de Inc. ii. 5.

and love, uniting things lowest with the Highest, human with Divine, through our nature, the least and last and sunken lower still, raising up the whole universe unto union with Himself, encircling and enfolding all with His love, and knitting all in one; and that, through us! Present with all His creatures by nature; present, in a way above nature, with all holy beings, by grace; He would become present in our flesh, in a way more marvellous still, in His Person, by taking it into God. And so close is this union of the Godhead and the Manhood in the One Person of Christ, that what belongs to the Man may be said of God. For so Holy Scripture speaks of "the Blood of God[j], "and "We preach Christ crucified, Christ the Power of God and the Wisdom of God[k]." Him Who was crucified, it calleth "the Wisdom of God, and the Power of God." These are the very elements of the faith; for the deepest mysteries are those "revealed unto babes." He then, the Uncreated Wisdom, was crucified; and so, in this exceedingness of mystery, we may say, "God died," "God suffered," "God was buried[l]." For Christ was not divided, nor shall His Natures ever be. He is One Christ, God and Man; what He did, He did, being All Which He is; the works of God, He did as God; the sufferings for man, He endured as Man; yet in both One Christ. "So great an unity was made of either substance," says a father[m], "that from the time that 'the Word was made Flesh' in the Blessed Virgin's womb, we may neither think

---

[j] Acts xx. 28.   [k] 1 Cor. i. 23, 24.
[l] See note i on S. Ath. c. Ar. iii. 9. p. 446. Oxf. Tr.
[m] S. Leo Hom. 54. de Pass. Dom. 3. init. (quoted ib.)

of Him, as God without this which is Man, nor as Man without This Which is God. There is which could suffer, there is Which can receive no hurt; yet His is the shame Whose is the glory. He is in weakness, Who is in power; He is subject to death Who subdues it. God then did take to Him whole man, and so knit Himself to him and him into Himself in pity and in power, that either nature was in the other, and neither in the other lost what was its own." And so S. Paul says, "they crucified the Lord of glory;" and our Lord Himself says, "The Son of Man *is* in heaven [n]," not because He was crucified in His Majesty, nor was at that time in heaven in His Human Nature, but that the same Jesus Christ being God and Man, God by His Divinity, Man by taking the Flesh, "the Lord of Glory" was said to be "crucified," because He, Who was Both, in His Human Nature suffered, and He Who was "the Son of Man," as God, came down from heaven, and as God was still "in the Bosom of His Father," and was "in Heaven." And so all His works for our salvation were blended, the Word working that which was of the Word, the Flesh performing what was of the flesh. Both acted in one, though Each that which belonged to Each; as it has been set forth [o] by aid of created things; steel glowing with fire, cuts by the nature of steel, and burns through the indwelling fire which fills it. So our Lord called Lazarus with a human voice [p], but raised him as God;

[n] See S. Augustine and S. Chrys. in Cat. Aur. on S. John iii. 13. Oxf. Tr. and other fathers in Pet. de Incarn. iv. 16.

[o] Maximus Disp. c. Pyrrh. and others from him, quoted by Petav. viii. 14. 11.   [p] S. Ath. c. Ar. iii. § 32 and notes.

made clay with the spittle through the flesh, opened the blind eyes as God; suffered as Man, atoned as God. He made our human flesh, our whole human nature, His very own; so that His Flesh was the Flesh of God [q], the Body of God [q], essentially joined with His Divine Nature; so that all the actions or sufferings of His humiliation were the actions and sufferings of Almighty God, although, as God, He suffered not. "Himself," says a holy father [r], "removed from suffering, yet willing for us to suffer, He clad Himself in a Body which could suffer, making It so His Own, that He might be said to suffer, since His own Body, not another's, suffered. All belonging to the Flesh was His, since He was in It; and the works belonging to the Word, He wrought through His own Body." And so of His Human Name, the Name of His humility, it is said, that He was from eternity.

[q] S. Ath. iii. 31. and n. i.
[r] S. Athanas. cf. Ep. ad Epict. § 6; "When His Body was struck by the servant, as Himself suffering, He said, 'Why smitest thou Me?' and the Word being by Nature intangible, yet said, 'I gave My Back to the smiter, &c.' For what the Human Body of the Word suffered, these things the Word, conjoined with It, referred to Himself, that we might be able to partake of the Divine Nature of the Word. And passing wonderful was it, that the Same it was Who suffered and suffered not; suffered, because His own Body suffered and He was in that which suffered; suffered not, because the Word, being by Nature God, cannot suffer. And He, the Incorporeal, was in the Body which could suffer; and the Body had in Itself the Word Which could not suffer, effacing the weaknesses of the Very Body. But this He did, and it was done, that the Word taking what is our's, and offering it in sacrifice, might consume it, and then enfolding us with What is His, might occasion His Apostle to say, 'This corruptible must put on incorruption, and this mortal put on immortality.'" See also Orat. c. Ar. iii. § 32. p. 446. and n. o. Oxf. Tr.

"Jesus Christ the Same yesterday, to-day, and for ever." "Yesterday [s] in His Divine, to-day in His Human Nature," yet in both the Same. And He Himself prayeth, "Father, glorify ME with that glory which I had with THEE before the world was." The Glory, which He ever had as the eternal Word, He had now too, although unseen. He, Who could not be bounded in space, nor severed from the Father, still was, He Himself says, "in the Bosom of the Father." He prays then that His Manhood should, after His Death and Resurrection, be in the same Glory at God's Right Hand, be in the essential Glory of God. And yet so truly is He, God and Man, One Christ, that He Who, as God, gave to His Manhood Its glorious gifts, prayed the Father, "glorify ME," that is, the Man Christ Jesus, "with that glory Which I," the Co-eternal Co-equal Son, ever "had with Thee," when in all eternity "the Word was with God, and the Word was God."

These thoughts are a safeguard against misbelief as to the Blessed Person of our Lord, which is around us now also, Satan tempting people to forget in the humble language as to His Manhood, that He ever was and is Almighty God, in the Manger, on the Cross, or when, as Man, He said, "My Father is greater than I;" or to imagine that God was united to the Man in a mere outward way; or again to be ashamed of His Manhood and confess Him only to be God; and not rather, "One [t] Christ; Christ in the Form of God, Christ in the form of a Servant; Christ

---

[s] S. Ambr. de Fide v. i.
[t] Vigil. L. iv. col. 512. quoted by Petav. 4. 16. 12.

equal to the Father, Christ inferior to the Father; the Same, God, and the Same, Man."

But now I would think of them, brethren, not only for the exceeding mystery of the loving-kindness of God, Who, the Essence above all essence, came down to take our clay, but for the high dignity which He has bestowed upon our dust, uniting it with Himself. If such was the glory in His humility, what is it now in such His Majesty! If, when His glory was veiled, still such was the hidden union, that God can be said to have endured whatever the Manhood endured, the Manhood to have done what God in It wrought; if, with a perfect human will, it was yet the Divine Nature in Him, which ruled and gave force to all His acts [u]; if even, when for us He was "the scorn of men and outcast of the people," His inward Majesty drew to Him His disciples by a word, at a word His enemies fell to the ground; what must it now be, now that the Godhead is not veiled in the Manhood, but the Manhood filled, overstreamed, overpowered in the glory of the Godhead; Itself visibly, as in truth It ever was, in God, and Deified [v]!

[u] See on S. Ath. c. Arr. § 57. p. 480. n. c. d. O. T. "In the nature which He took, the human mind being deified, there were not two ruling principles, God and the mind, but one, God Who had deified the mind." Maximus quoted by Pet. de Inc. 8., 12, 3. "His Will could in no wise be contrary to God, being wholly deified." S. Greg. Naz. Or. 30. c. 12. Yet, Maximus adds, not so as Moses or David, or any one who giving up his will to God, were acted upon by God and moved by His Will, but that "the God of all, having, without change, become Man, willed, not only as God, as became His Divinity, but also as Man, as became His Humanity." ap. Euthym. Panoph. ii. 18. referred to by Petav. l. c.

[v] See S. Ath. c. Arr. ii. § 70. p. 380. n. h. The words "Deified, In-Worded," (See ib. iii. 33. p. 448. n. y.) are used by the

Bliss of Heaven—Glory of the body. 331

What must be that union with God, that the Flesh, although created, exists not as a creature but in the Word ʷ; that although perfect Man, It never had being, save in the Person of Christ ˣ; that Christ, as Man, was not, as we are sons by adoption, but was by Nature the Son of God ʸ; that the Flesh, being the Body of God, is worshipped with Divine worship in God ᶻ,

fathers, of the Human Nature of our Lord, to express its union with His Divine Person. (see Pet. de Inc. iv. 9.) They are used also to express the dignity, which thereby redounds to our whole nature, (see ib.)

ʷ See on S. Ath. c. Arr. ii. 45. n. f. p. 344.

ˣ This Catholic doctrine stood opposed, in the East, to the heresies of Paul of Samosata, Nestorius &c.; in the West, to that of Pelagius. see Petav. de Inc. iv. 11.

ʸ See on S. Ath. c. Arr. ii. p. 47. n. i. p. 348. This follows from the preceding, and is opposed to the same heresies; for that could not be adopted, which never existed, save in Him, Who was the Son by Nature. See passages from the fathers in Pet. de Inc. vii. 3.

ᶻ See on S. Ath. c. Arr. ii. 45. n. f. p. 344. Opposed errors were anathematized by the Synod of Alexandria under S. Cyril, whose Synodical Epistle was received by the Council of Chalcedon and the 5th. General Council, which delivered it, " as the tradition of the Holy Church of God from the first." " God the Word Incarnate with His own Flesh was worshipped with one Adoration." See further, Pet. de Inc. xv. 3. 7. " Although the Flesh in Itself is of things created, yet It became the Body of God. But neither do we, severing off that Body, worship It through the Word, nor when we would adore the Word do we regard Him separate from the Flesh. But knowing that, ' the Word was made Flesh,' we know also, that in the Flesh too He is God. Who then so phrenzied as to say to the Lord, ' Depart from the Body, that we may worship Thee?'—Where then will the ungodly find the Flesh which the Lord took, apart, that they should dare to say, ' We worship the Lord with His Flesh, but we separate the Flesh.'" S. Ath. Ep. ad Adelph. § 3, and 5. p. 912. 914. quoted ib.

since Christ is not divided; and we, worshipping Him, separate not the Body from the Word, nor the Word from the Body, but worship our One Uncreated Lord, the Word, Who, for our sakes, took the Manhood into Himself, the Only-Begotten with that holy Temple which He came and took[a].

And now what must be the glory of that Human Nature of our Redeeming Lord, in the full Majesty of the Godhead, so united with the Everlasting Son as to have no being but in Him, as part of Him, more closely united with Him, than our body to our soul, since our body and soul may and will be severed, It never shall; our soul and body are imperfect, He is Perfect God and Perfect Man; "our soul cannot be called the body, nor the body the soul;" in His Blessed Person, "God and Man are so One Christ, that God may be called Man, and Man God[b]." Here, His Human Flesh was still liable to decay, although It was so raised that It saw not corruption; here to pay our debts It was liable to all our sinless infirmities, the punishment of our sin; It could suffer hunger, thirst, weariness, yea even (had He not of His own Will laid down His life) grow old and die[c]. Now It has passed into God. The truth of the Flesh remains; the glorious Scars plead for us in the sight of God; the sight of Them, radiant with that Light wherewith the Lamb is the Light of the Heavenly Jerusalem, shall fill our hearts with love and admiration for ever; but all which was corruptible is changed into incorruption, the mortal into immortality; a Body, as before; yet, glorified with that

---

[a] S. Epiph. Anc. § 51. quoted by Petav. de Inc.
[b] S. Bern. de Consid. v. 9.   [c] S. Aug. de Pecc. Mer. ii. 19.

glory which the Son had with the Father before the world was, "It is worshipped by the heavenly hosts [d]."

And this for us! For was it for Himself that the Eternal Word, ever resting in the Father's Everlasting Love, with Him Coequal and Coeternal, took flesh, "the likeness of our flesh of sin," our miry clay, in Him sinless, in us to whom He was likened, steeped through and through in sin? "For us men and for our salvation" He "came down from heaven," to take our death and give us His Life; to take on Him our sin and give us His holiness; to take our shame and give us His glory. For us He came down, lived here, died, rose, ascended; for us is His Human Nature at God's Right Hand, that, "where I am," He saith, "there shall My servant be." "What," says a father, "shall man be, for whom God became Man!"

To that glorious Body, brighter than the sun, shall, if we be His, our vile body be conformed, and that by the working of His Almighty Power. "He shall change," it says, "this our body of humiliation," change its fashion, and clothe it with another form, that it may be conformed to, and may be partner in the Form of His Glorious Body; and that, "according to the working, whereby He is able to subdue all things to Himself." To Whom shall this poor body be like? To Him "Who sitteth at the Right Hand of the Father," to Him Whom Angels

---

[d] "The Body then of the Lord arose incorruptible and impassible and immortal, and glorified with the Divine Glory, and is worshipped by the heavenly hosts; yet is a Body circumscribed as before." Theodoret Dial. ii.

adore, to Him before Whom stand the unembodied hosts, to Him Who is Himself by Nature the Image of the Everlasting Father, shall we through grace and glory be conformed; and, beholding His Essential Glory, be filled with It and reflect It, as It is indwelt by the Fulness of the Godhead. Then shall all defilement, all shame, all trace of sin, all deformity, be taken away. "It is sown in corruption," says the Apostle, "it shall be raised in incorruption; it is sown in dishonour, it shall be raised in glory; it is sown in weakness, it shall be raised in power; it is sown a natural body, it shall be raised a spiritual body." Great is the gift, that we should not again be liable to corruption, dishonour, weakness, but instead, have bodies whose beauty can have no decay, whose glory cannot be dimmed, obedient to the spirit, and so themselves spiritual, excelling in might, mighty as the Angels. But how much more that this beauty and glory and might and spirituality of our bodies shall be the likeness to the glorious Body of Christ; that they shall shine with His brightness, be spiritual through His indwelling love, be incorruptible through His life in the spirit, be swift through His drawing to Himself! Blessed will it be to have all our senses, which are here abused to vanity, there reformed. Blessed[c] with our bodily eyes to behold the Face of our Redeemer and the piercing beauty of His radiant Scars and the glory of all our fellow-citizens in bliss, and with the inward eye to see God. Blessed to hear the sweet Voice of our Lord, Who here called His sheep by name, and the melody of the heavenly harps and the Seraphim

[c] In this Rusbroch is followed and his language in part retained.

singing Holy, Holy, Holy, all voices as one in the full accordance of the harmony of endless Halleluiahs, yet each [f] touching the ear with its own sweetness of love, while the inward ear heareth the Wisdom and Truth and Word of the Father. Blessed to perceive the fragrance [f] of those heavenly odours from the golden vials, which, as S. John saw, each of the blessed held; and more blessed "the savour of that good ointment," which was shed through the whole world, for which "virgin" souls "have loved" Him, for which they have run [g]; which when they had received they became themselves "the sweet savour of Christ," through the Anointing which is the Holy Ghost [h], and "which shall draw us out of ourselves to the everlasting love of God." Blessed to taste the sweetness of God; sweetness which never decays, but over-streams the whole soul and draws forth the longings which it satisfies. Blessed—but how shall we in the flesh speak of that blessedness, when The Eternal Father shall enfold within Himself His returning prodigals, and they by cleaving to Him shall spiritually hold fast to, touch, God? "Truly is it a good thing to hold fast by God." "But what do I love," says S. Augustine [i], once a sinner, then, when converted, loving much God Who had recalled him to himself, "What do I love when I love Thee? Not beauty of bodies, nor the fair harmony of time, nor the brightness of the light, so gladsome to our eyes, nor sweet melodies of varied songs, nor the fragrant smell of flowers, and ointments and spices,

[f] S. Bernardin. T. 1. S. 57. Art. 2. c. 2. Art. 3. c. 1. 2.
[g] Cant. i. 3.   [h] S. Ath. ad Serap.
[i] Conf. x. 8. p. 186. Oxf. Tr.

not manna and honey, not embracements of flesh. None of these I love, when I love my God. And yet I love a kind of light, and melody, and fragrance, and meat, and embracement when I love my God, the light, melody, fragrance, meat, embracement of my inner man: where there shineth unto my soul what space cannot contain, and there soundeth what time beareth not away, and there smelleth what breathing disperseth not, and there tasteth what eating diminisheth not, and there clingeth what satiety divorceth not. This is it which I love, when I love my God."

But, in this Ocean of bliss, surely it is the very bliss of bliss, that it shall not be by any power of our own, that we shall enjoy that bliss, but through the inflow of Divine love: that it shall be, not out of God but in God that we shall see, hear, feel God Whom here we "feel after," hold Him Whom here we follow after, love Him Whom now we hope for; that soul and body shall be, by His Indwelling Spirit, conformed to Himself; that "by the inworking of His Mighty Power" our bodies shall be "subdued into a likeness with Himself." As on Mount Tabor His sinless Flesh was transfigured, and the inherent Glory of His Godhead gleamed through the veil of His Flesh, and made It all radiant with a loving Brightness, bright as the sun, (yet not as the sun repelling but drawing the eyes of the disciples, so that Peter said, "Master, it is good for us to be here,") so in bliss, shall the bodies of the Blessed be filled with glory, be "transformed from glory to glory," "be made like unto His glorious Body," because they shall receive Himself, and His glory in them shall make their bodies like unto His own. Not for His own sake was that glory which ever resided in Him, the Glory of His Divine Person, allowed once to pierce through the Flesh which He for us had taken; nor for Himself after His Resurrection, was His Body, Which, before, once only walked on the water, removed above the laws of natural bodies, and He passed through closed doors; was seen, yet could not be discerned until He gave the power to see Him; came and vanished as a Spirit, yet not being merely Spirit, but "Flesh of our flesh, Bone of our bone," as we are now by union with Him "members[m] of His flesh and His bones." Not for Himself was it, (as not for Him but for us were all His Acts and Sufferings,) but that in Him, as in a glorious mirror, we might see a portion of the glory and the bliss in store for the righteous. Like His, shall their bodies, too, through His indwelling glory, shine like the sun, in the firmament of the heaven; like His, shall their bodies also, when raised spiritual bodies, obey, unhindered, the spirit; their bodies too, not ceasing to be bodies, shall still have nothing of their earthly, sluggish, nature, but shall, swift as the spirit itself, serving, not hindering, obey God.

Such is our hope of glory, my brethren, even for these poor bodies. Blessed be His Goodness Who so cares for us, glorifies what in us is uncomely, dissolves what in us is decayed, abolishes what in us is defiled, that He may enrobe us with His own glory, giving us by grace what we can receive of the Glory which He has by Nature, "the Glory of the Only-

[m] Eph. v. 20.

Begotten Son of God," through His Indwelling. For so He Himself said, "the glory which Thou gavest Me, have I given them, that they may be one even as we are One; I in them and Thou in Me, that they may be made perfect in One." In Him, by Nature, in us by grace; in Him Eternally, in us, in time; in Him, as Man by Personal Union, in us by Indwelling; yet still that God should, in our degree, and as far as creatures are capable of, dwell in us, as He dwells in Him, our Head, Christ Jesus.

And shall any of us then, whoever has so done, again defile like the brutes that perish, by open or secret sin, that flesh, which for our salvation our Blessed Lord took and placed at God's Right Hand? Shall we bury in corruption and the mire and filth of sin, the flesh which God gave us, that He might make it like unto the glorious Body of His own Son; to be His very members by union with Him; to belong to Him, to glorify Him Who so dearly bought it; to be the temples of the Holy Ghost by His indwelling, as the Human Nature of our Lord by union with It was the Temple of the Eternal Word? Will ye again debase, sinking from sin to sin, bodies which He created, redeemed, sanctified, to raise in Himself from glory to glory, from faith to sight, and be filled with His glory?—more glorious far than the earthly sun; for that shines by created light, the bodies of the saints in bliss shall shine with Uncreated Light; the Light Which shall ever shine upon them, and which they shall reflect; the Light which shall ever shine within them through the indwelling of God. The sun is a mere creature[n], the soul of the righteous

---

[n] S. Anselm Elucidar. c. 18. de corporum dotibus in beatis.

shall be united with God, and His Glory shall fill His temple, the body.

What ye seek then, is not here. Ye seek, as it may be, beauty, or health, or life, or contentment, or ease, or sweetness, or love, or power, or transporting joy and bliss; for, bliss all seek. Why seek ye it here where it abideth not, and seek it not where it abideth? "Why seek ye the living among the dead," and life "in the land of the shadow of death,"—riches which burn out the flesh; beauty which decays; dead and deadening pleasures, which banish from the soul its Life Who is God, and deliver over to the second death? Why seek ye joy, where your Lord is not, and not where He is, that ye may enter into His joy?

"Oh!" says a holy man[o], once the chief pastor of this our Church, "what shall they have, what shall they not have, who shall enjoy this Good? They shall have whatsoever they will; not have, whatsoever they will not. For good will there be there of body and soul, which 'eye hath not seen, nor ear heard, nor heart of man conceived.' Why then wander up and down, thou hapless man, among manifold things, seeking good things for thy soul and body? Love that One Good, in Whom is all Good, and it sufficeth. Desire that simple Good Which is all Good, and it is enough. For what longest thou, my flesh? For what longest thou, my soul? There, there, is all ye love, all ye long for. Doth beauty please? 'The righteous shall shine like the sun.' Or speed, or strength, or freedom of body, which nought can let? 'They shall be like the Angels of God;' for

[o] S. Anselm Proslog. fin.

'it is sown a natural body, it is raised a spiritual body,' in power, though not in nature. Or long and healthful life? There, is healthful eternity and eternal health; for 'the just shall live for ever,' and 'the health of the righteous is from the Lord.' Or fulness? 'They shall be satisfied, when they awake after His likeness.' Or ebriety? 'They shall be out of themselves with the richness of the house of God.' Or melody? There the choirs of Angels sing in unbroken harmony to God. Or any, not impure, but pure pleasures? 'God shall give them to drink of the river of *His* pleasure.' Or wisdom? The Very Wisdom of God shall manifest Itself unto them. Or friendship? They shall love God, more than themselves, each other as themselves; and God shall love them more than they themselves; for they shall love Him, themselves, each other, through Him; He them and Himself by Himself. Or concord? They shall all have one will; for they shall have no will, but only God's. Or power? They shall have all power over their own will, as God over His. For as God can what He willeth, by Himself, so shall they what they will, by Him; for as they shall will no other than what He, so He shall will whatsoever they will; and what He willeth, cannot but be. Or honour and riches? God shall set His 'good and faithful servants, over many things;' yea they shall be called 'sons of God' and 'gods;' and where His Son shall be, there shall they too be, 'heirs of God and joint-heirs with Christ.' Or true security? Sure shall they be that these, yea That Good, shall never fail them; since, neither of their will, will they let Him go; nor, against their will, will God Who loveth withdraw that Good from them; nor ought more powerful than God sever, against the wills of both, 'twixt God and them. But what and how great shall be the joy, where such and so great is the Good! O thou heart of man, thou poor, longing, aching, sorrowing, overwhelmed, heart of man, how wouldest thou joy, hadst thou all this! Ask thine inmost self, could it contain its joy at such its bliss? But if one, whom thou altogether lovedst as thyself, also had this bliss, thy bliss would be doubled; for thou wouldest joy for him not less than for thyself. But if two or three or many more had that same joy, thou wouldest joy for each as much as for thyself, if thou lovedst each as thyself. So then in that perfect love of countless Blessed, Angels and men, where none shall love another less than himself, each shall joy for each as for himself. If then the heart of man could scarce contain his own joy at such his own Good, how shall it so many, so great joys? And since as each joyeth in another's joy in the degree he loves him, so in that perfect bliss, as each shall love God incomparably more than himself and all else with him, so beyond compare shall he joy in the bliss of God more than in his own and all beside. But if they shall so love God with the whole heart, whole mind, whole soul, that yet the whole heart, whole mind, whole soul, suffice not for the dignity of that love, they shall so love with the whole heart, whole mind, whole soul, that the whole heart, whole mind, whole soul, suffice not for the fulness of the joy.

"O my Lord and my God, my hope and joy of my heart, say to our souls, is this the joy whereof Thou tellest us by Thy Son, 'Ask, and ye shall receive, that your joy may be full.' This joy is full, and more than full. For when the whole heart, whole mind, whole soul, whole man, shall be full of that joy, still shall it, beyond measure, overflow. Not into those who joy shall that joy wholly enter, but they who joy shall wholly enter into that joy. Lord, say to Thy servant within, in his heart, if this is the joy into which Thy servants shall enter, who shall 'enter into the joy of their Lord.' But truly the joy of Thine elect 'eye hath not seen, nor ear heard, nor heart of man conceived.' I have not then said, as yet, or thought, O Lord, how much Thy blessed shall joy. Surely their joy shall be great as their love, and their love as they shall know Thee. How much, Lord, shall they know Thee then? how much love Thee? 'Eye hath not seen, nor ear heard, nor heart of man conceived' in this life, how much in that life they shall know Thee, shall love Thee.

"We pray Thee, Lord, let us know Thee, let us love Thee, that we may joy in Thee. And if we cannot fully in this life, let us at least advance daily, until it come to the full; let our knowledge of Thee advance, that there it may be full; the love of Thee grow, and there be full; that here our joy may in hope be great, and there in deed be full.

"Lord, by Thy Son Thou commandest, yea, counsellest to 'ask;' and promisest that we 'shall receive, that our joy may be full.' I 'ask,' Lord, what Thou counsellest by the 'Wonderful Counsellor;' may I 'receive' what Thou promisest by Thy Truth, 'that my joy may be full.'

"O God of Truth, we ask; may we 'receive, that our joy may be full.' Thereon meanwhile may our

Bliss of Heaven—Glory of the Body. 343

mind meditate; thereof our tongue speak; this our heart love, our soul hunger, our flesh thirst after, our whole substance long for; until we enter into the joy of our Lord, the Trinity in Unity, God Blessed for evermore." Amen.

O God, Whose Blessed Son was manifested that He might destroy the works of the devil, and make us the sons of God, and heirs of eternal life; Grant us, we beseech Thee, that, having this hope, we may purify ourselves, even as He is pure; that, when He shall appear again with power and great glory, we may be made like unto Him in His eternal and glorious Kingdom; where with Thee, O Father, and Thee, O Holy Ghost, He liveth and reigneth, ever One God, world without end. Amen.

SERMON XVII.

PROGRESS OUR PERFECTION.

(Tuesday Morning, Octave of the Consecration, Nov. 4.)

PHIL. iii. 15, 16.

"*Let us therefore, as many as be perfect, be thus minded; and if in any thing ye be otherwise minded, God shall reveal even this unto you. Nevertheless, whereto we have already attained, let us walk by the same rule, let us mind the same thing.*"

THERE is perhaps no more difficult form of spiritual blindness, than when men secretly act upon maxims, which they will not openly own, or would be the first, if nakedly stated, to disown. What they would disown, if asked in a way which should not bring it home to themselves, they will not believe that they are daily in life acting upon. They do not look into themselves, nor see on what principles they are acting, or whether upon any at all; and so suspect not themselves of acting blindly on what they would not act upon, if they saw. Thus, ask any person, whether he thinks he have already reached that perfection, which Almighty God intended for him? whether there is nothing more for him to do in this life? nothing to amend? nothing which might be more according to God's holy law, or our Blessed Redeemer's All-holy Pattern? and he would think rightly, that you meant to mock, or, by strong irony, to upbraid him. Yet take the same person in life. See him, day by day, without an effort, going on exactly as the day before, perfectly at ease and satisfied with his state, going through to-day, in a manner by chance, just as he did yesterday, having no object set before him, no aim, no Pattern by Which he reviews his acts, and to Which he strives continually to conform them,—what would be the meaning (if it had any) of all this unmeaning action, but that all is well with him, that there is nothing for him left to do in this life, except to remain just where he is? For if there be, why is it not done? why not strive to do it? The grace of God will not fail him. The acts belie the words. Such a course of life has too clear, solid, a meaning in it, deepened and wrought into the soul, day by day, by its daily action. It means, that it *will* not be at the pains to make any great effort; *will* not look into itself to see whether any great effort be needed; and so, in a random way, regardless of God's threats and promises, *trusts* that none *is* needed.

Meanwhile such an one little thinks, that he is not standing still. Advancing, of course, he is not. How should he advance, who never makes any real consistent effort? Yet if not, even heathen morality knew that in this life there is no stay. It knew that "not to advance is to fall back." And yet, this is no rare nor uncommon case. Rather, to judge by men's lives and maxims, the easiness of their ways, their aimless round of action, ever revolving amid the same failings, weaknesses, negligences, vanities, what heathens condemned is the very principle of the greater part of those who bear the Name of the Crucified, themselves in Baptism buried in His Death, and, if now living, living, in whatever degree, by His life.

And so, since this is so very fatal but common a snare, in order to take away all excuses from us, S. Paul is taught to give us his own example, to picture to us the course of his whole life. Elsewhere he had taught us what Christ had wrought in him; here, that all was not *yet* wrought in him: elsewhere, how "in all things he approved himself as the minister of God,—by pureness, by knowledge, by longsuffering, by kindness, by the Holy Ghost, by love unfeigned;" here, that there was that yet lacking to him, at which he had to aim. Who might not be scared from his listlessness, if S. Paul "had not attained?" Who might think that he might rest contented where he is, if S. Paul was not "perfected?" who stand still, when S. Paul knew that he must press onward, if he would attain?

Far, indeed, was the glorious Apostle already advanced, following his Master's steps, and by the grace of his Lord. But he had not yet come to the days, when he should say, "I have fought the good fight, I have finished the course, I have kept the Faith;" what he was, was not yet revealed to himself; he was nigh upon it, but as yet he knew it not; already was he "Paul the aged," aged yet more through the countless sufferings of the thirty years of his Apostleship, than by those years themselves; himself not as yet reaching the age of man [a], yet his life being measured out, not, as ours, by hours but by toils; not by the daily rising and setting of the sun, the daily death and birth of nature, but by daily deaths in himself; his life ever spent anew and expended for the Church, and anew revived; "always," at all times, "being [b] anew, delivered over to death for Jesus' sake;" living, as it were, many lives in one, through his multiplied sufferings and deaths; yea, rather, living one life through daily deaths; for he had died to himself and to the world, dying almost in the flesh, that he might "live through the life of Christ" within him. He had been nailed to the very Cross of his Lord, and crucified with Him; he had, by the virtue of that Meritorious Death imparted to him, been fitted to the Cross of his Lord, stretched out hand to Hand, side to His Blessed Side, foot to Foot, nail to Nail; had received in him the prints of His Wounds; "bore about in his body the marks of the Lord Jesus," burnt into him, as it were, by sufferings, a brandmark and token of reproach in the sight of men, in the sight of Angels glorious scars, the badges of his Apostleship, the ensigns of his noble soldiery [c], the pledges of his future inheritance in glory, the livery of his Master, the tokens of his predestination, that "having suffered with Him, he should with Him be glorified." With his Lord he

[a] Since he was "a young man" at the stoning of S. Stephen, even if this term were extended to thirty-two or thirty-four years; but the homily which assigns 68 as his age at his martyrdom, is not S. Chrysostom's. See Tillemont Art. S. Paul, Note 1.

[b] ἀεὶ εἰς θάνατον παραδιδόμεθα. 2 Cor. iv. 11.

[c] S. Chrys. ad loc. apparently speaks of the στίγμα as containing an allusion to the military mark.

had been scourged, been stoned, been carried to prison and to judgement; "all which was gain, he had counted loss for Christ;" he had, for his Lord, "suffered the loss of all;" all which was loss, he had accounted gains; he had been gladdened "by persecutions, by distresses, by stripes, by imprisonment," by want of all things; "infirmities, reproaches, persecutions, distresses for Christ's sake," had been his pleasure and comfort, and exceeding joy; his continual death and life alike were above nature; for his daily death was "the dying of the Lord Jesus" which he "ever bore about in the body;" his life in this "continual death[d]" was already the manifestation of the life that shall be; for it too was "the life of Jesus." And so having in him the virtue of the Death and Life of his Lord, the daily death of the Apostle was a channel of life to the Church; his weakness was their strength; "death worked ever in him and life in them." His Lord, Whom once he had persecuted, now endured in him. It was not enough for His exceeding love to suffer in the flesh only. Now, free from suffering, in His excellent glory, at the Right Hand of the Father, would He in His members suffer still; yea, so count their sufferings His own, that the sufferings of the Apostles were "the filling-up of that which was yet lacking of the Sufferings of Christ," which He vouchsafed to suffer, not in His own glorified Body, but in the Apostles'. In Christ, had he (as have all Christians) been crucified, been buried with Him; he had been with Him and by virtue of His Spirit, raised again; and now in turn Christ

---

[d] νεκρωσιν Lat. "mortificatio," what was continually bringing death.

Who lived in him, daily suffered; He drank anew in them and with them the Cup of His Passion in His "Father's kingdom." Yea, so did He make His own Death and Life the death and life of His servants, so gave to their death and life the virtue of His Own within them, that He, enduring in them their sufferings, gave them in their degree, the character of His, so that they, in Him, endured, no longer for chastisement, or trial, or purifying only, but "for the elect's sake, that they too might obtain the salvation which is in Christ Jesus, with eternal glory[e]." Well might the Apostle in this his outward death and hidden power of life, appointed, as it were, to a perpetual conflict with death[f], yet upheld in life by the Life of his Lord, so that it is not, he says, "I that live, but Christ liveth in me,"—well might he be a spectacle, not to the world only and to men, but to Angels, marvelling to see in our fallen race, a life like their own, the first-fruits of the Mystery of the Passion, the human partaking of the Divine, man living by and sharing the Life and love of his Redeemer and his God.

Yet he, who was a spectacle to Angels, was none to himself. He reflected not on his good deeds wrought in God; he counted not the courses he had run; two years after this, and by revelation of God, he knew that it was finished: now, what did he? He who "knew" his Lord, and "the power of His Resurrection" in himself, "and the fellowship of His Sufferings;" he, to whom those Precious Sufferings had been so imparted, that what were Christ's were, by His communicating, made common with

[e] 2 Tim. ii. 10.   [f] ὡς ἐπιθανατίους. 1 Cor. iv. 9.

him; he who had been conformed to His Death, had received the stamp of its likeness on himself and been "moulded into it [g];" what did he? "Brethren," he says, "I count not myself to have apprehended; but this one thing I do; forgetting those things which are behind and reaching forth unto those things which are before, I press towards the prize of the high calling of God in Christ Jesus." Of all the past, he recollected this only, that he, when fleeing from Christ, had been pursued, overtaken, apprehended, by Him; "for which also I was apprehended by Christ Jesus." And now, he had but one thought, One Object before him, One Prize hanging before his eyes on high, after Which, the more he had attained, the more he must strive in his course. It was on high, and he must see nought on earth; he saw, as though he saw not; heard, as though he heard not; had, as though he held not; suffered, as though he endured not; dead to all outward things; all, sight, hearing, soul, body, wrapt in that One Object toward Which he day by day strained and stretched onward, to Which he was, day by day, nearer; "if by any means," he says, "I might attain to the resurrection of the dead." For by that Resurrection should he be brought to Him Who had so loved him, Him Whom he so loved, when he should be raised aloft amid Cherubim and Seraphim [h], to hold that Prize on high, to Which he had stretched out; hold It for ever, by Whom he was held; might grasp in his hands, enfold with his soul, Him by Whose love he should be enfolded, God Himself.

But if S. Paul was not yet "perfect," how then

[g] S. Chrys.   [h] S. Chrys. Hom. 32. on Rom. p. 504. Oxf. Tr.

Progress our perfection. 351

says he, "as many of us as are perfect?" One is the perfection in the way, another is the perfection in our home[i]; one the imperfect perfection[k] of earth, another that, whereby they who shall attain, shall be perfected in Him Who Alone is Perfect and our Perfection[l], our Father Who is in Heaven; one, perfection on the part of the Giver; another, as it is bounded by the capacity of the receiver. We may

---

[i] Perfect and not perfect; perfect travellers (viatores) not perfect possessors, &c. S. Aug. Serm. 169. § 18. (on the passage) p. 870. Oxf. Tr. ubi pl. "They who make advances are on the way; although they who make good advances are said to be perfect as way-farers. But that is complete perfection, whereto nothing is to be added; when that, whither we now are stretching towards, shall be possessed." Id. de nat. et grat. § 13.

[k] "Being then thus minded, seeing that I am both imperfect and perfect; imperfect as not having yet received what I wish, perfect, as knowing what is lacking to me." S. Aug. in Ps. 38. § 15. "It may be too that one shall be accounted worthy of this name, (in Holy Scripture) not because there is no further point whereto to advance, but because he has advanced the greater part of the way; as one may be said to be perfect in the teaching of the law, even though some things are still unknown to him; as the Apostle calls those perfect, to whom he yet says, 'And if any be otherwise minded,' &c." Id. de pecc. mer. et rem. ii. § 22. "Unless there were a certain, so to say, imperfect perfection in this life, the Apostle would not say, 'As many as are perfect, let us be thus minded,' thus namely as he had premised, 'Not as if I had already attained, or were already perfect.'" S. Bern. in Ps. Qui habitat, S. 10. init.

[l] "Our end ought to be our perfection; our perfection is Christ. For in Him we are perfected, because we are members of Him our Head." S. Aug. in Ps. 54. init. "The end whereat we aim is Christ; make we what efforts we will, we are perfected in Him and by Him; and this is our perfection to attain to Him, for if thou attain to Him, thou seekest no further. It is thy End." Id. in Ps. 56. § 2.

imperfectly receive that which is perfect; nay, as far as we receive the Gift of God, we must so receive It, since the Gift of God is His Holy Spirit, Who, as God, is Perfect; and His love, which is the bond of perfectness.

We are then in one sense perfect, as having received that which is perfect, His Sacrament. In the words of a very early father, "Baptized [m], we are illumined; illumined, we are adopted as sons; adopted, we are perfected; perfected, we are made immortal. 'I have said, ye are gods, and ye are all the children of the Most High.' For in many ways is this work called; grace, illumining, perfection, the laver. The laver, whereby we wash away sins; grace, whereby the penalty of sin is remitted; illumining, whereby we are admitted to contemplate that holy and saving Light, that is, whereby we behold God; perfection, whereunto nothing is wanting. For what is wanting to him who knoweth God? For that were not meet to be called the grace of God, which is not full every way. Perfect must be the gift of The Perfect. For as, when He commandeth, at once all things are, so, in that He willeth to give grace, the grace is full; for what shall be in time, is already in the efficacy of His Will." "Perfect," he well saith, "are the gifts of The Perfect," although by us imperfectly received. Perfect is the principle of life imparted to us, but we receive it in "a body of death;" perfect and perfecting is the seal of the Spirit, if we but yield our whole clay day by day to receive Its Blessed Impress; perfect the life within us, for It is "Christ our Life," if we receive It, shut

[m] Clem. Al. Pædag. i. 6. init.

It not out by returning to our former death, but let It pervade our whole selves, take up our whole will, conscience, being, and doing, into Itself. Perfect are we in the purpose of God, and the loving-kindness of His good-pleasure, and the fulness of His good-will towards us, if, by a contrary will, we mar not the graciousness of His Will for us.

And as we are thus perfect in the purpose of God, so have we a sort of relative, an imperfect perfecting, in faith, in will, in temper, in love, if we give up ourselves without reserve to receive that perfect gift of God. It is a sort of perfection, to hold back nothing from the perfect grace of God. Thus our Lord, having taught us to love and do good to our enemies, to the evil as the good, says, "Be ye perfect, as your Father in heaven is perfect," both because such love, being His gift, is so exceedingly perfecting[n], as also because we thereby, conquering nature and withholding nothing, yield ourselves on all sides to receive His perfect love. So He saith, (as all have known,) "My strength is made perfect in weakness[o];" because then is His strength put forth in its full power, when man, owning his nothingness, mingleth nothing of his own, but yields himself as one, blind and helpless and powerless, to be borne along by the stream of Divine grace. So also as to knowledge, S. Paul says, "We speak wisdom among those that

---

[n] "Whoso then doth not return evil to those who requite with evil is perfect." S. Aug. in. Ps. 7. § 3. on our Lord's words. (Matt. v. 48.) "He calls them 'perfected in love.' What is the perfection of love? To love enemies, and to this end to love them, that they may be friends." S. Aug. in 1 Joh. 2. Tr. 1. § 9.

[o] 2 Cor. xii. 9.

are perfect;" i. e. to those who receive the "faith of Christ Crucified" wholly and entirely, so that it should penetrate and pervade their whole souls, keeping back nothing out of respect for man's philosophy, or the wisdom of the flesh, or his own imaginings, to these he declares the further mysteries of the faith. And again, "We preach Christ, warning every man and teaching every man in all wisdom, that we may present every man perfect in Christ Jesus;" i. e. we warn all against all evil, so purifying the soul, and teach to all all wisdom, that so they, dwelling in Christ and He in them, might be "presented perfect in Him." And again, "that ye may stand perfect and filled in all the will of God [p];" "for he that is filled," saith a father [q], "suffereth not any other will to be within him; for if so, he is not wholly filled." So also in S. James, "Let endurance have her perfect work, that ye may be perfect and entire, wanting nothing;" i. e. in unreserved conformity to the will of God, yield yourselves to His searching and purifying trials; let them cut, burn, wound as He wills; only withdraw not thyself from His healing Hand; so, fulfilling their own work, they shall wound, to heal; shall leave you "perfect and whole, lacking nothing."

This, then, is our perfection in our pilgrimage, to own our imperfection [r], and aim that the will of God

---

[p] Col. iv. 12.   [q] S. Chrys. ad loc.

[r] "Before, he had called himself imperfect; now, perfect. Why, but because this is the very perfection of man, to have learnt that he is not perfect, &c." S. Aug. Serm. 170. § 8. p. 878. O.T. "Thou canst not otherwise be perfect here, unless thou know that here thou canst not be perfect. This then shall be thy perfection, so to

be on all sides, in all things, in every part of us, at all times, equally fulfilled, to admit His holy Light into our whole selves, that there be "no part dark," "nothing hid from the heat thereof."

So says S. Paul here, "As many of us as are perfect, let us be *thus* minded." *Thus*, as he had himself said of himself. And what was this? Never to look backward, ever onward. Such was his whole life, from the time that Christ revealed Himself to him, never looking back to see what heights of virtue he had reached, never pausing to count the courses he had finished, or the victories of faith which he had won, never resting as though he had "attained;" but having God for his Pattern, his Aim, his End, his Everlasting Home and Reward, ever to strain onwards towards That which is Infinite; drawn upward the more, the more he followed on; caught up by Him Whom Alone he felt after, grasped, cleaved

---

have passed beyond some things as to hasten on to others; so to have passed beyond some, that there should be That Whereto, when passed beyond all beside, we must still pass onward. This is sure faith. For whoso thinks that he has already attained, sets himself on high, to fall." S. Aug. in Ps. 38. § 14. "Warning those who might think themselves already perfect in the fulness of that righteousness, he says, 'As many as are perfect, let us be thus minded;' as if he would say, 'If according to the capacity of mortal man, and the petty measure of this life, we are perfect, let us understand that this too belongs to that very perfection, that we should be 'minded' that we are not yet perfected with that angelic perfection which we shall have at the manifestation of Christ.'" S. Aug. c. 2. Epp. Pel. iii. § 22. add § 15. "In human nature, the one perfection is to know one's self to be imperfect." S. Bern. Ep. 433. fin. "So then an unwearied eager zeal to advance, and a continual straining towards perfection is accounted perfection." Id. Ep. 254. §. 3.

unto, with the unutterable longings of his spirit; until at last he should reach that blessed height, the last on earth reserved for him, where earth and heaven should melt together, when there should be no more falling, no more strife, no victory, for there should be nought of the flesh to rebel, but the chains of the flesh should drop off from the freed spirit, and he should rest not *in* the conflict, but *from* the conflict, contemplating what he had believed, possessing what he had ever hoped; enlarged, perfected, fulfilled in love; above what even he could here ask or think, the love of those, who shall be enfolded in the embrace of All-Perfect Love.

In nature or in grace there is no standing still; when the sun ceases to ascend, it sinks; when days no longer lengthen, they become briefer; when the sea ceases to flow, it ebbs; when all things fair cease to increase in beauty, they decrease; when strength is no longer enlarged, it lessens. On the ladder which reached to heaven, none stood still[s]; all were ascending towards God, or descending towards the earth. "Our nature being subject to change," says a father[t], "so long as this our mortality endures, although it be advanced to the very highest earnest love of all excellence, still ever, as it may fall back, so also may it grow. And this is the true righteousness of the perfect, that they should never presume that they are perfect; lest ceasing from their intentness on their course, while yet unfinished, they there fall into the peril of sinking back, where they laid aside the eager desire to press on." Who in Christ's

[s] S. Bern. Ep. 91. § 3. Ep. 385. § 1.
[t] S. Leo Serm. de Quadr. 2. init.

school is sufficient to himself, how can he be a proficient? how must he not become deficient[u]?

But these heights of virtue and glory, we may well feel, are for the Apostle and such as are nearest to him, as he unto his Lord. What are we to do, who are but on the plain, ever at the mountain-base, treading the same weary round of daily failings, infirmities, surprises, self-indulgences, listlessness; our earthbound souls scarcely able to rise, and view even from afar those blessed eminences; earthborn clouds hiding from us the tracks of saints and the Presence of our Lord. How shall we, so imperfect, gain the very thought of what growth and advance to perfection should be? The Apostle tells us, "God shall reveal it to you." "If in any respect ye be otherwise minded, God shall reveal even this unto you." And how? By holding fast, and advancing in what ye have, in order and in love. "Whereunto we have already attained, let us walk by the same rule, let us mind the same thing." He saith not, part we with what we have attained unto, but "whereunto we have attained, there walk we;" he saith not again, "there *abide;*" but "there walk." "See ye," says a father[v], "we are wayfarers? Say ye what is it, to walk? In one word, I say, it is to 'make progress,' lest if ye understand not, ye walk too slowly." And walk (so the word[w] means) straight onward, as men in a march, by the same rule as the Apostle, in the same mind, with the same love.

---

[u] "Nolle proficere, deficere est. Ubi ergo sunt qui dicere solent, sufficit nobis, nolumus esse meliores quam patres nostri?" S. Bern. Ep. 254. § 4. add Ep. 385. init. Ep. 91. n. 31.

[v] S. Aug. Serm. 169. fin. p. 870. Oxf. Tr.   [w] στοιχεῖν.

Yes! my brethren, wherever we are in the Christian course, as we have all one End, God; One Faith, in the One Object of Faith, the Everblessed, Coequal, Coeternal Trinity, as that Faith has been revealed to us and fenced round against every error in our Creeds; One Hope, to see Him; One Food of life, Himself in His Sacraments; One Spirit, Who is the Life of all the members of the One body, the life of all alike, although His gifts be manifold; so also for saints or penitents, there is only one Way to Heaven, to walk on in Him Who is the Way, to hold fast that ye have and to press onward. This is the remedy of all doubts in faith and practice. "One step[x]," it has been well said, "enough for me." To-day is thine, by the gift of God; to-morrow as yet is His. Fear not whither you may be led; see only, that you be now "led by the Spirit of God;" led, not going before, not holding back, not standing still, but "led."

It is the very part of faith, to go forth, as Abraham went, not knowing whither he went. He "leadeth" His own "by ways which they know not, even by a path which they have not trod with their feet." Hold fast what thou hast; act up to what thou believest; walk on in His strength; halt not; and what thou yet lackest, He has said, "He will reveal unto thee."

Thus alone, my brethren, may we hope that in doctrine, our sad manifold divisions will cease. Thus they must cease; for, He has said, "God will reveal it unto thee." Not by disputing, not by teaching alone, not by learning, not by reading Holy Scripture only, shalt thou know the truth; but by gaining, through God's grace a childlike mind; by cleansing

[x] Lyra Apost. No. 25. "Light in the darkness."

the eye of the soul; by obedience. Not by wisdom or prudence canst thou gain the knowledge of the things of God; from proud wisdom God hides it, and reveals it unto babes. "I am wiser than the aged," says the Psalmist, "because I keep Thy commandments." Well might he be wiser than the aged, whom God taught! But how taught He him? First, by His grace, He taught him to "keep His commandments," and then by keeping them, gave him wisdom to discern Himself, the true Wisdom. So saith our Lord Himself, "If any man will do His will, he shall know of the doctrine, whether it be of God," and "He that hath My commandments and keepeth them, he it is that loveth Me, and he that loveth Me shall be loved of My Father, and I will love him, and will manifest Myself unto him;" for in those who love Him and keep His commandments, should He Himself dwell by His Spirit, the Life of their life, the Spirit of their spirit; and so they should know things by a higher sense, not of reasoning or of inference, but in His own clear light, Whose Spirit dwelleth in their hearts by love.

And what if some have at all times used this doctrine amiss, and set up their private revelations against the Church, and through their belief of an inward light have rather gone astray from the true Light, which is Christ, and from that light which He has set aloft in the Church, that "it may give light to all who are in the house." It is of the very nature of error that it should look like truth; even as a false coin has the Royal Image set upon it, although it be base and adulterate. Mostly, it must be said, such have not gone the way of obedience and self-denial; have not followed painfully, step by step, the leadings of God and the tracks of His Cross. We see not on such systems "the prints of the Nails ʸ."

But S. Paul's words give a further test, "whereto we have already attained, let us walk by the same rule," a rule, plainly, without them, not within them; the rule of faith delivered to the Church from the first; embodied chiefly in the Creeds; made ours in Baptism; by contemplation, adoration, loving obedience, made a part of ourselves. For this has been the character of all heresy; it has not simply invented what is new, it has begun by parting with what was old, what "was from the beginning." The promise is to those who, as far as they have attained, walk on by the rule ᶻ, that they shall see what as yet is hidden to them, shall be guided on it, not to those who quit the rule and the road marked out by God.

And this might, as I said, bring us back from our manifold divisions to the one Truth. Where are so many discordant voices, all cannot be right. How

---

ʸ "The application of this vision [Satan, arrayed in glory and beauty, claiming to be received as Christ] to Martin's age, is obvious; I suppose it means in this day, that Christ comes not in pride of intellect, or reputation for ability. These are the glittering robes in which Satan is now arraying. Many spirits are abroad, more are issuing from the pit; the credentials which they display, are the precious gifts of mind, beauty, richness, depth, originality. Christian, look hard at them with Martin in silence, and then ask for the print of the nails." Church of the Fathers, end.

ᶻ "'God will reveal even this unto you.' How, but if ye walk and make progress in the way of right faith, until this pilgrimage be finished and we come to sight?" S. Aug. c. ii. Epp. Pel. iii. § 22.

then shall we discover the One Voice of our One Shepherd, Which His sheep hear and follow Him? He has taught us, Hold fast that ye have; walk ye on by the light of it; and what ye see not now, ye shall see; what ye see dimly shall be clear. He Who has touched your eyes, that ye now see perchance "men, as trees, walking," shall "put His Hands again upon your eyes and make you look up, and ye shall see every thing clearly." Would indeed that all could know the blessedness of believing that which has been ever taught, of receiving all on an authority out of one's self; of not enquiring, but knowing; not seeking, but seeing; not discussing, but living on the Living Truth, which we have received! Would that we, living in a Church founded by God, could all so live, day by day, in the devotions, Creeds, hymns of praise, preserved to us in her, as to imbibe their spirit in ourselves! This would be no uncertain voice to us, did we learn it in the Presence and the house of God. Words have a different meaning, when tossed to and fro in argument, and when prayed in the Communion of Saints, the voice of the one Dove, moaning to its Lord. The full heart, then, stints not the meaning of the words; thinks not how little they *may* mean, but how much; a ray of light falls upon them from above; we stand not without them, as judges, but within them as worshippers; He Who has taught the Church her prayers is present in our souls; and with His "Blessed Unction from above, Comfort, Life, and Fire of love," anoints both them and us. Disputing divides, devotion knits in one; for in it we pray to One, through One, by One.

But, meantime, whether within or as yet without [a], the Apostle's rule will guide us all in one. Our strifes every where are not about what we hold, but about what any do not hold. It has been said at times, "let us drop our differences, and hold fast what we have in common." Good were it and true, if it be not thereby meant, that any should part with any truth he holds. We need not, should not, part with any truth; but mere denials are not truths. It is a blessed truth that the Holy Eucharist is a Commemoration of the Sufferings of our Blessed Lord; they who have held most vividly truths beyond this, have been most melted into tears at the thought of this. It is a heavy truth, that "the world lieth in wickedness." that "whoso loveth it, hath not the love of The Father," that "such must be converted and become as little children:" they have most owned this, and the sadness of the depth of their own falls, who have most believed the might implanted by God in Holy Baptism. And so again, they are truths, that all works, seemingly good, without the grace of Christ, are but shewy sins, destroying rather than giving life; that of our own we have nothing but our sins and short-comings; that could we do all we are commanded, we should still be unprofitable servants; yet is it also true, that, under grace, "the love of God shed abroad in the hearts of those who believe," by the Holy Spirit Which is given them, "is [b] a law of faith and a spirit quickening him who loveth;" that "the law of faith

---

[a] This was said, it being likely that some, as yet severed from us, would be present.

[b] S. Aug. de Sp. et Lit. c. xvii. § 29.

saith, Give what Thou commandest [c]," "and command [d] what Thou wilt;" that what good we have, blessed be God, we have of Him, and therefore chiefly, if we have any good, do we love to have it, because it is His gift; but still righteousness is His real gift within us, and "whom [e] He crowneth, He crowneth *in* them His own gifts." And so in other cases, men deny plain, blessed, truths, because they think them opposed to other truths, which they are not; and which, would they only hold the truths they have, God would make plain unto them. Wouldest thou arrive at the whole truth of God; part with nothing, which the grace of God has worked into thine inward life; deny nothing, which the Church of God has not denied; whatsoever thou hast attained, seek by that grace therein to grow; pray that He perfect whatsoever be lacking to thy faith; and He from Whom thou hast what thou hast, will give thee what as yet thou hast not; He Himself has promised that " He will reveal it unto you." Pray Him to draw thee after Him, and He will give thee grace to " follow Him ; " and, " following on to know Him," thou shalt hear His Voice more distinctly, and know it from " the voice of strangers."

And so, and much more, in life. Think ye that when S. Paul " said, trembling and astonished, Lord, what wilt Thou have me to do ? " he foresaw the endurance, and labour, and sufferings, by which, with the other Apostles, he became " a spectacle to men and Angels ? " or that even that dim foreshadowing, whereby our Lord shewed him "how

[c] S. Aug. Ib. § 22.   [d] Id. Conf. x. § 45.
[e] S. Aug. oftentimes; " Deus in nobis dona coronat sua."

great things he must suffer for His Name's sake," was the same as when he actually followed his Lord, step by step, along a track of blood, and life was one daily death, whose hours were counted by sufferings, and the "jeopardy, every hour" in its turn brought with it? Or think you that the blessed S. John, when he said, "We are able," could imagine that lengthened banishment, more than the years of the life of man, from the Presence of Him he loved? Or that S. Peter, when he said, "Lord, Thou knowest all things, Thou knowest that I love Thee," foresaw that lasting sorrow whereby, night after night, he should, out of love, bewail his fall, or that suffering would be to him but as his meat and drink; the very life "whereto Christians are called," "no strange thing[f]," but the very substance of his joy? Yet all was wrapped up in those first words. With one earnest devotion, they gave their whole selves to their Master and their God, and He, step by step, unfolded to them the plan which His Fatherly Wisdom had prepared for them; He led them on from "grace to grace," from "strength to strength." He made weakness their strength; "the valley of tears" their fountain and refreshment; He drew them by each trial nearer to Himself, and Himself drew nearer to their souls; until they had reached that nearness which His love had chosen for them, and whom He had "guided by His counsel," He "received to His Glory."

And so will He, in our measure, with us. Give we up ourselves only with purpose of heart to have no will but His; desire we to be but led, as little

[f] 1 Pet. ii. 21. iv. 12, 14.

children, by Himself unto Himself; look we not what the way will be, joyous or dreary; pledge we ourselves but to this, to follow Him, and He will shew us what the next step shall be. And here again the Apostle's rule will be our guide. Hold fast what you have; act up to what you see; and what you see not God will make known to you. Alas! how many of us have just reversed this in our youth! How often happens it, that as soon as the young are left to act for themselves, they drop, out of impatience or negligence, pious practices which they learnt at their mother's knees! how amid the pleasures or business of the world is prayer or self-examination or daily reading of Holy Scripture laid aside! how many penitents, who have been brought back, have perished for ever, through the undoing of seemingly little links, whereby they were anew bound to God! "Whereunto we have attained, let us walk by the same rule." We should fear extremely to give up any thing, which God has heretofore blessed to our souls.

And then, would we walk onward, beware we how we reject any thing, which has been a means of holiness. See we that we are walking; not as some, who resolve, as it were, to stand still. If we see not what lies beyond, let us walk on where we see, and we shall reach it. Be it, that any cannot see fasting to be a duty, though sanctioned by the example and Word of our Blessed Lord, by Apostles and Prophets, by the experience of the whole Church. Happier were he, if he could take it up on their authority. Yet some sort of self-denial in food he will hardly think uncalled for. Let him try to practise this habitually; he will find fasting easier, and that it gives a substance to it. Does any think our weekly Friday-fast, or the observance of set "hours" of devotion which the Ancient Church ever kept in memory of our Lord in the great Mysteries of the Faith, a formal service? Yet can a Christian not meditate on the Passion of our Lord? Seek in earnest to do this, and you will be glad if the hours of the day, as they come, might, through their observance, by their very coming, remind you of the Mysteries of His Cross and Passion; you will find it gladlier to undergo privation with your Lord, than to feast with the world. Does any doubt of the value of some rule as to the means wherewith God has entrusted him, of the blessedness of liberal almsgiving according to his ability? Let him do in earnest something he does see, and God will teach him how blessed it is to lend unto Himself, how great the joy of self-denying love.

Nay, ye yourselves, brethren, wherever ye are in the Christian course, whatever ye have attained, know that ye would not, for the whole world, exchange what ye are for what ye were, when ye were less careful to do God's will. They, whose day is marked by seasons of devotion, or who have learned, in whatever degree, to "pray alway," can hardly picture to themselves the dreariness of existence, in which, from morning to evening, there should only be some chance thoughts of God. They who have learned fasting or simplicity or the blessedness of Lent, can hardly imagine to themselves day following day, in one round of self-indulgence. They who have learned, in strong purpose of heart, to have no will but God's, can scarcely imagine the misery of following blindly their own. They whose one longing it now is, to be approved to God, to gain God, oh what a dreary void, what a dismal blank, to see an existence spent on any thing which is not God, or for His Glory and Will!

Judge then by what ye know, of what ye know not. Or rather if ye have ever known any sweetness of the heavenly things, if, in any season of earnest purpose, ye have felt any thrill of joy, at the thought of the approach of your God, if, at any moment of persevering prayer, there has streamed upon your souls some ray of light, faint though it was and quickly vanishing, if, even in the refusal to "do" some "wickedness and sin against God," or on taking up again some neglected duty, or doing some deed of self-denying love, ye have, in some inward token of joy and peace, known some gleam of the bliss of being in one mind with God, oh, "whereunto ye have attained, walk" on with Him, and pray for perseverance to the end. They are the first faint dawning streaks of a glorious Day. Yea the richest brightness of earth's most glowing glorious light, as compared with the first gleams which just break through the darkness, were a faint image of the inward light of that soul, which makes God its only End, its Riches, its Delight, its All. For what were the brightest light, which God ever kindled in the soul of man, what the sweetness of those unutterable words which S. Paul heard, what the beauty of the heavenly Jerusalem which S. John saw, " which the Glory of God did lighten, and the Lamb was the Light thereof," compared to that Glory, and Sweetness, and Brightness, which not even Apostle's "eye hath seen, nor ear heard, nor heart of man hath conceived;" for It is God Himself seen face to Face; It is the Sight, the Embrace, the Love of God. Take that first step; break off the sin thou knowest; seek, by God's grace, to gain some one grace thou most lackest; pray to persevere to the end; and that Sight, that Embrace, that Love is thine.

"Faithful is He Who calleth you, Who also will do it."

Now unto Him "Who hath saved us and called us with a holy calling, not according to our works, but according to His own purpose and grace, which was given us in Christ Jesus before the world began," be glory and dominion, praise and thanksgiving for ever and ever, Amen.

Almighty and merciful God, of Whose only gift it cometh, that Thy faithful people do unto Thee true and laudable service; Grant, we beseech Thee, that we may so faithfully serve Thee in this life, that we fail not finally to attain Thy heavenly promises; through the merits of Jesus Christ our Lord. Amen.

SERMON XVIII.

DAILY GROWTH.

(Tuesday Afternoon, Nov. 4.)

Ps. cxxxix, 15, 16.

" Thine eyes did see my substance, yet being imperfect, and in Thy book were all my members written which day by day were fashioned, when as yet there was none of them."

GOD, being One, the Author of nature as of grace, worketh harmoniously in both His kingdoms. And as in other ways, so in this: in both He createth and hath created by a single act; in both He carrieth on His work, silently yet in Majesty. His work broke not His Eternal rest; His rest on the seventh day hindereth not His continued working. The creation of the worlds was but the action of His Will; He said, "Let there be light, and there was light." "He spake the word, and they were made; He commanded, and they stood fast." Yet although they stood fast by that command, He still "upholdeth them by the Word of His power." "My Father worketh hitherto, and I work." He still worketh, but Unseen; noiselessly, known only by the workings. His greatest workings are carried on in silence. It is, as though things acted of themselves. Hence the Heathen worshipped the heavenly bodies as though they were gods; and the wise of this world, though fools in God's sight, have said "There is no God." "Day unto day uttereth speech, and night unto night sheweth knowledge; they have no speech nor language, their voice is not heard; yet their line is gone out into all lands, their words unto the end of the world." Their silence is speech; all nature speaks, in that it is; yet it carries on its Maker's Will in silence. Sun, moon, and stars, roll their courses, day by day, year by year, and century by century; summer and winter, day and night, melt into each other, yet we scarce see how, we cannot tell when one begins and the other ends; we feel when one has ended, but it is not until the other has made some advance; the sun sets, but it is not yet night; it rises, but it has been already, for some time, morning: we sow the seed, but we cannot tell when it is quickened; unseen it unfolds its life; we "sleep and rise night and day, and the seed springeth and groweth up, man *knoweth not how*, for the earth bringeth forth fruit *of herself*, first the blade, then the ear, then the full corn in the ear[a]." We see their growth after a time, but are, again and again, amazed at it, how rapid; how this world, as by a resurrection, seems to awake from the death of winter into the new life of spring. Yet this amazing change is wrought in objects, to us countless; each blade of grass, each herb of the field, every leaf of every tree, has its own separate history; no two leaves unfold themselves alike; yet thus manifold as are God's workings, and countless His

[a] S. Mark iv. 27, 28.

works, all by one viewless harmony join together to set forth their Maker's praise.

So it is, our Lord tells us, in the Kingdom of God, both as a whole in the Church, and in each separate soul, each fruitbearing tree and seed within it. It was planted at Jerusalem, the smallest of all seeds; it gained strength, men knew not how; "they wondered in themselves, whereto this thing would grow;" yet day and night "mightily grew the word of God, and prevailed [b];" every thing aided its growth; to scatter the believers, was to spread the belief; the wind which would carry it away, and has ever since sifted the seed, but wafted it to new seed-plots. He Who holdeth the winds directed them; each grain sunk silently and noiselessly to the bed, which God "had prepared" for it; the ground, which by the tender showers of His grace He has softened to receive it. To shed [c] Christian blood was to water the seed; to cut deep into the choice Vine, was to make it put on fresh fruit; the seeds which fell singly, arose multiplied; the world found that the Church was every where [d], that it was around it, encompassing it, without, within it, mastering it, it knew not how, only it felt it. So had our Lord foretold; "the kingdom of God," He said, "cometh not with observation [e]." It was leaven hid in three measures of meal, working its way, and spreading silently and unseen, "until the whole was leavened." Our Lord sowed Himself, as a corn-grain in the earth, by His Precious Death and Burial; and It yielded much fruit.

[b] Acts xix. 20.
[c] See on Tertull. Apol. c. ult. p. 105. n. a. Oxf. Tr.
[d] ib. c. i. [e] Matt. xiii. 33.

He was "lifted up from the earth," and "drew all men unto Him;" He lifted them up, as He was lifted up, by the power of His Death, and the likeness of it, so that they too were, with Him, "crucified to the world," lifted up above it, Heavenward, to live to Him, and in Him, and through Him.

The same is mostly the history of individuals. God created us, gave us life once, and then preserves it. Men grow in stature, (blessed are they, if in wisdom too,) they know not how; they eat, they drink, they sleep, are nourished, they know not how; and so, day by day, and year by year, pass through the stages of life, through childhood, youth, to manhood, and mature years. So should it be in our re-creation. In Holy Baptism, He re-creates us in His own Image; passes His Hand upon us, puts the first germ of spiritual life within us, to grow, be nourished, expand, flower, bear fruit, until it take into itself all our old nature, and we become wholly new. It is a spark from heaven, which should be fanned into a flame by the breath of charity, and burn within us, until it has consumed all low desires, all selfish thoughts, every thing which offendeth; and yield us pure, a holy acceptable sacrifice unto God. Such should our Christian course be; such is the blessed course; a gradual daily growth, from the first hour when we awake to the thought of God and of our own deathless being, to our final passage, through death, to endless life. Amid manifold hindrances, it may be, will be this growth, sometimes slower, then with quickened life, with fresh impulses, starting into new life, yet, on the whole, even while we grieve over our slowness, one stedfast, should it

Daily growth. 373

be, though often unperceived, growth upwards, Heavenwards.

Such is the course in nature and in grace, in the Church and individuals, pointed out in the amazing words of that Psalm of endless depth, "Thine Eyes did see my substance yet being imperfect, and in Thy book were all my members written, which day by day were fashioned, when as yet there were none of them." In nature, they tell us how, within the dark grave of the womb, the formless substance [f] of the future being is day by day unfolded, woven unseen into the one curious and intricate interlacing [g] of our bodies, "clothed with skin and flesh, and fenced with bones and sinews," taking the from marked out for it in God's book, until it burst forth into life, each different from its fellow, yet as God before willed it to be. In grace, they tell us how the body of the Second Adam is formed, His Church, growing out of the formless and deformed mass of our race, in this our prison-house and land of death [h];

[f] גלמי "an unformed lump, rolled together," afterwards to be developed or formed. ἀκατέργαστόν μου LXX. Aq. ἀμόρφωτόν μου Symm. informe meum. S. Jer.

[g] רֻקַּמְתִּי, used, of variegated work, of the streaks in marble, tesselated stone, tapestry, the developement of the embryo in the womb or the egg. "Thou art a painting, O man, painted by the Lord thy God; a good Artificer and Painter hast thou; be loath to deface that good painting, glowing not with spurious colours but with truth, not wrought through wax but by grace." S. Ambr. Hexaem. vi. 8.

[h] "The lower parts of the earth," i. e. the grave or Ades, to which the womb is compared, Job i. 21. with reference to man's formation of the dust of the earth, and his sentence, Gen. iii. 19. In the spiritual sense, man's life here is the embryo of his future being; and this earth "a land of darkness," both in its mystery

consisting of perfected yet also of yet imperfect members, which are being perfected; each with its separate lineaments, and form, and office; some more, some less, honourable; yet all growing together into one harmonious body, intricate in its harmony, yet harmonizing in its intricacy; all needed for the perfection of the whole and all needing one another; each member, lay or clergy, teacher or taught, old or young, rich or poor, head or foot, having its separate functions and uses; all growing together into the one unseen mystical whole, in a secret way, unknown to the world and amid the world's darkness, but under the Eye of God; her destinies, hindrances, reverses, growth, all written in God's book; until clad with the full number of the Elect, having gathered and formed all her appointed members, and grown "unto the measure of the stature of the fulness of Christ," she, at her Maker's, Saviour's, Husband's call, be translated wholly out of this "land of the shadow of death," to live for ever with and in God "in the land of the living." And as of the whole Church, so they speak too of us, who, however imperfect, are yet His members; of us, who too often, by our manifold frailties, the wilfulness of our childhood or our youth, issuing in our present weakness and imperfection, are "spots and wrinkles," marring the Church's glory, and blemishing her who is the body of our Redeemer. Yet for us too, such as we are, if, "being imperfect," we yet are His, the Church awaits her perfecting; on us hath the Eye of God

and its trouble, as compared with the "land of the living;" yet the womb, wherein he is fashioned secretly by God for his endless life.

ever been, and even now resteth, quickening us secretly by His gracious Look, "guiding us by His Eye upon us[i]," recalling our wandering glance from straying amid the vanities of this world, to fix itself on Him Who hath looked upon us, and would hold our gaze, that we also, with Hagar, should look after "Him That seeth us[k]."

"Fearfully indeed and wonderfully are we made;" a marvel to the blessed Angels and to ourselves. Strange, out of what death they of us who shall live are brought into what life! what conflicting passions, feelings, appetites, powers, cravings, shall all have been fashioned by God's moulding Hand, until they all be gathered and curiously wrought together in one, as being held together by Him Who is One, all centre in One, and so, in His Unity, to Whom they tend, become one. Strange, through what variety of accidents, griefs, joys, terrors, fears, death, life, His encircling Providence girding us round shall have fenced in our way; and He Who has all creation at His command, shall have made all creation, good and bad, great and small, natural and moral, the holiness of Angels and men and the malice of Satan, work together to the salvation of His elect.

And this amazing everlasting work is going on continually. "Which day by day were fashioned." It is the very marvellousness of God's works in nature, in the Church, in each single soul, that they go on so noiselessly. "Axe and hammer are not heard[l]," but the house of the Lord is raised without hands. Day by day we rise, and night by night lie down, and see not, except rarely, the growth of others

[i] Ps. xxxii. 8. [k] Gen. xvi. 13. [l] 1 Kgs vi. 7.

or our own. We may count over our falls and bruises, and God's mercies in upholding us when we have not fallen; we may know our own secret groanings; that we are no other than we are, our yearnings, our looks to our gracious Lord to unmake us what we have made ourselves, and re-make us what He once made us, and wherein He would have us grow; the frailness of our prayers, and our longings to pray; our coldness and selfishness, and our desire to love; our pride and our desires to be humble; our struggles, surprises, the cloudings of our mind; how some besetting sudden sins have overtaken us unawares: we find ourselves angry, when we meant to rebuke aright; we meant to eat for health, and find we have been self-indulgent; to speak of self for profit, and fear it is vanity; to do good, and fear we have been too forward; to avoid injuring others, and fear it has been a cowardly keeping back of the truth; to rest from weariness, and find it sloth; our very duties perplex us, and we know not whether we have chosen aright; in prayer we fear lest we have omitted active duty, or active duty have displaced some measure of our prayer; we have to bewail our sins, and yet be of a cheerful countenance; penitents, but do our part as though we had been holy. Then how much of us is hidden from ourselves! Satan darts thoughts into our hearts, and we know not, whether we gave not a moment's assent to them, though, when aware, we loathe them; we scarce know, whether an angry thought have been our own, or our penalty and trial; much trial is withdrawn from us, and we know not what we should be, if again exposed to it; we dread lest we fall not, only because Satan is not permitted to try us in earnest; we feel ourselves encompassed with death, and see not how it is to end in life.

And so we must be content oftentimes to abide, uncertain about our issue; in fear, yet in hope; knowing what we deserve, and hoping what we do not deserve, for His sake Who deserved it for us; a mystery to ourselves as to others; "fashioned in secret," even from ourselves. This is our comfort and stay, that we "*are* fashioned;" "we made not ourselves, but He made us," and He, our Maker, re-makes us. It is our comfort that "we are His workmanship:" and so we trust, that His Spirit hath quickened us, and still indwells in the mansion He made, and is restoring its decay, although we see more of our own decay than of His blessed work. "He hath made us;" and so, we trust, that He will sustain us to the end. He maketh us that, for which we have no thought. Did we make ourselves, we might well be concerned that we see not what we are becoming; now we may trust, that, although in secret, still we are being fashioned into "a vessel fit for the Master's use."

Still although we know not where we are; how much has been, or is being wrought in us; what our progress; we must know that something is being wrought. Day by day are God's operations wrought; "day by day," unbrokenly, " are our members fashioned." They are *our* members which are fashioned, and not without ourselves, although by God; they are *our* wills, which are to be subdued; *our* appetites to be reined in ; *our* love to be directed and upheld in its One End; *our* actions to be conformed, one by one, to the Will of God. We may not be conscious, that we are growing in grace, but we must be that we are acting under grace. We may not see how direct our path is (that we shall see, as it becomes straighter); but if we are moving upward, we must make efforts, and feel them. Downwards, persons may float unperceived, but it is to the gulf; descent alone is quiet, easy, painless, but it is—to Hell. We cannot win our way without resistance, nor resist self without consciousness and pain. If we feel not the clog, which our sinful nature hangs around us, it is because we are following it. Moral natures cannot stand still, unless perfected. Whatever lives, grows or decays, until it has reached its term. Things live on, without growing; but decay, at first imperceptible, has begun; it may seem some uppermost bough only which is leafless, but death is at work at the very centre.

Such then being the universal law of God, that whatever does grow, grows continually, that things are continually, though silently, tending to one end, each day of our existence has an immeasurable value; because each day tends to that which is immeasurable,—an everliving life or an undying death. The careless world, alas! our careless selves, too often, have lived or live, as though our days were of slight account, that we might live on through them, thinking, purposing, hoping, to live well on the whole, but disregarding each single item of our time, as though of little moment. One day or many days we might give up to pleasure, to travelling, to refreshment, to our callings; nay, we might even pass whole days or all our days in an easy way, and yet on the whole do well. As though moment by moment made not up our hours; hour by hour brought not on the night, that "night wherein no man can work;" day by day made not up the sum of our days, the period of our trial, and brought not on the Day of account and of final retribution! As though we might be careless about each item of our worldly wealth, and our whole worldly estate not totter! As though we might, day by day, neglect to provide oil for the lamps wherewith we are to meet our Lord, and 'not be shut out!'

There is no mere loss. Days in which we gain nothing are not merely lost; they weigh against us and weigh us down; day by day our habits harden upon us; day by day we become more confirmed in habits of selfishness or self-denial, wilfulness or subjection of our will; reverence or irreverence; communion with God or thoughtlessness of Him. Day by day, we are nearer, as to the end of our lives, so also to that place wherein our lives will end, Heaven or Hell. We see not the approach of either; but day by day Death is nearer; day by day men's own feet are carrying them nearer to their everlasting doom.

But although day by day we must grow or decay, yet is not the amount of our growth in our power. By the grace of God alone can we grow; and that flows into us more largely or more scantily, according to what we have ourselves become. If we have allowed our hearts to grow cold, or worldly, much more if defiled, we cannot at once love or serve God, or repent, or have that alacrity and energy of faith, which is the blessing of His more faithful servants.

We are not masters of our own faith or love. We cannot expand ourselves to receive God. One step only is in our power, the next. We cannot at once have great love, or deep humility, or intense penitence, or an active soul, or a reverent spirit, or a devout mind. We can neither at once unlearn evil habits wholly, nor learn great virtues. We can rarely bound in our Christian course. Step by step is the toilsome ascent to be won. Single acts of virtue, wrought by the grace of God, are the steps to Heaven. If in these we correspond to the grace of God, He will give larger increase. It may be, He will bring us into some new trial, in which, if by His grace we conquer, He will make us other men. One decisive deed well done, solely for His glory and His love, one trial well surmounted by His grace, will often, through His mercy, lift men up at once far beyond their measure. On one heroic act, He has wrought the whole living habit into the soul. A whole life may be wrapt up in one single deed, which He hath given and crowneth. One fervent act of self-devotion to our Lord, giving ourselves for life or death, weal or woe, to His Blessed and Almighty Will, surrendering ourselves and all which is ours wholly into His Hands, without reserve, to dispose of us, wholly as He wills, and it may be, we shall find His gracious Hand on ours, leading us to follow His steps, although it be to Calvary. But as this deed or purpose itself, so all is of grace. The morrow of grace is no more in our power, than of time. The first act, for which He gives us grace, is ours; all beyond is God's. But as we use the present, He will give the future. Despair we not, then, when we see any grace of reverence, or deep love, or lowly humility, or instant fervent thankfulness, which we have not; nor yet must we attempt to transplant it at once full-grown into ourselves. Reverence we the gift of God's Holy Spirit in it, and yield we ourselves to His moulding Hand, day by day, to fashion us; yet must we beware, lest we become unreal by seeking at once to be what we reverence. Let us do what, by His grace, we can; but let us not act, as if we had, what as yet we have not. If we humble ourselves, that we can no more, it may be, He will look upon our humility, and give us what we are grieved that we have not. Pray we for the grace of God to do each single act, as He shall will, to His glory; and He will lead us whither as yet we know not.

But although God forms us day by day, yet are there, from time to time, seasons of larger growth, as in nature so in grace. God, in His mercy, gives us fresh starting points in our Christian race. Some such most of us perhaps have passed; too many, it is to be feared, we have wasted. Such are childhood's earliest trials. The bitter fruits we have felt in ourselves from some one sin of childhood, from some neglect of God's loud warning or His call, may make us sorrowfully estimate the deep value of such calls, had we obeyed. What a depth of misery has lain wrapt up in one childish sin! Into what a harvest of death has one seed of sin, through successive acts, been multiplied! And so, in God's chosen faithful ones, how has one faithful use of grace drawn down more grace, issuing anew in fresh acts of faith, and these again inviting larger gifts of grace, until God hath enriched the whole soul with large "fruits of righteousness." Such periods, again, when used aright, are Holy Confirmation and the first Communion. Yea, so full is this of the richness of God's treasure, that thoughtful persons have said, that none ever went far astray, whose first Communion was diligently prepared for, and received and treasured holily. And, when these and other seasons have been wasted, God in His mercy visits us anew, but mostly in an austere form. "A mighty and strong wind" must "rend the rock" of our stony heart "before the Lord," ere He can speak to us in the "still small voice." When the clouds of our sins have gathered to hide from us our true Sun, storm and tempest must mostly scatter them. Sickness, the near approach of death, bereavement, must shake us through and through to bring us to ourselves. The numbness of our spiritual life must mostly be quickened by some startling stroke of pain.

Again, in the Church's year, at some seasons, "the windows of heaven" seem to stand open, ready to "rain down Righteousness," if our earthliness be prepared to receive it. "I will hear," saith the Lord, "I will hear the heavens, and they shall hear the earth, and the earth shall hear the corn and the wine and the oil, and they shall hear Jezreel," the plenteous harvest which "the Lord shall sow." In the holy season of expectation of His Coming, or His actual Birth in the Flesh, or the blessed austere days of penitence, or the Passion or Resurrection or Ascension, or the Descent of the Holy Ghost, the wonders of old time are again renewed. He Whom we look for again cometh. He is born in the faithful heart which watches and longs for Him; their "eyes see their salvation;" the Virtue of His Fasting hallows theirs, and shields their soul from temptation; they die anew in His Death; rise in His Resurrection; ascend with Him; from Him receive the Promise of the Father. Such mysterious efficacy has His Incarnation, that the very seasons of His precious Acts and Sufferings are full of blessing. "The tracks of Thy chariotwheels drop fatness [m]."

And to you, brethren, this week, which to-day brings to a close, has, we hope, in some sort, been some such period of blessing, not for the ministry of the preachers, but through the Presence of Christ, Whom here ye sought. And yet even such as I, if I, in myself too poor, have not been able to "bring out of His treasury things new and old," yet have I sought at least to bring before you what was old, and what aforetime has yielded fruit. Yet whatever any of us were, that whereof we would speak has been in itself the most solemn sermon to your souls. Not the words wherein we speak of them, but the eternal truths themselves, are the aweful preachers to man. The deadliness of sin, the sinner's death, final judgement, eternal woe, penitence, the Cross, the Sight of God, the bliss of Eternity, surely the very names might startle us from our listlessness, and bid us gird ourselves to more devoted service. Are they not the very Voice of Christ to wake the dead? Him too have many of us sought at His mercy-seat, where He feedeth us with Himself, and "washeth," we trust, our sinful "souls with His own Precious Blood."

[m] Ps. lxv. 11.

And now this solemn time is over; much sweetness had it while it lasted. God grant that its fragrance may not pass away, but may remain, " as the smell of a field which the Lord hath blessed," "a sweet savour of Christ" unto life everlasting. Yet that it be so, we must take some pains, by God's grace, to fix that grace in our souls, that it evaporate not in these our feelings whatever we may have had, nor even in expressions of thankfulness towards Almighty God Himself. Nor be we disappointed, on the other hand, if we see not as yet in ourselves the fruit of these our solemn services. So it is in God's work in nature. The life-giving nourishment of the tree riseth within, swells branch and bud ready to bursting, ere yet one leaf unfold itself. And so we trust that His grace has risen within our souls, although as yet we do not know what He has been doing with us; save that we hoped that while " our hearts burned within us," at thoughts of His endless love, or our own, but for His mercy, endless shame and misery, He, although unseen, was nigh. But holy acts fix holy thoughts. As yet perhaps these very services have come so close upon us, or we again have been led into them half unawares, or led on in them, or in part we have been joying in peaceful, happy, thankfulness for God's gracious acceptance of this work, that we have had hardly time to form more than some general purpose to give ourselves more wholly unto Him. But the life of religion is in single acts. Acts, within or without, are our steps to heaven. Whether, inward, of faith or hope or love, breathed from the soul to God, or secret self-control in which by God's grace we hold down and keep under our besetting sin, or unknown self-denial, or self-humiliation, or silent suffering, resigning ourselves wholly to His Fatherly Will, or meek silence in reproach, undeserved of man; or outward acts again, in deeds of self-denying love, or peace-making, or active service, or humility, or religious worship or abstinence.

And to this end, of fixing our purpose of more stedfast warfare under Christ's banner, it may by His gracious aid be of some help, now at the close, to name some few simple rules, familiar perhaps to many of you, which yet to some, who are beginners, may be useful. And yet, if any have not begun to live under rule, burden yourselves not with too much at once, lest it oppress or weary you, or you tire after a time, or it become mechanical, and you become distracted by thinking of your rules rather than of Him, under Whom you would thereby bring yourself under rule, Whose Holy Will you wish to make your Rule.

Above all, whatever you attempt, impress on the mind and pray God to write there a deep consciousness of your own helplessness and inability to begin or continue or hold on in any good. And this, not in the way of *formal* acknowledgement, (for this all ever make,) but impressing it and stamping it upon your inward souls, and acting upon it, whatever else you are doing, in continual, quick, instantaneous prayer for the aid of God. This very habit itself plainly cannot be gained at once. For, gained, it is to live in heaven, in continual intercourse with God; we ever breathing up to God and in God, His pity ever descending upon us. It too must be His gift; as, when it is given, it is the key to all His other gifts, and the treasuries of His love. Yet this too He will bestow upon us, in degrees, as we use faithfully His secret drawings to look up to Him.

But, first, in order of time, will perhaps be that searching of the heart, whereof I have so often spoken, both in order to gain a clean heart, by pouring out our whole selves in penitent confession to God, and also to know more clearly, what are our chief enemies. And these, indeed, we cannot expect to know all at once, as neither can we all our past sins. The eye must be cleansed, in order fully to behold sin, as well as to see God. Subtler and spiritual sins we shall not perceive, until we ourselves are becoming spiritual. Such are seen only in the full rays of the Sun of Righteousness. There might we behold the slightest specks floating to and fro, not settling, as it were, upon the mind, yet still not leaving it pure in His sight. More shall we ourselves see, as more light is poured into our souls; and more will be poured in, as we faithfully use what we have, and withhold wilfully no corner of our souls from its dread beam. Meanwhile, we may without fear commit our "secret faults" to His pity, by Whom we trust they will be "cleansed." We shall have enough at first to do with overt sins. First, we should declare a deadly, inveterate, war with these.

And when we have surveyed them, then it is advised, to select some *one*, by God's grace, to exterminate. In so doing, we shall not neglect the rest. Give we ourselves with earnest purpose to destroy one of God's foes within us, and He will for the time keep the others chained that they hurt us not. Wage we war in His Name, and He Who drove out the seven nations before Israel by little and little, will withhold our seven deadly enemies, the deadly sins, that they press not too heavily upon us. Only to this one end direct we all our strength. It is not a common easy warfare to which we are called, but one by which we are to uproot, one by one, all which rebels within us against the Lord our God, root and branch, so as to leave neither name nor remnant. We single out one foe, only that we may utterly destroy it. We track it out, that no remaining fibre of it may again shoot forth, to choke our vineyard.

To this one conflict then, we should bring all our spiritual force to bear. "Goliah fallen, the Philistines fled." The same sin will shew itself in different forms. How, for instance, will sloth or vanity poison or mar every action of our life! Resist we it then in all; mortify it in all; in every victory giving Him the glory. Be this the object of our earliest thoughts. In the morning, consider we the occasions wherein we are likely thus to be tried; about midday, if we can, (it much lightens our task at night,) review minutely our progress or defeats in it, and again, at least, at night; meditate we on the opposite Virtue in our Blessed Lord; let us gaze on Him, until we be ashamed to be proud or vain members of Him, Who so watched, toiled, was wearied, in seeking us. Then strive we, not only to uproot the sin, but to implant the opposite grace. This is often easier than simply to combat sins. It is even easier, for instance, to become very meek, than simply to restrain outbreaks of anger; for so must we throw ourselves, more out of ourselves, wholly upon the grace and strength of God. Then for this grace pray we fervently; for this ask, that when in the Holy Communion He vouchsafes to "come under our roof," He would bring it to our souls; on this let us meditate; to this, be the reverential reading of Holy Scripture directed; be we on the watch, how to practise it; take we shame, if we may without scandal, for any thing connected with our fault; own we it; put on ourselves something irksome, if we fall, that we be in earnest with ourselves; heed we not rebellious thoughts, but, by God's grace, crush it in the act. If not at once, it will slowly bleed to death. But let every step be, in "mistrust in self, and trust in God."

Yet whatever we would gain, seek we, as the first, best, gift of all, the gift of love. For "love is the fulfilling of the law." And then shall we gain real victories, when "faith worketh by love." Would we, as the outset, gain real penitence, pray we for loving penitence, or for penitent love; pray we, "Lord, for love of Thee, I would grieve that I ever offended Thee." Or humility? let it be humble love. Or love of our neighbour? seek we to mortify self-will and idle partialities, behold Christ in all, and so desire to love them with a superhuman love, as loving Him in them; let us love all, our friends in Him, or, if any hate us or speak evil of us, for Him.

And as we make progress in our spiritual conflict, we shall see what occasions are most hurtful to us, in what way our sin most steals upon us or assails us; and so we can either by ourselves, or by help of some who has the care of human souls, form rules to ourselves, how we can keep off the occasion, or be strengthened under it. For to come into temptation with no fixed rule to guide us, nothing to appeal to against our biassed judgement, is to give ourselves over to defeat.

You will at once feel, my brethren, what an aid in all our conflicts must be, a brief thought on our Lord, if it be but daily in our prayers, to look unto Him, " the Author and Finisher of our faith," and that, Crucified for us! or some brief recollection of the solemn hours of the mysteries of our Faith, and of His Precious Sufferings, if but with the use of the Lord's Prayer, in thought of and in union with them; or frequently to place ourselves in the Presence of God, by an act of the mind, " Thou, God, seest me;" or to take occasion of things of sense to rise up to Him our Creator; or to have some brief aspiration through the day, to which our minds may often recur, forming in our souls a secret cell, in which, retiring from the world, we may even amid the world, hold brief converse with our God. Or again, what a treasure that is, to count nothing small, wherein we may please God, to seek in all our thoughts, words, or acts, to please God Alone, to do little things, to accept each little or somewhat greater cross, for His Will's sake; to seek in all things to conform our will to His, and to count all things gain to us, which are permitted by His Righteous Will.

But, above all, as ye began with God, so with Him would ye end. " He that persevereth unto the end shall be saved." Perseverance to the end is the crowning gift of God, and given to all who pray for it, to none perhaps who do not pray for it.

Again and again we begin well, but again and again after a time we grow weary, or other imagined duties or employments interfere, and we lay aside what we had begun well and found good to our souls, not because it ceased to be so, but because we had not bound our unstable souls fast unto Him, the Unchangeable, by constant prayer for perseverance. Pray God then daily to "strengthen the thing which He hath wrought in you;" pray Him daily, in Whose "Hands are the issues of death" to be your "guide" unto and "over death."

And now, brethren, in the Name of God and with His blessing, Farewell. Gladly might we have lingered on in these solemn services, had other duties permitted. But there is a time to meditate in stillness, and again a time to carry out into life what in stillness we have gathered. Blessed and sweet to the soul is the memory of these hours, in which we have together meditated on some of the most solemn subjects relating to our salvation and our endless end in God, and together daily partaken of the Bread of Life. We shall not pass away, I trust, from each other's memories; but each, where God has placed them, shall in His Holy House, in the Communion of our Church, and at His Holy Altar, remember the one the other, that, by His grace persevering to the end, we may together rejoice in His Presence in endless glory.

"And now the very God of peace sanctify you wholly, and I pray God your whole spirit and soul and body be preserved blameless unto the Coming of our Lord Jesus Christ." "Faithful is He that calleth you, Who also will do it."

Lord of all power and might, Who art the Author and Giver of all good things; Graft in our hearts the love of Thy Name, increase in us true religion, nourish us with all goodness, and of Thy great mercy keep us in the same; through Jesus Christ our Lord. Amen.

𝔗𝔥𝔞𝔫𝔨𝔰 𝔟𝔢 𝔱𝔬 𝔊𝔬𝔡.

Note A on p. 13.

Any one who should read the history of the three anointings of our Blessed Lord, without any knowledge that any difficulty had been raised as to the sacred narrative, would, probably, look upon them as the act of the same person. And this is, in fact, the earliest impression which we find with regard to them. For Origen, in alleging grounds against it, speaks of it as the opinion of "many" or of "the many;" apparently, the current opinion of his time. He mentions also as the common ground of those who so understood the history, apparently, the "naturalness" of so taking it. The histories of S. Matthew and S. Mark have, in common with that of S. Luke, the mention of the "woman with the *alabaster* box of ointment," and that the anointing takes place in the house of one "Simon;" the history in S. John has in common with S. Luke, "the anointing of the *Feet* of Jesus and the wiping them with the hair of the head;" and these two circumstances S. John mentions (c. xi. 2.) as characteristic of "Mary." Yet they would not be characteristic of her, had they been done by another also, (as is supposed by those who distinguish Mary Magdalene from Mary the sister of Lazarus,) of a very different character. The difficulty has arisen from considering them, not as the act of the same person, but as the same act. If we look upon them as different acts of the same person, this, so far from raising any "apparent contradiction" in the Scripture narrative, (if one must so speak,) makes it the easier. For all are agreed now, that the history in S. Matthew, (c. xxvi.) S. Mark, (c. xiv.) and S. John (c. xii.) are the same; but of these S. Matthew and S. Mark relate the anointing the Head of our Lord only; S. John that of the Feet. But S. John relates the anointing of the Feet, as the characteristic of Mary. (c. xi. and xii.) This it is, of course, very remarkably, if this was the action of faith and humility, upon which she received her pardon. S. Matthew and S. Mark would thus relate that part of the anointing, which signified the nearness, with which she was allowed to approach our Lord, and His gracious acceptance and favour towards her, in that she was permitted to anoint His Sacred Head; S. John records that part of the action which betokened her continued humility, which he had before spoken of. Each part of the action had, thus, its special meaning. And so there is not even the appearance of contradiction in them, but rather an inward harmony amid the outward variation, which strikes every one on the first reading, that S. Matthew and S. Mark, relating the same anointing with S. John, mention the anointing of the Head only, S. John of the Feet only. This explanation is given by S. Ambrose (ad loc.) in relation to the difficulty; his first impression being, that it is the same person. "This woman then, S. Matthew mentions pouring ointment on the Head of Christ, and perhaps on that ground would not call her a sinner; for the sinner, according to S. Luke, poured ointment on the Feet of Christ. She *may* then not be the same; lest the Evangelists seem to relate things contrary. The question, however, may be solved by the difference of advancement and of time, in that, in the one case, she was yet a sinner, in the other, more perfect." S. Augustine has exactly the same view; "that it was not another woman, who, a sinner, then approached the Feet of Jesus and kissed them and washed them with tears, and anointed them with ointment, to whom the Lord, using the parable of the two debtors, said, ' her many sins were forgiven because she loved much;' but that the same Mary did this twice, once namely which Luke related, when first approaching with that humility and those tears, she obtained remission of sins. For this John also, although he does not, as Luke, relate it as it happened, mentions, in praise of Mary, when he had begun to speak of the raising of Lazarus, before He came to Bethany. ' Now a certain man was sick, named Lazarus, of Bethany, the town of Mary and her sister Martha. It was that Mary which, &c.' In saying this John accords with Luke, who relates that it took place in the house of one Simon, a Pharisee. This then Mary had already done. But what she did again in Bethany is different, not belonging to the relation in Luke, but related alike by the three, John namely, Matthew, and Mark. Of these there is no doubt that they relate the same act," &c. (de Cons. Ev. ii. 79.) And certainly S. John's words, ' It was that Mary which anointed, &c. whose brother Lazarus was sick,' are much more naturally interpreted of a previous than of a subsequent action; of an act which S. John was not going to relate, and which would not otherwise be known to belong to this Mary, than of one which he was; as giving us an intimation of some previous relation, in which she had been brought to our Lord, rather than an anticipation of an act which, in a manner, flowed out of this very history of the raising of Lazarus.

On the other hand, the very Fathers who suppose the women who anointed our Lord to have been different, illustrate incidentally their sameness. As Origen owns, " There is a great likeness and sort of affinity as to this woman in the four Evangelists." (Tract. 35. in S. Matt. § 77. Lat.) Thus, although in this place, Origen says, that there must have been three, distinguishing that in S. Matthew and S. Mark from that in S. John, as well as from S. Luke; yet, elsewhere, he distinguishes two only, " the sinner, who poured the ointment upon the Feet, and her who is not called a sinner, who poured it on His Head." (Tract 1. in Cant.) And again (Tract 2. in Cant.), he expressly identifies the woman " not a sinner" in S. Matthew, S. Mark, and S. John, distinguishing S. Luke only; but in yet another place (in Matt. tom. xii. § 4.) he speaks of the sinner, in connection with " Simon the leper," thus identifying the history in S. Luke with that in S. Matt. and S. Mark. S. Chrysostome, says (Hom. 80. in S. Matt.), that it "appears" to be the same person in all four Gospels; he thinks not; but still identifies the person mentioned in S. Matthew, S. Mark, and S. Luke, as distinct from her in S. John. Thus even Origen and S. Chrysostome, while they distinguish the history of S. Luke and S. John, together identify them with the same third history. S. Jerome (in S. Matt.) adopting (as it seems) the remark of Origen, inserts a word, which seems to imply that he (as does S. Ambrose above,) thought that the two histories might belong to the same person at different times. " Let no one think that it is the same who poured the ointment upon the Head and upon the Feet. For that one both washes with tears, and wipes with the hair, and is explicitly called a sinful woman (meretrix). But of this one nothing of this kind is written. Neither could a sinner of that sort (meretrix) *at once*, become worthy to minister at the Head of our Lord.

On the whole, then, the identity of the individual who anointed our Lord, seems to follow from the most natural explanation of S. John xi. 2. to have recommended itself to the minds of simple Christians, and, unless it be supposed (which is the opinion of Origen only, and very improbable) that there were three acts of anointing, or three women who anointed our Lord, the narratives of S. Matthew and S. Mark are harmonised most naturally with that of S. John (c. xii.), on the supposition that the anointing related by S. Luke was a distinct act of the same individual. This opinion, which appears (as was said) to have been the most common before Origen, is adopted in several places by S. Gregory the Great from S. Augustine, and, partly perhaps from its naturalness, partly from having been received in the Roman Breviary, has been prevalent in the Western Church. The alleged difficulties as to the Scripture narrative are occasioned solely by the supposition, that one act, not two different acts of the same person are related. See further the very interesting observations of Mr. Williams in his harmony of the Gospel Narrative of the Passion, " Mary Magdalene."

PRINTED BY THE SOCIETY OF THE HOLY TRINITY,
HOLY ROOD, OXFORD.

www.ingramcontent.com/pod-product-compliance
Lightning Source LLC
Chambersburg PA
CBHW022115290426
44112CB00008B/686